D0768928

Why Do the Jews Need a Land of Their Own?

Why Do the Jews Need a Land of Their Own?

Sholom-Aleichem

Translated from the Yiddish and Hebrew by Joseph Leftwich and Mordecai S. Chertoff

Beth Shalom-Aleichem, Tel Aviv

A Herzl Press Publication
New York ● CORNWALL BOOKS ● London

Cornwall Books
440 Forsgate Drive
Cranbury, NJ 08512

Cornwall Books
25 Sicilian Avenue
London WC1A 2QH, England

Cornwall Books
2133 Royal Windsor Drive
Unit 1
Mississauga, Ontario
Canada L5J 1K5

Herzl Press
515 Park Avenue
New York, New York 10022

Library of Congress Cataloging in Publication Data

Sholom Aleichem, 1859–1916.
  Why do the Jews need a land of their own?

  Translation of: Oyf vos badarfn Yidn a land.
  "A Herzl Press publication."
  1. Zionism—Literary collections. 2. Zionism—
Addresses, essays, lectures. I. Title.
PJ5129.R2A26 1984   839'.0933   83-45297
ISBN 0-8453-4774-8

Published in the original Yiddish as *Oif Voss Badarfen Yid'n A Land?* (Tel Aviv: Beth Shalom-Aleichem and, I. L. Peretz Publishing House 1978) and later translated into Hebrew and published as *Leshem Mah Tzrichim Hayehudim Eretz Mishelahem?* Beth Shalom-Aleichem and Dvir Publishers, Tel-Aviv, 1981.

Printed in the United States of America

Contents

Foreword

As with the previous Sholom Aleichem works (in Yiddish) published by Beth Sholom Aleichem, we have laid stress on preserving the uniform character of subject matter, so as to present a well-rounded picture of a branch of Sholom Aleichem's creative work that few of his readers know anything about.

It will be a discovery to many readers to see the extent to which Sholom Aleichem devoted himself to the problems of Shivat Zion, of Zionism, and of Palestine. And this during his most creative years. Naturally there were zigzags and inconsistencies in his ideological conception, discrepancies in his writings on this theme. But above all there is his real bond with the Shivat Zion aspiration, understanding for the Zion motif and the ancient longing for the Land of Israel.

This book contains nearly everything that Sholom Aleichem wrote on this theme. It is the Chovevei Zion climate of that period, the lovely dream of Eretz Israel, with all the endless dissensions and quarrelings between Zionists and Jews who believed that the Redemption must come from elsewhere. And all of them seeking to save the world and having their effect on the Jewish condition and shaping the Jewish destiny.

When you read these writings of Sholom Aleichem's, some of them written more than seventy–eighty years ago, you are really flabbergasted by the amazing way in which he feels the Jewish reality. This is the Jewish social truth of over two generations ago. But what is more, how this unique genius in describing the Jewish way of life succeeded in his narrative style in foreseeing the Jewish road. Thus the descriptions, all his most diverse stories, conflicts, and characters, are not only the literary fixing of a past epoch, they have the fresh breath of life in them, as have all Sholom Aleichem's people. They speak to us very often about our problems today, anxious about Jewish continuity, worrying most of all about the younger generation—what Eretz Israel should be, and how to get Jews to go there and live a full Jewish life. Some of these writings read as if they had just been written. That is the power of true creative art.

The book contains different kinds of work: descriptions of a way of life, stories, one-acters, a short novel—the description Sholom Aleichem gave his "Messianic Times," which, incidentally, was left unfinished—political essays, records of a Zionist Congress, and a stack of Menachem Mendel letters. These are works not only of different periods (1888–1913) but of different character and manner. Yet altogether they constitute a marvelous, colorful mosaic of

Sholom Aleichem's Zionist outlook, his Jewish nationalist conception, his thorough acceptance of the social and political ferment in Jewish life up to the start of the First World War, which changed not only the map of Europe, but also the entire Jewish social and demographic situation.

Clearly, it is a long way from the journalistic material, like "The Jewish Congress in Basel" (1897), "Why Do Jews Need a State?" (1898), "To Our Sisters in Zion" and "Dr. Theodor Herzl" (1904), which first appeared as separate pamphlets and were distributed in tens of thousands of copies—to the well-formed descriptions and tales, the Menachem Mendel letters, and Menachem Mendel's pronouncements about Zionism; the descriptions of the congress, and the pictures of the Zionist leaders. Sholom Aleichem was trying to acquaint the Yiddish-speaking man in the street with the ideas of Zionism, and the concept of Shivat Zion, to introduce him to the leading Zionist figures. Because of this mission which he had taken upon himself (when he was already a great and venerated name in literature) there is a strong propogandistic tone in these writings.

For the same reason, there is much repetition in this work. Even so, Sholom Aleichem's colorful light and warmth fall upon his page. Here too we recognize the hand of the master narrator. Nor must we forget that Sholom Aleichem wrote all this popularizing stuff at one and the same time as he wrote his stories of a Zionist nature—to say nothing of his other works of these years, like "Homesick" (1902). This marvelous tale of the Zionist ferment, with Reb Yosefl's deep emotion on receiving the Zionist Bank share is still today a chef d'oeuvre. So is the story of Selig Mechanic and the chapters on the red Little Jews, which were written in 1900, only a few years before he wrote the pamphlet, "Dr. Theodor Herzl," with his glorification of the Herzl figure.

There are two different styles here: a simple, propogandistic style, direct to the common folk, and a polished, literary style, charming and gentle. A compromise emerged: Sholom Aleichem the artist and Sholom Aleichem the writer; the wizard word-master and the bearer of the Shivat Zion idea.

True enough, there were zigzags in Sholom Aleichem's Zionist outlook, ups and downs in his relationship to it, that did not affect the great essential. There was a wavering about his faith in the possibilities. It was in the early days when Sholom Aleichem joined the Chovevei Zion. As far back as 1888 he wrote his well-known letter to Leon Pinsker, the Chovevei Zion leader, asking to be enrolled as a member. It is interesting that two years earlier, in 1886, he had written to Ravnitzky and Frankfeld in response to their invitation to contribute to the Chovevei Zion volume, "Der Veker"—"I want your idea to be adopted no less than you do yourself. But what can I do, knowing my people Israel as I do, that I can't believe it will take it to heart? You see what I mean? I can't believe. Not I don't believe. That makes it much worse for me than if I didn't want to believe! Why it should be so—there's a lot to say on that subject. I only wish God help you to have many people thinking as you do and doing what you are doing, and that your effort be not in vain."

Here you have Sholom Aleichem the doubter. At times, no less than in his writings of that period, we find the Shivat Zion sentiment, his belief in the Zionist necessity, expressed in letters to contemporary writers and personalities. One letter is so characteristic that it deserves quotation. It was dated 27 April 1906 and addressed to Israel Zangwill. It was written in Yiddish, but in Latin characters: "Revolution! Would that our brothers could and would bring such enormous sacrifices for a bit of land of our own, as they do for a land where they think and believe they will, at some time, be invited to the festivities."

Sholom Aleichem accepted gratefully and with satisfaction the achievements of the Zionist ideal. He lived and breathed with it. How happily he responded to the news: "My Kiev friends have thought it over, and have a sum of several thousand francs, to buy me a house with a small garden on the shore of the Mediterranean in the Jaffa region, in Eretz Israel." (From a letter to Dr. Gershon Levin, Nervi, 15 January 1909.)

Unfortunately, nothing came of the idea, although Sholom Aleichem was fascinated by the possibility of settling in Eretz Israel. He even wrote to several friends about it. Nothing came of the plan. What has remained is Sholom Aleichem's great and conquering creative work.

ABRAHAM LIS

Why
Do the Jews
Need a Land
of Their Own?

Sholom Aleichem the Zionist

Dr. J. Klausner

The Chovev Zion

Sholom Aleichem became a Chovev Zion as far back as the beginnings of the movement, around 1883. He was captivated by the idea. A year later he wrote a novel in Russian, "Vperiod" ("Forward"), picturing an idyllic life in Eretz Israel, in one of the colonies there. It was not published. Later he cooled down a little to the idea. In 1886 when the Odessa Chovevei Zion decided to publish a collected volume, "Der Veker," devoted to the idea of Yishuv Eretz Israel, they turned to Sholom Aleichem, asking him to contribute a story with a Zionist trend. He wrote to Ravnitzky, the editor: "Writing to order is no damn good! I can't tell someone to believe when I have little faith myself. I want your idea to be adopted, no less than you do. But what shall I do when I know my people Israel so well that I can't believe it will take it to heart."[1] There is a second letter to Ravnitzky where Sholom Aleichem explains that he is no assimilator, nor is he a Palestiner. The idea is holy to him, but he draws a distinction between the theory and the practice.[2] He had recently reread the last chapter of his Russian novel, and tears had come to his eyes. So as we see, Sholom Aleichem was Zionistically inclined, but he could not envisage the movement developing to anything big. He sent a story to the "Veker," but it was not one of his successes.

In 1888 there was another change in Sholom Aleichem's attitude. He decided to become officially a member of the Chovevei Zion movement. He sent a further letter to Dr. Pinsker, the chairman of the Chovevei Zion in Russia: "I, Sholom Aleichem, the youngster of the group, send you herewith a 25 rouble note, and ask you to enroll me as a member in the Chovevei Zion, and to bill me annually to this amount of 25 roubles. Greetings to all Lovers of Zion, and to all the Children of Israel." One of the Lovers of Zion, "not on paper, but with all my heart, as it should be."

Sholom Aleichem was at this time (1888–1890) editing the literary collections

1. Ravnitzky, *Memories of Sholom Aleichem* (Petrograd, 1918).
2. I. D. Berkowitz, *Memoirs* (Tel Aviv, 1937).

of the Yiddish Folkbibliotek. Its contributions include several Zionist articles. S. L. Zitron, for instance, has an article in the first volume tracing the road of the writer Levanda to the Chovevei Zion movement. The second volume has an article by the then young Moscow Zionist Ussishkin. Sholom Aleichem was one of the most active members of the Kiev branch of the Chovevei Zion. By the end of 1889 he was made the leader of the branch. He did all the correspondence of the branch, collected the funds, organized an inner study group for the problems of Palestine colonization. About this time things began to look up for the Chovevei Zion. Alexander Zederbaum, the editor of "Hamelitz," obtained from the government the legalization of the Chovevei Zion in Odessa. Plans were made to increase Jewish colonization in Palestine. Sholom Aleichem flung himself into this work with enthusiasm. The Kiev branch wanted to provide the funds to establish its own colony, Gedera. It also decided to raise a fund of one thousand to two thousand roubles for supporting the colony. Shalom Aleichem undertook to collect the money. There is a letter to Samuel Joseph Finn in Vilna, one of the treasurers of the Chevra Chovevei Zion, where Shalom Aleichem informs him (28 February 1890) that the Kiev branch will send five hundred roubles as deposit for the legalization and two hundred roubles as a thanksgiving to Zederbaum, in the form of subscriptions for twenty copies of "Hamelitz."[3]

When the first General Assembly of the legalized Chovevei Zion met in Odessa, Sholom Aleichem was there as a delegate from Kiev. In April 1890 he announced that he intended, with the help of the Odessa committee, to publish a collective volume in Hebrew and Yiddish, devoted to the problems of the movement. The proposal was adopted, with appreciation and thanks, but the book never appeared.

After the session in Odessa Sholom Aleichem became more active than before. On Ussishkin's invitation (Ussishkin was in charge of the propaganda for Chovevei Zion in Russia) Sholom Aleichem set out upon a tour of Russian towns and shtetlach—Borislav, Fastov, Biale Tzerkov. In Biale Tzerkov they made arrangements for a literary evening to benefit Jewish colonization in Eretz Israel, with readings from Jargon (Yiddish) books. And Sholom Aleichem would read something of his own.

Sholom Aleichem tried also to keep the Kiev branch active during the summer months as well, when he went to his summer home outside the town. Among the visitors who came there then were the young Ussishkin and the venerable Bialystock rabbi, Reb Shmuel Mohilever. The rabbi made a tremendous impression on the Chovevei Zion in Kiev.

The work of the Chovevei Zion in Kiev grew tremendously as a result, and Sholom Aleichem could not give it as much time as before. So he asked the young Yiddish writer Jacob Dineson to be the paid secretary.

---

3. The letter, in Hebrew, is in the Schwadron collection in the Hebrew University in Jerusalem.

Sholom Aleichem left Kiev after that and went to live in Odessa.[4]

During his Zionist period in Kiev Sholom Aleichem wrote a Zionist story, "Selig Mechanic." It came out first as a pamphlet (44 pages, Kiev, 1890. The original title was "Yishuv Eretz Israel." Sholom Aleichem changed it afterwards to "Selig Mechanic" and included it in his collected works, published in Warsaw in 1904.) All proceeds from the sale of the pamphlet went to the Kiev branch of Chovevei Zion.

The Herzl Epoch

When Dr. Theodor Herzl appeared on the Jewish horizon Sholom Aleichem was one of his first adherents. He became an active worker in the movement. He published Zionist propaganda pamphlets, weaving Zionist motives and ideas into his literary work, and he started writing a Zionist novel. In response to Ussishkin's call he went traveling through the towns and shtetlach, speaking at Zionist meetings, a Zionist propagandist. When the First Zionist Congress met in Basel, Sholom Aleichem had gone back to Kiev. The congress made a powerful impression on him. He translated into Yiddish and edited a long report on the congress by Dr. Mandelstamm, "The Jewish Congress in Basel," a pamphlet of thirty pages. It sold twenty-seven thousand copies. The wide circulation this pamphlet obtained showed that there was a demand for such pamphlets in Yiddish. Sholom Aleichem wrote two other such pamphlets, "Whay Do Jews Need a Land?" and "To Our Sisters in Zion" (22 pages, Warsaw, 1898). The pamphlet "Whay Do Jews Need a Land?" is an exposition of the Zionist case, explaining the Zionist idea in good homely Yiddish folk tongue. In the pamphlet "To Our Sisters in Zion" Sholom Aleichem tells Jewish girls and women not to feel ashamed of their Yiddish tongue, their Jewish names, and their Jewish appearance, urges them to read Jewish history, where they will encounter a galaxy of remarkable women, and generally to acquaint themselves with Hebrew and Yiddish literature.

During this period Sholom Aleichem wrote a Zionist novel, "Messianic Times," which was printed in Berditchev, in the print shop set up there by three young people, Moishe Kleinmann, Yehuda Fogel, and Mordecai Perlmutter. They wanted to do Zionist propaganda in Yiddish and turned for that purpose to Sholom Aleichem, Bal Machshoves, Avrohom Reisen, Ravnitzky, Joseph Klausner, and Dr. Nathan Birnbaum. They all agreed to join the enterprise and sent manuscripts for publication. Sholom Aleichem wrote "Messianic Times" for them. It was their first publication and was intended to appear as a serial in pamphlet form. Two pamphlets appeared in the summer of 1898. No further issues appeared. Kleinmann explained afterwards (in 1935 in "Haolom") that the editors had not liked the form in which Sholom Aleichem had cast his tale. Too much witticism and too much feuilleton style. This unfinished novel, included in this volume, definitely belongs to the field of Zionist literature.

---

4. "Goldene Keit" (Spring, 1950).

Contributor to "Der Jud" and "Die Welt"

The publishers of "Ha-Assif" started in 1899 a serious literary journal, "Der Jud," with Dr. Joseph Luria as editor, and the best writers of the time among the contributors—Mendele, Peretz, Avrohom Reisen, Reuben Brainin, Morris Rosenfeld, Ben-Ami, Bialik, Spector, Sholom Asch. Sholom Aleichem became one of its principal contributors. Between 1899 and 1902 he published there feuilletons and stories that belong to the best of his creative work, like Menachem Mendel's exchange of letters with his wife Sheine Sheindel, and with Sholom Aleichem himself, and the Little People of Kasrilevke. It was here that he started publishing his Tevya stories and his "Jewish Children." Into all these contributions Sholom Aleichem interwove Zionist sentiments and ideas. He also printed there his "Millions," an exchange of letters between Menachem Mendel and his wife Sheine Sheindel about Zionism.

Sholom Aleichem was also invited to contribute to the official paper of the Zionist Organization, "Die Welt," which appeared in 1900, also in Yiddish. There he published a story called "Lunatics," about a Zionist utopia. One of the red Little Jews visits this fortunate land for the Sabbath and relates afterwards the kind of life led by the Jews there. When "Die Welt" in Yiddish stopped publication, Dr. Herzl asked Sholom Aleichem to contribute to the German weekly, "Die Welt." So his feuilletons and his stories appeared there in German translation. They were also translated into other languages and printed elsewhere in Zionist publications.

Journeys to Zionist Gatherings

Menachem Mendel Ussishkin, the official representative of the Zionist Organization in the Ekaterinoslav region invited Sholom Aleichem in 1902 to visit the towns and shtetlach of the region, to appear at Zionist meetings arranged there. Sholom Aleichem did it with the same alacrity as twelve years previously. One sees this in a letter Sholom Aleichem sent to Ussishkin from his campaign center, Alexandrovs, "When I arrived from Jerusalem, I mean Ekaterinoslav, there was a deputation of Zionists waiting for me at the railway station. The police officer on duty showed me great respect. He didn't dare to approach the Jews, and he remained content to watch us from afar. I was taken to a Jewish hotel, Central. There was no samovar that evening, but there were bed bugs aplenty. In the morning I saw a lot of people, mostly Jews, walking along the street. I asked where they were going. To the market, they said. To get tickets. And when it was dark we had a flood. A miracle—thick mud. So they put on galoshes. And by the time they brought me to the hall it was packed full, full of people, men and women, all in the same image, like you don't see it in our parts. But I doubt if they had the same understanding as ours. As is written further herewith. Right at the top sat a rabbi, a real rabbi, not a government appointed rabbit, with a hat on his head. And facing me women, all sorts of strange-looking women, dressed-up women, and all looking at me, all eyes on me. And when I went up to them they started clapping, made a lot of noise. It scared the rabbi, the real rabbi, not the government appointed rabbi. And when I had finished my speech, the crowd laughed, rocked with laughter. The rabbi, the real one, not the one appointed by the government, didn't understand what they were laughing at. He probably thought they were laughing at me, so he was sorry for me. And when I got down from the platform the crowd went on laughing and clapping, and calling, Bravo! At this, the rabbi, the real one, not the government appointed one, couldn't feel any sorrier for me, and he went away. As for me, they called me out ten times and tormented me till one o'clock in the morning. It was terribly hot. Hotter than in the steam bath. And much hotter than in Ekatorinoslav, at the round table where Litch-insky and his clique kept denouncing Herzl, belittling him and making nothing of Ussishkin. And all the time strange creatures in the image of human beings kept coming up to me, to ask me to explain whom I meant with the word "Tepel," and whom I had called "Yente," and whom I had referred to as "Gnessi." And had I used the word "Geese" to mean the Zionists? And lots more barbed questions like that. The whole crowd clapped wildly. And at the end they gave me a banquet, in my little hotel room. With sardines and sweet wine. No bread. And in the whole town no rolls, except two egg bagels. So we ate sardines and egg bagels, and washed it down with sweet wine. It wasn't very good. So they begged me to stay over for the Sabbath, and to speak again on Saturday night, after Sabbath's end. But I had a telegram from Charkov. Telling me that I must be in Charkov. And the train rattled and shook. So I can't write. So I cut it short. My greetings to your wife and children and the whole family. Sholom Aleichem."

The Herzl Memorial

When Dr. Theodor Herzl, the Zionist leader, died, plunging the whole Jewish world in mourning, Sholom Aleichem wrote a Herzl Memorial tribute, which was printed in Odessa as a pamphlet of forty-six pages. "Millions of Jews followed his funeral cortege, millions of Jews, almost the whole Jewish people . . . one of the greatest, the best and the most loved, the dearest of our people."

At the request of Dr. Bodenheimer, the director of the Jewish National Fund, Sholom Aleichem wrote a call for "A Monument for Herzl." The Herzl Forest.

Israel Zangwill

Though Sholom Aleichem was now fully occupied with his literary work and worried about his health and doing a lot of traveling, he retained his strong

Zionist feelings, continued with Zionist writings, and attended Zionist congresses, as a delegate or a guest. When he arrived in Galicia early in 1906, his old friend Moishe Kleinmann, who was then editor of the Lemberg "Togblatt," arranged a big welcome reception for him. The Zionist students also gave him a banquet. His family remained in Lemberg while he traveled the towns and shtetlach of Galicia, and after that of Roumania. From Roumania he planned to come to London. He wrote to Israel Zangwill from Galatz. In Yiddish, with Latin characters.

"Dear Colleague, forgive me for writing to you in my language. You can answer me in the same way, in your language. It would be a pity if I did not understand you. In brief, I am coming to London, and I am already flattered by the thought that I will be getting to know the great Zangwill."

Sholom Aleichem came to London, got to know Israel Zangwill, stayed a few days as his guest at his home in East Preston. There was a reception for him in London, with Zangwill in the chair. From London Sholom Aleichem went to Paris. While he was in London he had met the Zionist leaders, Joseph Cowen and Chaim Weizmann.

On 9 June 1906 Sholom Aleichem wrote to his friend Moishe Kleinmann in Lemberg: "Have traveled, or to put it better, have flown from Switzerland, and today I am back in London. So I use the opportunity to send you my warm friendly greetings, from me and from my whole republic to you."

"You surely see the London Jewish press. I also had two evenings in Paris. Splendid! London was a great occasion. Zangwill presided. I shall be staying another month in London."

Continuing his use of Zionist themes Sholom Aleichem published in "Dos Yiddishe Folk," a Zionist weekly started in 1906 in Vilna, "Chava, a new story about Tevya the Dairyman." In the summer of 1906 he wrote in Switzerland a Zionist play "David Ben David." It was written for the great Yiddish actor Jacob Adler in New York. But Adler found the play unsuitable for the stage, and it remained unpublished till recently, when the "Goldene Keit" published it in the year of Sholom Aleichem's centenary.

"The First Jewish Republic" is another Zionist-inspired Sholom Aleichem story (1909). It was printed in 1909 and reprinted in 1912. It is set in a supposed desert island, after a shipwreck, with thirteen Jews, survivors, trying to build a Jewish state, only to find themselves trapped by the old established inhabitants and deported. "What a great God we have, who has created such a big world, and no bit of earth, not a corner for His Chosen People!"

Zionist Congresses and Conferences

At the end of 1906 Sholom Aleichem went to America. He returned to Switzerland in the summer of 1907, when the Eighth Zionist Congress was held at The Hague, in Holland. The Zionist Organization of America appointed him its delegate to the congress. There he met several old friends, writers like Ravnitzky, Levinsky, and others, and there for the first time he met and became friends with Bialik.

After that Sholom Aleichem returned to Russia. When David Wolffsohn, Herzl's successor as the Zionist president, went to Russia with Nahum Sokolow, Sholom Aleichem spoke at the banquet given them in Vilna. In 1908 when Sholom Aleichem's twenty-five years in literature were being celebrated, the Zionists joined in the celebrations. Sokolow, then editor of the Zionist official organ, "Die Welt," wrote a very fine article about Sholom Aleichem. And some of Sholom Aleichem's writings appeared in the Zionist press throughout the world. Sholom Aleichem attended the Tenth Zionist Congress in 1911 in Basel and wrote it up in the Warsaw Yiddish daily, "Hajnt," in a series of articles under the title, "Marienbad."

Sholom Aleichem did not live to hear about the Balfour Declaration and to see the beginnings of the establishment of the Jewish National Home. He died in New York in 1916, at the age of fifty-nine.

The Western Wall

"So tell me, please, exactly how—you mean to say that you yourself, with your own eyes, have seen the Western Wall? That's what it's called? You really saw it? Please tell me, how and what and when!"

That's what I heard my rabbi plead with a Jew just returned from the Holy Land, from Eretz Israel, from Jerusalem. "Please tell me, describe it to me exactly, how and what and when!"

The Jew from Jerusalem described it to him exactly, how and what and when. My rabbi swallowed his words, rejoiced, swelled visibly, like a man getting greetings from someone near and dear to him in a far off land.

The rabbi watched his face, hung on his lips. He was so absorbed that he didn't notice us, one after the other, stealing out and sliding on the ice.

When we came back we found them sitting together. "The Western Wall!" our rabbi said to the Jew from Jerusalem, "the Western Wall! That's what is left to us of our entire Temple, our whole state! The Western Wall! The Western Wall!"

And our rabbi wept.

Selig Mechanic

1
He Prepares for the Road

"Zelda, my girl! I'm off! This very day! No excuses! Pack my things! Everything I'll be wanting on the journey. I'm going to Yehupetz for a few days. Get a move on, Zelda love! Time doesn't stand still. And Leizer is rushing me off my feet. He's got all his passengers ready to go. Only waiting for me! Be a good girl, Zelda! Hurry up! Please!"

That's how Selig, the tailor, or Selig Mechanic, as people call him in Mazepevke, burst into his home early one winter morning, returning from the market place. Zelda couldn't make out at first what he was saying. "The only thing, he must have had a drink with some of his pals in the tailors' guild. But no! Selig was as sober as you'd wish all drunkards to be!

"Listen to me, Zelda! We have a great God! A living God! A merciful God! He has had a good look round and he's come to realize that it's no way to be always at his poor little Jews. He has reached this conclusion—All right! says he. Bang your head on a soft pillow! You don't want to be bully-boyed down here. Then pack up and go back home, to your old Mother, Eretz Israel! Now, aren't I clever? Didn't I tell you Messiah is coming? Can't be anything else!"

At these words Zelda felt faint. She rejoiced, and she was frightened. Rejoiced, because it was such good news. Salvation was coming to the Jews. And frightened of the words "Messiah is coming." She had often heard those words from her husband. Messiah is coming? Good! But why today? It seemed to her too sudden. What would she do with her geese now? Hadn't she just bought a whole coopful? What would she do with them? Where would she put the plucked geese and the goose fat she had prepared for Pesach, and the goose feathers?

"Tell me," said Zelda. "He's already arrived? Or is he just setting out?"

"Oh? The ukase? It's already issued, and all arrangements made for us to put our names down now to go to Eretz Israel, in accordance with the regulations."

Zelda felt a stone lifted off her heart. She had no wish to question him again now—"What ukase? And what is it to do with her husband?" These things she always left to him. One of those things of no concern to her. She always hated interfering in his affairs with the higherups. Or with the affairs of his trade guild. "Those things are not for me!"

But she did venture one question: "The horses are waiting? Can't they wait till after the Sabbath?"

Selig folded his arms, standing like that in the middle of the room, shaking his head, in the way of one saying, "Argue with a woman!"

Zelda got his meaning immediately and busied herself packing his bag. Everything he would need. She only asked: "Be away long, Selig?"

"Didn't I tell you? A few days. Have I so much to do there? Just put my name on the register and get a ticket for the journey to Eretz Israel. That's all!"

She didn't dare to ask any more questions. Something about these things she had already heard from him, and for the rest, she left that to him. Though her husband treated her with respect, and she was the mistress in the house, in "such matters" he had the say. "If that's the way he wants it, he knows what it's about." In such things she left everything to his judgment.

2
He Hobnobs with the Young Men and Becomes a Chovev Zion

Not only Zelda, who is his wife, has this high regard for Selig. All the craftsmen in Mazepevke have. They look up to him as a man with brains. In his own circle he has the reputation of a scholar, a man who can read the small print and knows what is going on in the world. The people in his tailors' guild pay him respect, as he deserves. They like him. He has been for years the president of the Tailors' Synagogue. Though if you look into it further, the post is neither so exalted nor so enviable. Quite often, in the synagogue, mostly Simchas Torah, during Hakofes, during the procession with the Scrolls of the Law, Selig gets his face slapped. But a slap in the face is soon past, and the presidency will last. In the end Selig has the last word. He decides who goes where in the procession. So it's not surprising that he is looked up to with respect, and that they call him Reb Selig. Selig sets great store by that, for let's not fool ourselves—why shouldn't he? to tell the truth Selig didn't himself know the exact difference between Palestine and Eretz Israel. He had a sort of idea that they might be one and the same. He felt ashamed to go and ask those young men who read the newspapers. But in the end that's what he did. And he found that they really were the same. Palestine was indeed Eretz Israel, the Land of Israel, which had once been ours, and now belongs, for the time being, to the Turk, that Eretz Israel where we had once had our Kingdom and our Temple, of which we had been left only one wall, after the Temple was burned down, standing nearly two thousand years, that Eretz Israel which will one day be returned to us, with interest, in God's good time, when Messiah will come.

When Selig found that out, it made him very happy, and those young men, though they were not such religious Jews, gained favor in his eyes, and he was prepared to sacrifice himself for their sake and stand day and night listening to what they told out of the newspapers.

3

Selig Carries the Idea Deep in His Heart and No One Wants to Understand Him

"Cabbage" is a term common among tailors. It means pieces of cloth left after the shears have done their work. What Selig knew about Palestine was no more than a kind of cabbage, bits and pieces of the tales he had heard told in the Beth Hamedrash. Nothing definite, nothing firm. For the reports that came from the outside world to Mazepevke were so twisted and distorted that one conflicted with the other. Everyone had his own story. One said that in all right and proper towns they had formed societies for "Yishuv Eretz Israel." These Yishuv Eretz Israel societies were making money grants, registering everybody's name who wanted to go "out there" to work on the land, and providing funds for the costs to take you all the way there.

Somebody else said they were taking only craftsmen. No others. That started a row. Why only craftsmen? Eretz Israel isn't America. America is a foreign country. But Eretz Israel is ours, our own. Did you ever hear such a thing?

Just at that time luck brought along Baron de Hirsch with his fifty millions!

It was so ordained that Jews should be caught up in a new quarrel, more troubles for Mazepevke. The people in the Beth Hamedrash soon split up in two camps. One said here. The other said Eretz Israel. One wanted schools for general education. Others wanted Talmud Torahs. And there were voices demanding fair shares. Divide up the money among the lot. They forgot that the Baron also had a say in the matter. Luckily the millions existed only in the newspapers. Everybody screamed and shouted, and in the end they were left fooled.

That was in Mazepevke. But in Yehupetz—so Selig had heard—they already had a Society Yishuv Eretz Israel—a hundred members. Others said two hundred. They were only waiting for things to be confirmed. As soon as the confirmation arrived they would buy land in Eretz Israel and put their names down to go there.

"You see," Selig said one day to Zelda, "Yehupetz is a town! A proper town. But Mazepevke—can anything ever happen here? It's a dead end! Sodom and Gomorrah! It should be burned down!"

Zelda's answer was, "You've got nothing else to do but to carry the whole world on your shoulders."

"Go on with you, woman! Let's consider the whole thing. All-around—our own bit of land, over there, in the Homeland. Can you see it? Our own garden. Cabbages, garlic, cucumbers, our own fig tree. Camels. And mules! Zelda, my dear! Summer holidays! People going out into the fields, singing Jewish songs, bringing in the corn and the ripe fruit, to Jerusalem! Aren't you a little fool! Bringing it all to the High Priest, for his blessing!"

"Yes," says Zelda. "That's all very well! But must you give yourself to it more than all the other tailors in the town?"

"Long hair, short on brains! Talk to a woman!"

Another time Selig said to Zelda, as he sat over a job of work: "If I had the money now I'd make the journey for a few days to Yehupetz."

"That's a good one! You'd be poking around, here and there, with no idea what it's all about!"

"Don't be silly! About that matter—."

"Yes, I know. About the Messiah. I have already got a hole in my head hearing about your Messiah! By my life! If he's coming he'd better make it quick. Otherwise he'd better stay where he is!"

"Zelda! Zelda! We are talking about Yishuv Eretz Israel, and you go on about the Messiah! You really are a little donkey, Zelda!" said Selig with a dismissing wave of the hand. There was nobody, he reflected, he could talk to! Nobody to understand him! Not even his own wife! Even she didn't want to know where it hurt him. Deep in his heart he carried the holy idea, after listening to all the discussions, all the talk about it, especially with those young men who read the newspapers.

4
He Becomes a Man of Hope

Those young men who read the newspapers didn't behave properly to Selig, the tailor. Not the way young gentlemen, Maskilim, should. Selig's intervention in their discussions seemed to them stupid. Absurd, silly. They laughed at him, fit to split their sides. "Eh, Reb Selig," they said to him when he was questioning them not always very straight to the point, "Eh, Reb Selig—leave it to your enemies to do the talking. Better for your health to keep quiet."

These young men who kept saying, "The People! The People!" seemed to have forgotten that Selig, the tailor, was one of the people, the people whom they invoked at every opportunity, the people they were so concerned about, about whose plight they wrote so eloquently and elegantly in their newspapers, these Mazepevke Maskilim. They were so devoted to "The People," worrying about their welfare, from a distance, with a joke about it all, making fun of the whole thing.

"The People," meaning Selig, the tailor, made nothing of it. He took their laughing and jeering good-naturedly. "Let them laugh! As long as something is being done. As long as they have that in mind. As long as something comes of it."

And that something was really being done was clear to Selig from all that he had heard the young men discussing after reading their newspapers. They said it was not only in the big towns like Chmielnick, Gontiarsk, Guilolopiaterke, and Tetrogetz, but even in small places like Yampele, Makerevka, and Strisht (imagine a forsaken hole like Strisht!) that they already had societies for Yishuv Eretz Israel. There was only one thing he couldn't make out—could outsiders also put down their names for Yishuv Eretz Israel, or not? If they could, he would put his name down immediately, together with his whole household, with his two poor brothers and his sisters and several other tailor families with whom he had already discussed the matter, and it seemed likely that they would join him, if only they were helped with enough money for the journey to take them there. Selig tried several times to discover from these young men how it could be arranged, throwing in a casual word, by the way.

"About what you say regarding Yishuv Eretz Israel. There's word going round in the guild. There's no work just now. We've got no money. Poor as can be. So the guild members ask—'Reb Selig! When and how?' They want to put their names down for Yishuv Eretz Israel. They want to know from me whether there's something in the idea, or it's just a dream."

And Reb Selig's eyes were fixed hungrily on these young men. Trying to read from their faces what was nagging him. He didn't miss any change of expression. He was waiting to hear something good for the people, and they fobbed him off with next to nothing. These things, they told him, must not be talked about openly, must not be written about in the papers, not yet. You have to wait for the confirmation. When the confirmation comes, we'll know what to do. Meanwhile it's a matter of waiting, like waiting for the Messiah. The only thing to do is to pray for the confirmation. "Please God, help us that the confirmation should come soon."

Selig repeated that prayer in the tailors' synagogue, among a ring of people.

And the people of the tailors' guild placed their trust in Selig's words. "If Selig Mechanic says so he knows what he's saying." Their minds were made up. They had faith in Selig, and when the time came everything would come right. God would have mercy on his poor Jews, for it was high time for salvation to come to the Jews!

Meanwhile, like poor sheep when a disaster hits them, they huddled together, one against the other, seeking help from themselves. So these poor Jews, sad and disconsolate, without any proper livelihood, met together every evening in the synagogue, with mouth and ears wide open, listening to the lovely stories about Jews who had been saved and comforted and that salvation was coming also for them.

5
There is Much He Finds Obscure and Confusing

One thing Selig Mechanic couldn't understand on any account, and it gave him no peace. "How is it that the rich Jews are keeping quiet?" Surely, if a rich man like Reb Michael Melech Michols, for instance, wanted to, they could, he and Mottel Moshe Myers and some others like that, buy up the whole of Eretz Israel with the Turks and everything that goes with it. Selik had made it his business to stand near several times and overhear what these rich men talk about when they get together in the Beth Hamedrash. He had listened to them talk about this and that, one thing and another, about Yehupetz and Boiberik, everything in the world, but never a word about Yishuv Eretz Israel. Not a word! And if the young men tried sometimes to start a conversation with them about it, they listened with half an ear, blinked their eyes, combed their fingers through their beards, shaking their heads, and said not a word that would answer his question, as though it didn't concern them. But it was very much the concern of poor Jews, humiliated, downtrodden, unhappy souls praying for the Deliverer, the Redeemer, to come and release them from their misery. How to explain this silence of theirs?

That thought kept nagging Selig. Those rich men of Mazeppevke. If he, Selig, had an approach to Reb Michael Melech Michols, he would make an issue of it. He would put the whole question before him, fair and square. After all, what difference would it make to a man as rich as he was to put half his fortune on the table—half and half, and say—"Here you are, brothers! Let me earn eternal life, my reward in paradise!"

"If I were in Reb Michael Melech Michols's place," Selig told himself as he sat at his work, "if I had his money, I'd soon know what to do with it. The beginning of wisdom—."

"Go through your pockets, Selig. You may still find a couple of copper coins. Or will you? We've got to get fuel for the stove, and we haven't the money."

Of course, just then his wife Zelda was sure to come in and disturb his thoughts.

"Yes, Zelda dear! You always come along with your needs and wants. One groshen and another groshen. Only a groshen!"

"Yes, I know, Zelda. We've got to get this, and we've got to get that!"

"We've got to get potatoes to put in the pot for supper, haven't we? How am I to get them?"

"Always the stomach, Zelda! You want the worms to have plenty when our turn comes!"

"At it again! It's always the same! It's either the Messiah or the worms!"

"You might at least say L'Havdil, you silly goose!" And this time Selig is annoyed. Zelda flounces out of the room, and Selig returns to his thoughts, all sorts of plans, all the things he would do if he had the money, how pleased everybody would be with what he was doing, God and man. But Heaven had ordained things so that the money should be with Reb Michael Melech Michols, and he, Selig Mechanic, should be a poor tailor, going cold and hungry with his wife and children, God forgive me for such talk! A Jew must accept everything with good grace, for it is all but a trial—God trying us, whether we can withstand our troubles or not. So we must hope for a better time coming, in God's own good time.

And with such thoughts a tear stole down Selig's face and dropped on his middle finger, which was working the needle in and out. Selig swayed to and

fro over his work, humming a tune, and his thoughts carried him far away—
over there, over there.

6
Selig Travels with the Rich in the Same Coach and Makes an Error in His Calculations

Traveling in the same coach with the rich men of Mazeppevke was no easy matter for Selig. Sitting in Leizer's coach he thought to himself—nothing to do. Plenty of time. Thirty-six hours on the journey. No business. A clear head. So how to avoid talking about present day Jewish troubles and getting finally to the subject of Yishuv Eretz Israel. Especially now, when we already have the confirmation—.

Selig happened to be sitting on the box seat, with his back to the driver, just facing Reb Michael Melech Michols. There were some other fine rich men in the coach, but compared with Reb Michael Melech Michols they were like small tallow dips against a big seven-branched menorah. Everybody had moved closer to make more room for him, to make him more comfortable. Watching every flicker on his face, to read what was in his mind. And most of all Mottel Moshe Myers, a young man of much wealth. Whatever Reb Michael said Mottel responded:

"Yes, true! Absolutely true! Sure as I'm alive!"

The subject of the talk in the coach was completely above Selig's head. They were discussing corn, wheat, timber, milk, sugar, spirits, exchange rates.

"Nothing I understand! Might be talking Turkish for all I know! What a to-do! Like a fair in heaven!"

Every time Reb Michael said anything witty, everybody laughed, Mottel Moshe Myers louder than the rest.

"They may well laugh, those rich folk," Selig said to himself. "They don't have to go short of anything! They can laugh! Well fed, satisfied, with fur collars on their coats. Well stocked larders at home—flour and everything you need, plenty of wood for the fire. So why should they worry about Yishuv Eretz Israel? Not like us poor devils!"

Thinking like this Selig reminded himself that he had left Zelda at home without one copper coin. The three groshen coin, all there was, he had taken himself, and here it was going on Thursday, with the Sabbath to prepare for. They had a big unpaid bill in the grocery shop. There was no straw in the house. And the frost showed no sign of abating, though it was more than time— with Passover on the doorstep. Pesach! Sholom Aleichem, Uncle Pesach! Nice how d'you do, isn't it!"

As the coach traveled on, Selig's sadness grew. The dark outside was closing in. The sun was setting between the clouds that looked like dirty rags in the grey sky. The wind whistled in Selig's ears, stole under his collar. Selig put up his collar and rubbed his ears with both hands. And these young men in the coach laugh as though everything was just fine.

"Time for Mincha!" said Reb Michael Melech Michols, yawning.

"You're right! True as I'm alive!" put in Mottel Moshe Myers, also yawning, and he started saying the Mincha prayers, softly, under his breath. Selig joined in with a will, sitting down and swaying to and fro, easing his joints and warming himself with the movement. He stood up for the Shemono Esra, keeping his eyes closed and repeating the words with great fervor in his usual way. He rolled the words lovingly on his tongue—"And to Jerusalem, thy city, return in mercy and dwell there." "Yes, in mercy return and dwell there! Speedily, dear God, Lord God, merciful Father!"

Bits of cloud spread over the whole expanse of sky. It was getting warmer out there. "The thaw has started!" Leizer, the coach driver, calls across to Selig, as though he feels the news would please him most. But Selig did not respond. He was straining his ears to hear the rich young men in the coach talking about Jewish troubles, about Jewish poverty.

"There!" says Selig to himself. "Never underrate a Jewish heart! These men really mean it. It worries them. You'll see, Reb Michael will soon jump to his feet and call out—'Why don't we do something about it! What's stopping us? Where's the difficulty? Money? We've got enough money! Let's only get the people who want to go there!"

But Selig was wrong. Reb Michael Melech Michols did nothing of the kind. True, he did at first heave a deep sigh because of the troubles of Israel. But the next moment he was back to his money. "The best cure, I tell you, Reb Mottel, is money. What do you say, eh Mottel?"

"Right! You're absolutely right! Sure as I'm alive!"

"Yes," Reb Michael went on, "Money will buy anything! Isn't that so, Mottel?"

"You're right! Absolutely right!"

And after that the travelers in the coach went back to talking about corn and wheat and timber, milk and sugar and spirits and all sorts of affairs.

7
He Dreams Strange Dreams and Arrives

The jolting of the coach over the frozen ground and the talk of the passengers in the coach sent Selig off to sleep, and he dreamed all sorts of strange dreams—Yishuv Eretz Israel, vineyards and olive trees, oranges and pomegranates and figs. Jews with fine beards and satin caftans riding on camels and mules, young men and girls beautifully dressed, dancing, and Reb Michael and Mottel standing some distance away, looking on enviously. Their dress torn and tattered, their boots twisted out of shape. He felt like going up to them and feeling sorry for these poor rich men. Then a sudden knock on the head woke him. Leizer was talking to him. "It does send you off to sleep, this talk, doesn't it, Selig?"

Selig pulled his hat over his ears and went back to sleep. Another dream. A huge crowd of people, like an army of locusts, blotting out the light of day. Jews running, in flight. And behind the Jews an immense mass of moneyed men. And Selig himself flinging open his coat and running to catch up with the rest. Where to? No questioning! Everybody's running, so he's running too. He recognizes lots of people he knows among the runners, friends of his, tailors like himself, with shears and irons, with wife and children, with bedding and linen and household goods. He could swear that one of them is Michael Melech Michols himself. He turns his head to look more closely and gets another knock on the head. "Please, Reb Selig! Please move an inch or two. Or you'll knock a hole in my head, shaking to and fro the way you do!"

That's Leizer again, shaking him awake.

"Tell you what, Reb Selig! The best way to keep yourself from going to sleep is to walk a bit. Get out of the coach and walk behind it. That'll keep you awake. I'll come with you. The road here is mostly uphill, and the horses know the way."

So Leizer, the coachman, and Selig Mechanic got out and walked for a while behind the coach, one on each side. The horses swishing their tails and pulling the coach uphill, to the accompaniment of heavy snoring from inside.

"How they do snore, my passengers, bless them!" said Leizer to Selig. "Fast asleep, as though they were at home in their own beds. What rich people can allow themselves! I've been a coachman for more than thirty years! Thirty, did I say? Nearer forty. And I've traveled a good part of the world by now. The length and the breadth of it! I've lived under all sorts of conditions! Been burned down twice. Married off my children. And what I tell you, with more than thirty years of coachman's experience, is this: 'Pawn your trousers if you want, but stay rich!'"

With a rush and a roar Leizer's coach drove into Yehupetz the next day, a little late in the day. After midday. All the passengers got out, one by one—one here, one there. Only Selig Mechanic stayed in the coach, not knowing where to go. He found it strange that he couldn't tell even Leizer, the coachman, where he wanted to be dropped.

"What was it you came here for?" Leizer asked Selig. "A tailoring job?"

"Yes," Selik echoed dispiritedly.

"Nothing to be ashamed of," said Leizer. "A job of work to do! Why not? A man's got to make his living! No crime in that! Stealing is a crime!"

And that ended their conversation. Selig took the loaf of bread and two onions he had brought in his Tallis and Tephilin bag and bit into them. After that he went out into the town to look for a Yishuv Israel society.

8
After Many Attempts He Does at Last Find a Society for Eretz Israel

"If I were a man with a pen," Selig told people afterwards, "I would write up the whole story of what I went through in Yehupetz before I got to the local Society for Yishuv Israel. People I stopped in the street looked at me strangely. They couldn't understand what I was talking about."

The Yehupetz Jews seemed to him absolutely mad, running around all day the way they did, busy with their affairs in a way Selig had never seen people so busy before. They either didn't answer his questions, just turned away and walked off, or they stopped, listened, shrugged their shoulder, as if to say—"Ask me something easier!"

He tried it another way. "Where's the synagogue here?" And the people answered, "Not round this way. No synagogue here!"

How was that possible? A town full of people and no synagogue! "Yes," they answered with a smile, "you may well ask!" And with that they hurried off, as much as to say, "Don't bother us with your stupid questions!"

Selig realized that asking a sensible question in a sensible way wouldn't get him anywhere. So he stopped a man in the street, put his question, and the man thoughtfully scratching his beard, said, "Yishuv Eretz Israel? You must mean the crowd that meets to listen to the Magidim? Those who want to improve the world? What do you want them for? What business have you with them? Get out of my way, Reb Jew! We are not allowed to discuss these things out in the street. Look, there's a policeman coming now! It's forbidden to stand about in the street."

"Mad!" said Selig to himself. "Absolutely mad! A town full of Jews, and they haven't got a synagogue!"

So Selig kept stopping one man after another and got no help from any of them. Everybody told him to try somewhere else. One or two gave him an address where he might try. But he had no luck there either. Either the man wasn't home yet, or he was having his midday meal. Or he was on his way back to the office after his meal. He had just got his bank statement, and he was worried about it. Timber had taken a bad knock. His customers were not paying their bills. Or else the man's wife was in bed ill. Or the children were down with the measles.

Or there was the man who told him to come inside—quickly. People were not supposed to stand talking in the doorway. "What do you want? Is it about that forest? For lumber?"

But this time Selig wouldn't go away. "I must talk to you. About something very important. I wouldn't have come all this way if it wasn't important. Let me come in, and I'll explain."

"All right then! Come in! Let's hear what you have to say!" And the man showed him into the parlor, a big room, beautifully furnished. "So they're sending you on your travels, eh? Not enough having you sit in the office, sending out letters to us! You have to come knocking at the doors? Your people don't care about our difficulties! How we can make ends meet! You have to come into our houses and lift the money out of our pockets! Is that the way to behave! It's scandalous! Come on now, tell me what you want! How much!"

"I'm sorry," said Selig, "but I don't know what you are talking about. I haven't come to you for any money! Not a copper coin!"

"Then what have you come for? To look at my face? To give me your bless-ing?"

"No! Nothing like that! It's about the confirmation! If it wasn't for the confirmation, I would never have come here! I thought to myself—there's a coach going, and I know the coachman. The fare isn't much. All this talk about the Society for Yishuv Israel. So I decided to take a day off and come here and look into it. What do I get for that? You go for me, about money I never asked you for!"

"So you haven't come about that timber deal? Your name isn't Alter?"

"No! My name is not Alter! Selig is my name. I come from Mazeppevke. I've come here to find out about your Society for Yishuv Eretz Israel. I want to put my name down to go there. My family, and several other families of craftsmen, like me."

"Then why didn't you say so?"

"You didn't give me a chance! You kept shouting at me all the time. So I waited till you stopped shouting. What I wanted to ask you is this: There are several craftsmen's families who want to go to Palestine. We want to make our application through you. Please put us on the register. Put our names down for working on the land.

But the man was no longer listening to Selig. He was shouting and storming at his servant for having shown Selig into the house. When he quieted down a bit he wrote down for Selig the address of the chairman of the Society.

"That's where you should go," he said. "That's the man who can tell you all about it. Believe me, I can't do a thing. I'm a sick man! Leave me alone!"

So it was not till late in the evening, after Maariv, that Selig found himself at last in the presence of the big man, the chairman of the Society, spoke to him in his study, and got to know more about it.

9
Selig Has a Long Talk with the Right Man

But the right man was by no means as important and impressive looking as Selig had imagined him. He was a clean-shaven youngish man with no sign of a big boss about him. Some leader for Yishuv Eretz Israel! Selig thought to himself. And to the "big leader" he said: "So you're the head man here of the Society for Yishuv Israel? I'm from Mazeppevke. I've just come from there. People in Mazeppevke are talking a lot about the Society. They say that you keep the register, with all the names in it, all the tickets issued to everybody who wants to make the journey to Eretz Israel. So I've come to you to ask you to register me and my household and several other households as well, craftsmen families like my own."

"All right, Reb Jew!" the man said to Selig, looking him up and down. "Please sit down! What is your name?"

"Me? You want to know what they call me?"

"Yes, you!"

"They call me Selig Mechanic! That is to say, my name is Selig. And my work is tailoring. We've got plenty of tailors in Mazepevke. More than enough! I wish there were enough work to do as there are people to do the work. It's a question of making a living. Things are slack just now. We envy the man round the corner who's got a steady job to go to."

"No! That isn't what I asked your name for, Mr. Selig. What I wanted to say is that you are not the first to come here to put down your name on the register for Yishuv Eretz Israel. We get people here from all the small towns, ten, twenty a day. True enough, times are bitter bad now. Jews are terribly poor. So they turn to anything that comes up. Perhaps—"

"But they say you give—"

"That we give money. Our Society has no money to give. At least not yet! And if there would be any money there are plenty of poor people here at home."

Selig tugged at his little beard and said: "Forgive me for asking! But what has your Society got if it has no money?"

"Signatures! Just now we are collecting signatures, holding meetings, getting together, discussing things. And in time we'll have money, too. When we have a good deal of money collected, I mean donations from each of the people registering, then we'll know what to do. That's what we've got a committee for!"

That answer made Selig feel quite confused. He couldn't understand this business of collecting signatures. What did they want signatures for?

"Yes, that's what I've been wanting to ask you. What's all this about signatures? You mean the people who want to go to Eretz Israel, over there?" And Selig stretched out his arm to point the way there—all that distance.

"No, Reb Selig! You're wrong. The names of those who have some knowledge of things to do with Yishuv Israel, people who want to help us in some way, here on the spot. Each one in his way. With his own work. With proper guidance. The right way. Those are our signatories. They come to our meetings when we call them. It's a bit of a Mitzvah!"

One wouldn't say that Selig was exactly elated by this answer. He had a lot more questions on the same lines to ask, lots more! But it seemed too much to burden a stranger, a man he saw for the first time, with all the questions they kept directing at the Mazepevke Maskilim, and their unsatisfactory answers. Especially when the man was treating him like a gentleman, answering the questions he put to him courteously, civilly. Yet he couldn't resist putting one more question to him.

"Forgive me worrying you with my stupid questions. In our town, Mazepevke, nobody knows the answer. How much money do we have to put down, all round, if we want to buy all Eretz Israel? How much does each man need for his share? How much?"

"The first thing we need," came the answer, "is that Jews shouldn't ask such questions, shouldn't busy themselves with calculations like that. I've alreay told you that we don't distribute any money. We collect money. We must first be sure that those colonies that already exist and look for our help are secure. That is our first consideration. When we've done that, we'll go on to our next job, making calculations. What we have to do next. Meanwhile we need money. Every Jew must contribute, as much as he can, each according to his means. So that each should have a share in the colonies, that everyone should be a partner in carrying out the sacred ideal of Yishuv Eretz Israel, which will not be realized in a year or in ten years. That when a Jew gives a rouble, he shouldn't think he is going into a business which will bring him profits. He doesn't do anything more than give a donation for a particular object, but for a common purpose, for his children and his children's children. Now do you understand me, my friend?"

10
Selig Gives a Donation and Goes Home Rejoicing

By his silence Selig showed that he needed no more explanations. He had gotten the hang of it. Only one thing still worried him. Why must it take so long? All right, whatever the consequences there was one question he must still ask. So here it is.

"You say all Jews should contribute. That's what you say. All Jews! Very well! Here is my contribution! A three bit. If every Jew gave a three bit would that do it?"

"Look, Reb Selig," the other said with some asperity, rising from his seat, "that's a story without an end. I'll argue, you'll argue, everyone will argue, all of us will put our arguments, and that's where it'll stop. Good night to you! Have a safe journey back! My greetings to everybody there!"

So Selig got up from his chair, buttoning up his capote, at the same time getting out his wallet and producing a creased three bit note, the only one there, and passing it with both hands.

"I didn't come here just for a chat," Selig said. "I really mean it. With all my heart. I want to have a share in a Mitzvah like this. I'm not a rich man. I can't afford much. That's all I can manage."

The big man of the Yehupetz Society stood still in the middle of the room with the three bit note in his hand. Reb Selig's last words had completely confused him. Had shown him that a poor little Mazepevke tailor could respond more readily than a rich man in Yehupetz.

"Look here, Reb Selig," he said. "I'm taking your note and I'll give you a receipt. But I must repeat what I said before—don't think we are going to allocate land with it in Israel, as folk in Mazepevke seem to expect."

"God forbid!" said Selig.

"I don't want you to think, Reb Selig, that things like this are done as quickly as talk about them."

"So we've had a talk. And we're not out in the rain."

"I would like you, Reb Selig, to tell the people in Mazepevke that we've taken your money as an advance. It's a big undertaking."

"What a man you are!" said Selig. "Do you think we don't know that! As though we had no brains!"

And with his face beaming Selig pocketed the receipt, pushing it deep down in his wallet. And into his capote. And off he went happily out into the world of coachmen, to spend the night in the coachmen's shelter.

"Judging by your face, Reb Selig, you've struck lucky in Yehupetz. A good business deal, eh? The only trouble with Yehupetz is that they won't let more poor Jews stay in their town. As soon as night falls they boot us out. May they be paid out for it!"

Thus said Leizer, the coachman, sitting on his box seat, talking things over with Reb Selig, on their return journey to Mazepevke, his eyes on Reb Selig's beaming face, suggesting to all and sundry that he must really have struck a good bargain in Yehupetz.

This time Reb Selig was not sitting on the box seat, squeezed in against Reb Leizer, the driver, but comfortably at ease inside the coach, feeling in his own mind better off, richer than even Reb Michael Melech Michols. He felt for the wallet in his capote, where he had deposited his receipt for the three bit note, which would find its way to Eretz Israel. A long time since a note like that had achieved such a good stroke of business as this with the Society for Yishuv Eretz Israel. He had certainly achieved something in Yehupetz. And so discussing things with Leizer on his box seat, talking about this and that, Reb Selig slipped off into a comfortable sleep, dreaming about the Land of Israel, about the colonies and the colonists, vineyards, camels and mules, fig trees and olive trees, about the other side of the Jordan, a new world, a world of prosperous Jewish farmers, and he, Reb Selig, one of them. He could swear he heard one of them speaking now, Reb Michael Melech Michols's voice:

"Who is this new farmer, sprawling comfortably full length in the coach?"

"Over there? Why, that's Selig!"

"Selig who?"

"Selig Mechanic of Mazepevke!"

The Jewish Congress in Basel

Be proud, my children, let your light shine far and wide
Upon the sacred name that was in olden times your
pride,
It was your glory before God and man.
Guard and protect your honor, on your throne,
The dear and precious name of Zion.

—Frug

This year, in the month of Elul, a Jewish congress was held in Basel, Switzerland, a gathering to which delegates came from every corner of the world; from Europe, Asia, Africa. From America came great men, Jewish professors, doctors, lawyers, and also rabbis, as well as just fine cultured people. They came together and devoted themselves to Jews and Jewish affairs. They discussed and considered our position in different countries, tried to find ways and means to help our poor brothers and sisters who have been for so long pulling the heavy cart of our Exile. They talk about important matters and adopted statutes, with which you will be made acquainted presently.

You will ask: Why suddenly in the midst of everything a Jewish Congress? Who called this congress? I must explain it all to you in the proper way. Our brothers abroad dreamed a sweet dream. After the great troubles and persecutions that Jews suffered over there for centuries, when the bright light of liberty, Haskalah, and humanity shone over the whole world, Jews too would have to enjoy the same privilege among the nations, and the Jews did receive all these rights—on paper. It means that they were notified that they are now equal with all people.

There was joy and jubilation. A light had dawned for the Jews. Rejoicing. Great rejoicing. And as usual with Jews, when they are let off the leash for a while, they became puffed up with pride, thinking that they really and in fact had become equals with everybody else, from tip to toe, till something like this happened: The nations had second thoughts and repented the marriage bond into which they had entered, and the Jew grew to be a bogeyman in their eyes. As once before, in the time of King Ahasuerus, another Haman arose and proclaimed that the Jews must be destroyed. Other Hamans rose up in other places—a Stoeker, a Drumont, a Lueger, who spread lies about Jews and called themselves anti-Semites. There is this People among us, they said. They are wiser than we are, and stronger. More able. If we don't get rid of them, if we don't drive them out from here, they'll make an end of us.

So they took to persecuting us, hunting us on all the roads and byways, deprived us of our livelihoods, incited everywhere against us, throwing stones, smashing our windows, and enforcing all sorts of hostile ordinances. It brought panic, as always among Jews when they get knocked about and hurt. They always remind themselves at such times of the ancient Jewish God, the ancient Jewish Torah, and the ancient Jewish land—Eretz Israel, the Land of Israel.

What shall I tell you? Our brothers abroad woke from their sweet dream. There was an upheaval. Lords and professors, doctors and lawyers, students of all sorts beat a retreat—back to the ancient Jewish God, to the ancient Jewish People, to the Jewish land, to Zion! And a new organization was formed—Zionists.

There is a man in this Zionist Organization named Doctor Theodor Herzl from Vienna. Dr. Herzl is a young man, thirty-seven years old, one of the outstanding German writers, one of the editors of the leading newspaper in Vienna, "Neue Freie Presse," a man of culture, a true aristocrat, an orator and a diplomat, and a man of wealth as well. At first Dr. Herzl was little interested in Jews, till the anti-Semites started digging under us. Then he came to see that things were really bad for the Jews, and he took to thinking about it. Two years ago he published his book, *Der Judenstaat* where he shows, proof positive, that Jews can and should set up a state in Eretz Israel. This book caused a sensation among Jews and Christians, and it made Dr. Herzl world famous.

A year ago Dr. Herzl was in Constantinople, discussing Eretz Israel and the Jews with the Grand Vizier. He showed him how useful Jews could be in all directions to Turkey. The Grand Vizier presented Dr. Herzl to the sultan, who conferred an order on him. This summer Dr. Herzl started issuing a paper for the Zionists, "Die Welt," and on Rosh Hashona Eve he convoked the First Jewish Congress in Basel. He put forward his plan how to go about things, and what should be done to realize the exalted idea of the Zionists to bring about the good of the Jewish People. This First Jewish World Congress has been written up in all the most important Russian and foreign newspapers, so that it is only right to put it forward also in our poor Yiddish language, for our people, in Jargon.

Here is what we are told about this congress by one of those who was there, one of the two hundred delegates, our highly respected Dr. Mandelstamm, who read to us the other day in Kiev the very fine paper he had composed about the congress.

Dr. Mandelstamm's paper begins:
    When I took my seat in the train going to Basel, I was, to tell the truth, deeply apprehensive. I went to the Congress with a heavy heart. Not because I had doubts about the aim of the Zionists. Not because I had no faith in the idea of Yishuv Eretz Israel, like those Smart-Alecks of ours who make fun of it and say that settling Jews in Eretz Israel is as feasible as trying to

settle Jews on the moon. No! My heart was heavy because I knew how hard and bitter was the plight of my brothers here, where they find themselves in larger numbers than anywhere else. On one side paupers—poor devils! Down and outs, beggars, sunk in misery, so full of daily cares and troubles that they have no mind left for big ideas and big hopes. They have grown apathetic, have stopped thinking, no longer feeling their poverty. On the other side a considerable class of wealthy Jews who don't want to look and who say they are doing quite enough by maintaining our own poor here where we are, at home.

Then we have another class of Jews who call themselves Maskilim, intellectuals. The educated, cultured people, who draw knowledge and wisdom from all the foreign wells, but not from our own Jewish well. They know the history of every foreign nation, but not our own Jewish history. Not our own Jewish literature. These are our assimilationists, who want to merge and melt with the nations, hug and kiss them, though they are told to "Wait! What's the hurry?" That, I said to myself, is the kind of material our People is made of, poor material to build a house with. Hard to carry out such a lofty idea with such people. It needs an immense effort. The right people! And where are we to find them?

Those were my thoughts as I traveled to Basel. And now I am back from Basel, I can tell you, brothers, I have no regrets that I went to the congress. On the contrary, I am sorry you didn't all travel with me to Basel. Because had you been there I would have seen straightaway that "Jacob is not dead," that there are still Jews among us who are good, honest, decent folk, truly cultivated, with good Jewish hearts, prepared to sacrifice themselves for All-Israel. I saw it clearly, I tell you, And my hopes grew bright.

I arrived in Basel at night. The next morning I went to the Casino. This is a hall belonging to the town, where the congress was to meet. The town had the flags out, posters in the streets pointing out the place where the Zionist Congress was to meet. Entering the hall I saw a very interesting picture: several groups of people in their Sabbath best. One wore a frock coat and white tie, another in a long Hasidic capote and a velvet skull cap. A third was dressed like a Turk. All of them, of course, were Jews, from different countries. Except for half a dozen Christians interested in the idea, of whom more anon. And there was something in the faces of all these Jews that is difficult to describe; it can't be conveyed in words.

The gallery, too, was packed with people, men and women, people who live in Basel, and Jews from outside, who had come to the congress. There was a long table to the right where the journalists reporting the congress would sit. Facing the door was a platform, for the presidium. At nine o'clock Dr. Herzl, the president, arrived, with Dr. Max Nordau, the vice-president, and several others who would be speaking. The audience was already seated. There was complete silence.

The first speaker was Dr. Karl Lippe, from Jassy, the oldest Zionist, who opened the congress and proposed sending a telegram of thanks to the sultan for his friendship to the Jews of his country. Next Dr. Herzl. "Honored assembly," he began. "as one of the conveners of this congress it is my privilege to welcome you here. All in all we have only three days in which we have much work to do. We are going to erect a great building here, and it has fallen to us to lay the first stone."

"In the first place," Herzl went on, "we shall acquaint ourselves with the condition of our brothers in all countries. It is not a happy condition. The nineteenth century which has achieved so much in discovery and invention could not achieve the miracle that the damnable Jewish Question should at last be wiped out, that people should stop busying themselves with the Jews, the question of anti-Semitism, which means hating Jews, now just when we had started considering ourselves human beings, on a par with others in this world. Anti-Semitism has driven us back home, back to Zion. Zionism means returning to the Jewish people before we return to the Jewish land. Zionism has produced a miracle here. It has bound together all Jews in all countries, of all classes. That alone is proof, if proof is still needed, that Jews are a People, are a nation. That is why our congress should devote itself first of all with raising our national spirit, that we should no longer be ashamed of being Jews, that we should hold our heads high, raising our Jewish flag.

"Fifteen years earlier," Herzl continued, "the Chovevei Zion already gave their attention to this matter of Yishuv Eretz Israel. They founded colonies in Palestine. It was a start. Our approach though is different. We don't want to slink into Eretz Israel. We want to go there openly, by arrangement with the Sultan, showing him how our settling in Palestine is of benefit to the country and the state, both with money and with learning, with Haskalah, as well as in other ways. That brings us to the point that this is a matter that must be spoken about openly, without concealment, as an undertaking treated seriously by all nations and states, with us as fully responsible people, speaking and behaving openly and frankly, without fear, for in this regard we must realize that in some countries the Jewish Question is indeed a real misfortune to the countries concerned, who would gladly get rid of it themselves.

"We don't mean transporting all Jews at one go, out of Europe to Palestine. Only allow us to settle freely in the Land of Zion, and anti-Semitism will disappear also in other countries, and the Jewish Question will be at an end also in other countries. What should interest us here is not the fact that the number of Jews outside keeps decreasing, but that the number of Jews in Eretz Israel is increasing. When that happens it will be better for us everywhere.

"Zionism is something that no one can have anything against. On the contrary, both our friends and our enemies should help us, should sympathize with us, feel with us. What one man wants can easily be washed out, made to naught. But when there are thousands who want it, millions, a whole nation—that you can't push aside. We must keep together, united, not working at cross-purposes, one in this direction, and the other in the opposite, our Zionist Congress should be our permanent center, our rallying point. We need to come together so as to realize our national idea, to carry our ideal into effect.

"Now we are in Basel. Where will we be a year from now?"

Dr. Mandelstamm's account notes that Theodor Herzl's speech aroused a great deal of enthusiasm and brought lots of applause, and goes on to describe the next speaker, Dr. Max Nordau, the vice-president.

Who is Dr. Max Nordau? He has come from Paris, and he is one of the most famous writers in Europe. His books are translated into almost every language, and they bring him countless honors and big sales and royalties. His ancestors came from Spain, refugees from the Inquisition. He is the son of a rabbi. Till a short while ago the world didn't know that this famous Nordau was a Jew, though he never concealed the fact. "I was for a long time," he has confessed, "far away from Jews and Jewish affairs. Anti-Semitism made me a Zionist. I am proud of my People and my land."

When Dr. Nordau stood up to speak, the whole gathering clapped and cheered. It was a marvelous speech. More or less, this is what he said:

"From the reports that will be presented here by the delegates, each speaking for his own country, you will see how terrible is the condition of our brother Jews among the nations! From their reports you will be able to paint a picture that might be called Jewish Need. It means Jewish Misery, Jewish Wretchedness.

"There are two kinds of suffering—material, like poverty, disease, hunger, cold. And suffering of the spirit, like dishonor, humiliation, frustration, resentment. Besides the material suffering, lack of bread, inadequate proper food, especially in those places where Jews are herded together in millions, they have in addition their own special Jewish suffering, such as no other nation can know. They are the sufferings in civil life, the sufferings Jews have to bear everywhere, even in those countries where they are supposedly equal in status, since all the rights the law has granted them exist only on paper. Essentially however, they show us at every step that these are Jews.

"As if to provide evidence for these words France came up around that time with the Dreyfus Affair and the Zionist Congress meeting then in Basel drew the logical conclusion from the position in which our brothers in France found themselves that it was the same with Jews all over the world. We learned three things. One, they hate us everywhere in the world. Two, things are now so bad that it can't go on much longer. Three, we must find a way out, but only such a way that it will be really effective.

"Let's consider it carefully, this question of why we are so hated. Among ourselves (we don't have to pretend to each other) we know well enough that we are no better and no worse than the others. We have all the qualities and all the faults that everybody else has. And if we happen to overdo it in one direction, we have, on the other hand, enough good qualities to outweigh ever so many faults. There is only this: They hate us so much, and their hatred goes so deep, that they refuse to recognize our undoubted qualities, and they do everything they can to stress our faults.

"Where does this hatred come from?

"We won't go into lengthy arguments, turning the pages of history to get to the bottom of it, to discover the real source from which this hatred grows. It is an old, lasting disease, inherited over generations, from one generation to the other. Indeed, our enemies very often are unable to say themselves why they hate us. It is a tragedy, God's chastising us over the ages. And indeed, to come back to our question, why should people love us? Can we demand of people that they should love us? Who are we among the nations? What fellowship have we with all the other nations in Europe, that they should love us?

"Who are we? Sons of Abraham, Isaac, and Jacob, who had our own land, and because we sinned we were driven out, were exiled, dispersed throughout the whole world. And so we wander around among the nations for nearly two thousand years, like a lost orphan tolerated only out of pity, thrown a scrap, a crust, a bone. And one doesn't choose one's words too mildly when speaking to him. If you want to say something to him, you say it directly, straight from the shoulder, without concealment, and if he doesn't understand, you follow it up with the stick.

"What does the orphan do then? He pockets the blow, takes the slap in the face, wipes his lips. For he knows well enough that no prayers will avail him. After all, he is only a poor orphan, come without an invitation, a stranger everywhere, an imposition. The fact is that wherever there are *our own* and *strangers,* so long as *our own* feel comfortable, live well, make a good living, so long the *stranger* can fit in, more or less. But when *our own* begin to feel cramped, suffer from the competition of the *stranger,* then the *stranger* is told very bluntly, in no uncertain terms, that *all our troubles* are your fault, *all because of you.* Then the people start murmuring against the *stranger.* At first, quietly, subdued. Then louder and louder. 'What do we want these strangers for? What use are they to us? For all the good they do us, let them go elsewhere. We can manage without them! Get out!'

"When it reaches that stage it only needs one voice to be raised, and everybody else will follow. No arguments will avail. All the evidence you can bring that the *stranger* is a human being, just like you, with a belly to feed, and that he can be of use to you is dismissed out of hand. They don't want his good help! Let him take it somewhere else! 'We don't want him here! Get out!'

"That's the way it is! We are strangers! Everywhere strangers! Then there is a second question: What are we? Are we a People, a nation, or not?

"What is a nation? What are the signs of a nation? A nation must first of all have a land. A nation must have an ideal, meaning an idea such as the whole nation must share and towards which it strives. Be devoted to it, heart and soul. We have lost our land. Where is our ideal? In order to have a land we must first want it—it means, we must, all of us, have one wish, one desire, one will, one overriding idea. That means unity. All right! We have the unity. We know it. Our enemies keep reproaching us all the time that there is too much unity among us. They repeat the saying, 'All Israel are brothers!' And 'All Jews are as one Jew!' Of course, we know how far that is true. I would wish that sort of unity on the anti-Semites! Who doesn't know that we've got the very opposite of unity among ourselves. What we have got is something altogether different—when one says yes, the other says no. If one says kosher, the other says treif. The same with liking somebody. Have you ever seen two Jews of one mind? Two Jews are sure to have three minds. How much more so when we are dealing with an idea which should unite us, bring the whole nation together. What is after all an idea according to the reasoning of our nation? Take a ride, for instance, to Berditchev, a Jewish town, stop a Jew in the street or in the synagogue and put the question to him: 'Tell me, begging your pardon, Reb Jew, what is your ideal? What do people here say about Zion and Zionism?' He'll look at you as though you were some busybody, with nothing better to do. Ideal-shmideal! What Zionism? What Zion? And he tries to turn the conversation to what he calls brass tacks. What do I get out of it? How does it help me to turn an honest rouble?

"I chose Berditchev, not as a chapter, but just as an example, an illustration. The same could be said about Kovno or Riga or Shnipishok, or what you will. They say the whole world is like one town. And I'm not saying that everybody in Berditchev is exactly the same.

"We get very unhappy reports from Roumania, with its quarter of a million Jews. They speak there of pogroms. Most of them are destitute, paupers, deprived of every opportunity of earning a living. In Galicia our brothers live under frightening conditions. A Jewish population of eight hundred thousand of whom 70 percent are reduced to the state of beggars. In Austria the Jews are not so well placed as people think. Of twenty-five thousand Jewish families in Vienna fifteen thousand haven't enough to pay their taxes. The anti-Semites are busily at work there. And things are getting worse from day to day. The same kind of reports are coming in from Bulgaria. The Jews have all the rights on paper, but no rights in actual fact. Want and misery and not a hope of anything better.

"The condition of the Jews in Hungary is better than in many other countries. But there is a hatred there of the Jews, deeply concealed, but only awaiting the opportunity to leap into a fire.

"I have nothing to say about the Jews in Morocco and Persia. We no longer hear of Jews complaining in these countries. They have got used to it. It is only rarely when things have gone too far, that we hear a voice rising there that tears your heart strings.

"All the Jews together in these countries number up to seven million. Seven million souls without human rights, poor, wretched, oppressed, despondent, paupers most of them, penniless, beggars, with no hope for improvement. In the countries where Jews are much less in number, they have indeed their livelihood, their crust of bread, and they earn it with less humiliation and indignity, with less pain. But does a man live by bread alone? Every man wants to be on a level with other men. But it's a futile hope. Where the Jew, under the law, is free, the people as a whole are against him. 'I am a man, a human being,' the poor Jew cries, 'a man like all other men!' 'No,' comes the answer. 'No! You are a Jew!'

"Here I must utter my most bitter word: The nations which emancipated us, gave us Jews equality, were supposed to have given us all the rights, did this, not because they recognized it as something due to us, something we were entitled to, but because there was a new fashion—emancipation, which means all equal. This strange emancipation did not do us much good. It transformed the character of the Jew completely. Previously, when the Jew felt an alien among the nations, he was a nation on his own, had his own world, his ghetto, his Beth Hamedrash, that were more precious to him than anything else. Here he was his own master. Here he was in his own place, with learning and erudition, charity and good deeds—what had he to do with the nations? Like yesterday's snows!

"Well now—we've got emancipation. It means that what was on paper was given us as our rights. We were made equal with all the nations. There was jubilation, festivity, Jews and Christians were both liberated. We were drunk with joy. Jews forgot almost everything. Till suddenly the fire of anti-Semitism flared up. And Jews again saw that lovely inscription, *No Admission for Jews!*

"And Jews woke from their sweet dream. What a tragedy it was when they realized how distant they had become from their Jewish brethren, how detached and strange from their Jewish background, and their Christian brothers refused to know them. They had departed from the old Jewish ghetto, and the new Fatherland would not admit them.

"Our enemies have besmirched us Jews so much that we have ourselves begun to believe all that our detractors say about us, that we are a people full of faults and wrongdoing, full of wickedness and evil deeds, that Jews are the scum of the earth. Till Jews began to be ashamed of the very word Jew. They had lost everything, faith and hope. A few even went away, deserted us. But where they went to they did not find what they looked for. And so we got a new type of Marrano, like at one time in Spain. The difference is only that the Marranos of old were forced, compelled. That is why they had hiding places, cellars, secret holes where they served God. The present day Marranos slipped away of their own will from our People, without faith, without hope of anything better, disillusioned, frustrated, with hate, with discontent.

This is the civilized, cultured Jewish need, the sufferings of the spirit. And this is the real, the true actual state of our brethren among the nations at the end of the nineteenth century."

It will be a criminal act, Max Nordau's address continued, after he had said his say about our enemies, the anti-Semites, not forgetting on the way our plutocrats, our millionaires, who stand aside and do nothing to save our poor Jewish People—it will be a great wrong, he said, a wrong against all of us if attention is not paid in time to the unfortunate, unhappy Jewish People, who cry out for help for hundreds of years, a People with good customs and capabilities, a People that could still bring much of great use to the world. The present condition of this People is bitter and gloomy, and a road must be found along which effective aid can be applied—that is the task of this congress.

After that, after the various delegates had read out their reports, each from his own country, about the condition of the Jews in his own area, Dr. A. Saltz of Tarnov in Galicia, Mr. Jacob de Haas from England, M. Jacques Bahar from France, Dr. Pineles from Roumania, Dr. Mintz from Vienna, Dr. Schauer from Germany, Professor Belkovsky from Bulgaria, Mr. Adam Rosenberg from New York, Dr. Nathan Birnbaum from Vienna, Dr. David Farbstein from Warsaw, and others, we had the program read out to us, as the committee had worked it out.

These are the resolutions adopted at the congress:

Zionism seeks to create a place in Palestine for the Jewish People secured by public law. The congress contemplates the following means to the achievement of this end:

Gradually settling the Holy Land with Jewish land workers, artisans, and merchants; binding together all Jewry through institutions in accordance with the laws of the country; strengthening the national sentiment of the Jewish People; taking the first steps to secure authority from the government for them to agree to the Zionist idea.

A plan was also worked out at the congress for how to organize the Zionist bodies in these ways:

1. The center for the Zionists is the congress which assembles each time in a different country.

2. Every Zionist who wants a say in selecting delegates to the congress will pay every year a coin of the realm not less than half a shekel. A hundred Zionists elect one delegate.

3. The congress chooses from among itself a committee for carrying out what is decided in congress.

4. The seat of the committee is in Vienna, the committee consists of 23 members, of whom 5 are permanently in Vienna, and the 18 will be divided among all the countries—1 Austria, 2 Galicia, 1 Bukovina, 2 Germany, 4 Russia, 2 Roumania, 1 France, 1 England, 1 America, 1 Serbia-Bulgaria, 1 Palestine, and 1 from the other Eastern countries.

About the program of the Zionists, the congress found it necessary to say that, so long as legal permission is not obtained from the sultan, no emigrants should be sent to Palestine, but meanwhile the earlier settlers should be helped. There are in Palestine now up to seventy-three thousand Jews, and it should be noted that even the Chalukah Jews who have looked out till now only for alms from us are beginning to show a liking for work and send their children to work in the colonies.

On the third day the congress was busy with many other matters of concern to the Zionists, about Jewish schools where people could learn Hebrew, helping Jewish literature, Jewish newspapers, etcetera.

In Dr. Handelstamm's words, "Everybody had to air his own opinion, but in the end all came to the one opinion, to one mind, and what the congress has decided, so it remains."

During the last minutes of the congress the rabbi of Basel, Dr. Cohn, a devout Jew (orthodox) mounted the platform as the delegate representing all the orthodox rabbis in Germany, and he addressed the congress with these words:

"I have not been a Zionist till now, and I am now, too, not completely convinced. But the congress has opened my eyes. I see that we have not understood the Zionists, have not valued them as much as would have been right and proper. As a rabbi of the orthodox sector I greet you and I hope that this national movement will be a transition to religious Judaism. It means that Jews should be good and devout. That makes me ask the committee—how do the Zionists stand with the faith, with our religion? If there is no danger from that quarter, I promise you that I will with all my abilities extend the area of the Zionists among all of my religious colleagues, the rabbis in Germany."

To this Dr. Herzl replied:

"I thank the rabbi for his frankness, and certainly I can assure him that the Zionists are not, God forbid, against religion, and do not in general devote themselves in any way to things that would harm the Jewish religion."

Dr. Herzl went on to thank very handsomely Switzerland, the country that had received the congress with so much friendship, whose president had attended some of the congress sessions, and the five Christian Zionists who had come to the congress, John Mitchell, the Reverend Hechler, Baron Manteuffel, and Colonel Bentinck, and M. Dunant, the founder of the Red Cross.

"Nobody knows what will happen," Dr. Herzl went on. "But that our getting together all in one place has brought and will bring benefit to our People—that everyone will admit. We want to give the poor, dejected, hopeless Jewish People a spade in their hand, to work with. Let's ask the Jews—what would you rather, be in Golus, downtrodden, starved for a bit of bread, or follow the plough over there, in the land of the patriarchs. Ask yourselves."

Dr. Mandelstamm followed with a good, short speech, thanking the whole congress, especially "that giant in Israel," Dr. Max Nordau, and Dr. Herzl, the founder of the congress.

At that point Dr. Herzl rose and said: "The First Zionist Congress is concluded."

What have they achieved, the Zionists? And what will happen when all Jews
will be Zionists? Where will we find all that money to settle all the Jews in the
Land of Israel? What do our millionaires say?

Who are the people to make the journey to the sultan? And when will they
go?

Jews will ask lots of other questions. Some will say: "So you've had a congress! Psha! Not worth a pinch of snuff! A lot of talk, speeches, speeches! That's
where it will all end!" Others will make fun of the whole affair. "What do you
think about it? About those Zionists, who want to bring Messiah down!" And
some will fly into a rage, as though someone had upset a good business deal for
them. "Atheists! Disbelievers! Want to hold back the Redemption!"

So here we are, reckon it up, and draw your conclusions.

"What use was the congress in Basel?" asked Dr. Handelstamm.

To begin with, we took the unhappy Jewish Question out into the open,
into the great wide world. We have protested openly against the wicked
ones, the anti-Semites. We have said what we mean, and what we want,
openly, aloud, for everyone to hear. Not like before, when we used to shout
and write, and we had to read it ourselves, poor us. Now the world had to
listen to us, listen to what we said, and the world paid attention and is
thinking about it. The big European newspapers are full of it, all our enemies
are talking about us, seriously, no longer as a joke, like they did before.
People have seen that we are on the move, using our limbs, they have seen
that we are not just vagrants, gypsies, with no national feeling. The Jews who
were at the congress were not ashamed of what they are. They did not make
excuses for being Jews. Our funds were not as big as those of our enemies.
We did not scold and curse. We told no fairy tales. We spoke seriously, from
the depths of our heart. I am convinced that the further and the deeper our
idea will reach among our people, this matter of Zion will be not only our
matter, but the matter of all the nations and of every state.

We have also convinced ourselves of the fact that we are a People, a nation,
which may hope to be one day a real nation, for itself and for those others
who came to Basel from all the corners of the earth, drawn from all classes,
from all sorts of people, holding all sorts of ideas and beliefs and yet all of one
mind and one will—Zion.

But there is a great difference in many regards between Dr. Max Nordau
and the Chassid from Tarnov, in his long capote. They are indeed far away
from each other, like east and west. Yet there, in Basel, they understood each
other and felt close to each other, like brothers, because they are both Jews,
equally distressed, equally persecuted, equally defeated, this one in this way
and the other in another way. And having convinced ourselves, having
shown ourselves at the congress, demonstrated to the world that to assimilate
means to mingle and merge with the nations, and is no plan at all for us. It

will never happen. So since people can't stand us, don't want us, we have to look somewhere else for a place where we can be endured, where we can have our own bit of land, where we can exist and work. And if we are looking for a country where Jews can live, what country is there for us if not Eretz Israel?

Meanwhile we must see to it that our idea should spread, should spread out, broaden, dig its roots deep down among our People, so that the idea of Yishuv Eretz Israel should be the idea not only of a few select Chovevei Zion people, devoted lovers of Zion, but the main idea, the wish and the will of the whole Jewish People. That is what the Zionists ask, for the present nothing more.

And when the time comes to do something, it will be done, sure and certain, for there are people working at this now, grown, serious people, not callow youths. The Zionists only have to keep an eye on the time, to see that we use the auspicious moment, for speaking to the Turkish government. Judging from the reports we read in the foreign press, it is not as far off as we think.

And when the time comes for us to need money, the money will be there. For where there is the will, and the idea embracing the whole of our People, the money will be found. It's no use looking to our rich men. They are not the only ones. We have a large section of middle-class people who will not refuse to help, to help themselves and their impoverished brethren, con-tributing each according to his means.

Of course, things don't move as fast as that. We have a long, hard road before us, hard work. It is not your duty to complete the work, but neither are you free to desist from it.

There are those who make fun of this whole affair and roll off a few glib phrases, like "Jewish State," "Jewish Cabinet Ministers," "Jewish Brass But-tons," Smart Alecks—cocky youngsters, who have no thought for the sad plight of their luckless brethren.

When Columbus set out on his voyage and discovered America, he had little idea of where he was going and what he would find. They had their scoffers then too, disbelievers, who laughed and sniggered at Columbus. We too sent out people to find a land—not America, Palestine! We sent out Chalutzim, and they are still there, our brothers, the colonists, a goodly number, thank God, several thousand of them. And they call to us to join them, but we stay where we are, joking and scoffing, ridiculing our entire enterprise, while our People sink lower and deeper. You repeat three times a day, "And to Jerusalem Thy city return in mercy."

And Dr. Mandelstamm concluded his speech with these words: "You cry aloud three times each year, Next Year in Jerusalem! See to it that these do not remain mere words. You should mean what you say. Mean it in real earnest. With all your heart, Next year in Jerusalem!"

It now remains to say a few words to those who raise objections with refer-ences to the Messiah. We could show them with passages from the Bible and from Talmud that our sages have said in many places that when Jews again settle in Eretz Israel and cultivate the land, then Messiah will come. We could show you many such writings, with the approval of more than a hundred rabbis and sages, and with passages from the Torah stressing that it is a great Mitzvah to devote ourselves to Yishuv Eretz Israel.

But why argue? Do we need endorsements for Yishuv Eretz Israel? Listen to what the great rabbi of Bialystock said, the Gaon Shmuel Mohilever, in his letter to the Basel Congress. Out of all the tens of thousands of telegrams and letters sent to Basel from all the corners of the earth, only one, the message from Rabbi Shmuel Mohilever, was read out to the congress, and the congress was so moved that it was decided to print his message, and a telegram of thanks was sent to him. This is the message, translated from Hebrew into our poor Yiddish folk tongue:

"Because of my health I could not carry out your wish to have me come to your assembly in Basel. Instead of me I send you my grandson to show you that my spirit is with you. From the depths of my heart I pray to God for you—Dear God, be with the messengers from your People Israel. Show them what to say, and make them understand what to say, that they should not sin with talk against our Holy Torah, or against the governments. Help them to carry out their idea, to the good, that they should win favor in the eyes of the kings and great men, so that when they come to ask for compassion for your People and your land, give all Jews a new mind and a great love for their unhappy brethren in the land. Amen!

"Now allow me to draw your attention to several things that will come up among you at the congress.

"A. Regarding the congress itself, it is enough to translate the words of your own communique. 'The congress wants only what is possible; everything that will be said and done there will be open and will not be against the laws of any country. We pledge ourselves that everything will be in accordance with the idea of the Chovevei Zion in Russia, and the laws of the Russian government.'

"I am sure you will keep your word. I only wish to add that most of all we must move the Turkish government to allow Jews to buy land and to build houses with no kind of prejudice. The whole existence of our colonization work depends on that.

"B. The congress will, of course, elect a committee, a center, probably abroad. We must see that the people in the center should be dedicated to our purpose, heart and soul.

"C. It is necessary to make it known that Zionists must all live like brothers, in friendship and love. They may belong to different classes, with different ideas in the matter of our religion. The religious people, who hold that the freethinking class are heretics must understand that when there is, God forbid, a fire in their home, they are themselves in peril, they and their goods and their lives, and when one of the freethinkers comes and wants to save them, their lives and their goods, will they not receive him with joy and friendship? In such a situation we are all brothers now. There is a fire raging around us. We are in great danger. Our enemies grow in number from day to day, and but for the fear of the government they would devour us alive! Now, when brothers come and want to help, which of us will dare to turn them away? Let all consider it well, that our unity should not be disrupted.

"D. All Zionists furthermore should be convinced and fully believe that the

Mitzvah of Yishuv Eretz Israel is one of the greatest Mitzvot we have in the Torah. Some of our early authorities say that this Mitzvah is over and above the whole Torah; and the reason is simple, because it is the basis, the very ground for the whole existence of our nation. The Jew who believes and is convinced of this is a true Chovev Zion, heart and soul. The Jew who does not believe this and is a Zionist is no more than one of those who give alms for charity, to get it over and done with.

"E. The basis of Shivat Zion is to guard the Torah as it is, not diminished and not increased, not added to. I don't mean by that to reproach anyone. Our sages said long ago, 'I don't know how one can reproach another these days.' I am saying this only in general, that our Torah, which is the source of our life, needs to be a basis in the revival of our People in the land of our forefathers.

"F. We have to build, not to destroy. Therefore it is not for us to intervene in regard to the Chaluka Jews in Jerusalem. There are tens of thousands of men living on Chaluka funds. So far they have no other livelihood.

"G. In order to spread the idea of Yishuv Eretz Israel among our People we should have traveling preachers, good speakers. We should bring booklets for the people, in Hebrew, Yiddish, Russian, and all other languages, explaining our idea in clear, simple language, with warm words and straightforward meaning. Such booklets are sadly lacking now. It is a fault that we must put right.

"H. About money. We must work in Paris, and also with other rich Jews, to establish a separate National Fund.

"I. The congress, as I see it, should send a letter of thanks to Baron Edmond de Rothschild, for his benefactions to Yishuv Eretz Israel. For he is the first of our brothers who responded to this great idea, and he has already spent millions for the idea. He is prepared to do more and more. He deserves it, that the First Zionist Congress, the First Jewish Congress, should tell him what we feel.

"At the close of my message I turn to my brothers with an appeal from the depths of my heart. For nearly two thousand years we have been waiting for Messiah to redeem us, to bring us out from all the four corners of the earth and settle us, each under his vine and under his fig tree. This hope is our only consolation in these hard and bitter times. True, in the last century such have arisen among us who derided this, who expelled 'Jerusalem your city' from the prayer book. But most Jews, the whole of our People, believe it and repeat it three times each day, finding them a comfort in their troubles.

"May God fulfill the words of the Prophet Zechariah: 'Thus sayeth the Lord of Hosts, Behold I will save thy people from the east country, and from the west country, and I will bring them; and they shall dwell in the midst of Jerusalem; and they shall be My people, and I will be their God, in truth and in righteousness.'

"In your day and in ours, Judah will be saved and Israel will dwell safely. And the Redeemer shall come unto Zion.

"From your brother who cherishes you,"

　　　　　　　　　　　　　　　　　　　　　　　Shmuel Mohilever

Have you ever heard such words from rabbis, gaonim, religious Jews (orthodox), and from great scholars, professors, doctors and the like? All of one opinion, all with one thought—Zion!

That leaves us with the last word—what is the conclusion? What was our intention? What do we want? And what do we ask from you?

Our answer is this:

Our intention was indeed no more than to convey to you in our simple Jewish tongue all that was done and was said in Basel, at the congress, and all the other things that happened after the congress, and what will probably happen and of which we will inform you in time.

As for what we ask from you—now we want only one thing. We want this that we have been telling you about not to go in one ear and out the other. We want you to bite on it, to chew it over, and to give your mind to our present sad condition all over the world and to realize that our help lies only in ourselves, and that if we ourselves won't help ourselves, then in God's Name, no one will. If you want it then, this great and holy idea, this lofty idea of Zion will be your one and only thought. It will serve you as a bright star to light your way and to show you the road to the only true happiness for our People. Amen!

1897

Why Do the Jews Need a Land of Their Own?

"For the Lord will have
compassion on Jacob,
and will yet choose Israel,
and set them in their own land."
Isaiah 14:1

What do Jews need a land of their own? Some question! There are people who would add another question. And they would be right. Why should Jews not want a country? If Jews are a nation, why should they be worse than all other nations? It's as though they were asking you what do you want a home for? Naturally everyone should have a home. What else? Stay outside? If you consider it at bottom, properly, it isn't just like that. The question is, what does one want a home for, a home of his own? Does a man need a home of his own?

Jews have a saying for it—better a rich tenant than a poor landlord. But when does that apply? When there are houses galore and houses are cheap, and landlords fight each other to get you as a tenant. Everybody after you, wants you! But what if the boot is on the other foot? What if you've been a tenant all over the place, and you've got a reputation—between ourselves—as a bad tenant, so that you can't get into a house anywhere, and you have nothing left but to stay outside, under God's Heaven! What do you do then?

More than eighteen hundred years we have been dragging around as tenants from one house to another. Have we ever tried thinking seriously—how long? How much longer? What will be the end of it?

In these eighteen hundred years we have gone through all sorts of times. There was a time when houses were plentiful, and everyone was happy to have us as a tenant (Nobody, indeed, came to blows over us). It didn't last long. They soon got fed up with us, and we were told to pack up and clear out. Go and find another lodging!

In these eighteen hundred years we have had all sorts of times. Occasions when we pulled ourselves together and recovered from our wanderings, hoping that any minute now Messiah would come, we would get over all our troubles, and be on a level with everybody else. It didn't last long. Before we could look round to see where in the world we were, we were again miles under, in the depths of despair.

That's what happened with us in the last few years, when people became

49

wise, and the world was full of knowledge. The word haskalah (education) brought us a lot of new words, noble, high-sounding words, like humanity, justice, emancipation, equality, brotherhood, and suchlike words that looked good and fine on paper and did your heart good to look at them.

What came of all these fine words you know by now. And if you don't know, try and read Dr. Max Nordau's speech at the Zionist Congress in Basel, and you will see that all these fine words remain no more than fine words. At bottom our position remained bitter and black. Worse than before.[5]

That our position is bitter and black we had known before. We heard the story from our grandfathers of old, terrible, wonderful tales, of a Pharaoh in Egypt who had plagued us, a Haman who had ended up in disaster, a Titus who had collapsed in ruin, an Inquisition, and the expulsion of the Jews from Spain and Portugal and other places. And more such tales with which our history is full. We witnessed many of them ourselves. Seen them with our own eyes, read about them in the newspapers. Only those who went to the congress opened our eyes, painted a picture of our position all over the world, and we discovered that even in those countries where we envied our brothers, thought they were living happily, it was nothing of the kind. We had been mistaken. It turned out that things are nowhere good for us; they are terribly bad. We are hated everywhere. They can't stand us anywhere. And as if to provide evidence for what we say, France came out with the notorious Dreyfus trial, and the hatred whipped up against the famous French writer Emile Zola, who wanted to put right the injustice committed against this innocent man Dreyfus. Who of you all hasn't read about that amazing trial? Who among you has been indifferent to the injustice committed before our eyes now at the end of the nineteenth century? And where? In France! "Spit on Zola!" "Death to the Jews!" That's what the anti-Semites shouted in Paris.

The Jewish Congress in Basel drew the right conclusions about the position of our brothers throughout the world, and considering these conclusions we learned three things:

1. They hate us everywhere, in the whole world.
2. The situation is so bitter and black that it can't go on any longer.
3. We must find a way, but one that will work.

A. Let's consider it well, why do they hate us? We ourselves know (we don't have to pretend among ourselves) that we are no better and no worse than the rest. We have all the good qualities and the bad that all people have. And if it happens sometimes that we go a little too far, we have, to compensate, other qualities that outweigh the faults. Only what? The hatred against us is so great and so deeply ingrained that no one will consider our good qualities, and our faults are flung at us at every step, all the time.

---

5. "The Jewish Congress in Basel," report by Doctor Mandelstamm, Yiddish by Sholom Aleichem (Warsaw, 1897).

What is the cause of this hate?

We won't go into long discussions, turning the pages of history, to get to the bottom of it. Where does this hatred come from? It is an old, persistent disease, an epidemic, God forbid! that goes by heritage from generation to generation. It sometimes happens that our enemies can't themselves say why they hate us. It's a real tragedy. God's own curse that has come down on us these many, many years. And going back to this question, let us make a strict account. Why should they love us? Can we demand of people that they must love us? Who are we among the nations? What are we, and what big noise do we make amongst the other nations in Europe that they should love us?

Who are we? Sons of Abraham, Isaac, and Jacob, who once had our own land. We sinned and were driven out and dispersed over the whole earth, and so we wander about among strange nations for nearly two thousand years, like a lost orphan child, who is kept only for pity's sake. He is thrown a crumb, tossed a bone, and little notice is taken of him. If there is anything someone wants to say to him, it is said straight out, without mincing words. And if he doesn't catch on, he gets it in the neck.

What does the orphan do then? He hides. He pockets the blow and wipes his lips as if nothing had happened. He's a stranger! Everywhere a stranger! So as long as the native, the one who belongs, finds things going well and easy, feels comfortable, earns enough for his needs, the stranger can get by, more or less. But when the native feels cramped, crowded out, with competition growing, and his earnings going down, then the stranger assumes enormous bulk, looks gigantic. All the troubles in the land seem to stem from him. And people begin to murmur. At first under their breath, then louder and louder. "What do we want these strangers here for!"

It only needs one to say it first, and the others follow. No arguments will help. No facts and figures, to show that the stranger too is a human being, that he has also to eat, and that he can help in the common task, can be of use. Nobody will listen. Nobody wants his usefulness. Take it somewhere else, they say. We don't want it. Get out!

So what are we? We are foreigners, aliens everywhere.

Now there is a second question—who are we? Meaning, are we a People, a nation, or not? What is called a nation, and what are the signs of a People? A People should first of all have a country. A People should have an ideal. That means an idea, a thought towards which the whole People will strive, devoted to it heart and soul.

We lost our land. Where is our ideal? To have a land we must want it. That means we must all have one wish, one will, one idea, one thought. That is unity. What unity we have now we all know well enough. Our enemies accuse us from the start, saying that we have too much unity. They say about us that all Israel are brothers. All Jews are one Jew. We, of course, know how much truth there is in that. Wish it on the anti-Semites to have our unity. If one of us says yes, the other will say no. If one says kosher, the other will say treif. And what one finds pleasing, the other dislikes. He wants it, so I want the opposite. Two Jews have three opinions. When one says this, the other says yes, but not like that. The other man's opinion isn't worth a pinch of snuff. No need to listen when somebody else is talking. There is no elder, and surely no wiser. Because we are all wise. Kulone Chachomim. We are all wise men. We all know what is going on in the world. We knew it long ago, long before that other man is trying to tell us. So what's all this about an idea that will link us all together—our whole People? Take a ride, for instance, to Berditchev, a Jewish town. Stop a Jew there, in the street or in the synagogue and put the question to him— Excuse me, Mister Jew, what is your ideal? And what's going on here about Zion and Zionism?

He'll look at you as if you were mad, a man with time to think about ideals, a loafer, a drifter, a waster of time. Ideal, shmideal, Zion and Zionism. You tell me rather how's business! Have you anything in your mind to turn an honest rouble?

I said Berditchev not as an exception. But as an example. The same sort of place. The same sort of thing will hold good in Kovno, in Riga, in Shnipishok, anywhere you like. They say the whole world is one town. And I'm not saying that all Berditchev Jews or all Shnipishok Jews are all so taken up with the chase after the rouble. Or that nobody there is interested in Zion and Zionism. I'm only saying that most Jews are miles and miles away from such things, things that don't contribute to their takings. And if there are Jews in every town who devote themselves to things like Zionism, they are no more than a few single individuals.

The argument is that Jews are poor, badly off. They must all chase after the rouble to keep going. But that argument is false. To begin with, not all Jews are poor. Thank God, we have plenty of wealthy Jews (and I am not speaking of the magnates, the really, truly rich, for where does it say that aristocrats like these, millionaires, must read little booklets written in Yiddish?) I'm talking of the middle-class Jews who have both time and the mind to devote themselves to such things as Jewish affairs. And on the other hand, the worse things are with Jews, the more and more often they have to think of these things on which their own happiness and the happiness of the entire Jewish People depend. Bad times and bad conditions getting worse every day demand that all Jews must come together, be driven together, all with one wish and one will, one purpose, one ideal. Brothers, there is something missing. The spirit is missing, the folk-spirit that we lost all this time that we have been dragging around here and there.

So what are we? Well, we have our religion. We have our own language. And, of course, there are a few million of us, people who pray from the same prayer book, who keep the Sabbath, eat matzoth at Passover time, hamantaschen at Purim, a smear of honey at Tabernacles, and—

That's all? Nothing more? If so the world is almost right when it says we are not a nation, but just a lot of stiff-necked, stubborn people—what we are told we are, every day!

Again, what are we? How about our ideal? Where is our "Jerusalem thy city" that we repeat day by day? What of "Next year in Jerusalem" and Ani ma'amin"?—Our "I believe"—our principles of Jewish faith? And our form of greeting to each other—"Live to see Messiah"!

True! Only we mustn't fool ourselves. We know well enough how a Jew speaks these words. Our question is, what has he in mind while he speaks those words—his shop, his mill, the forest where he has a lumber lease from the landowner, or his shares on the stock exchange, or far away in Yehupetz, at the Market Day Fair. As for living to see Messiah—good! Why not? If Messiah comes riding along to collect Jews and take them to Eretz Israel at his expense, on condition that each of us, all of us must go on that journey, and the moneyed ones go first!

Jews have such a delightful sacred ideal, and all they do is make fun of it!

No, brothers! We remember Jerusalem every day, but what we have in our minds is Yehupetz. Eretz Israel has till now been a place where old Jews go to die. Zion till now was a word, a fine, beautiful name that we find in our holy books, with other lovely old names, like Wailing Wall, and Mother Rachel's Tomb—all names that should move our hearts, should evoke memories, conjure up pictures of our glorious past.

"Zion, how fare your wandering children?" That's a line from a poem by one of our greatest Jewish singers and patriots, Rabbi Judah Halevi. That was his question to us!

But the words, alas, fly by swiftly, leave an impression with us for a moment, and vanish.

Judah Halevi was drawn to Zion all his life, till he went there and was killed there. "Where shall I find wings," he asked, "to fly there, to bring my broken heart to Zion, to the Holy Land? That I should fall with my face to the ground, embrace the holy earth, kiss the dear stones, the sacred dust, the holy graves!"

And that is where he was killed.

Unhappily, our Jewish People know little of this great Jewish poet and his intense love of Zion. Our people no longer feel what they once felt about this majestic name Zion. It seems that the wound must be so old that the pain is no longer felt, insensible. That is not surprising, for after all, this long Golus, this wandering from one land to another, suffering such things as the Spanish Inquisition, and more, much more, and still retaining some fragments of humanity, is itself an achievement, a miracle. Such a miracle as only God can work, God and his Torah, this little Pentateuch, our spiritual Fatherland, this community of soul!

This fact alone, that we hold on to our Jewishness so long, that we have not been wiped off the face of the earth like many others nations who have left no trace behind—that itself is proof that we can and with God's help will be a nation with all the signs and symbols of a nation.

That leaves us with the third question. What bonds have we with the other nations? No bonds at all!

There were times indeed when there was some talk of our being kindred, having bonds. Shem and Japhet wanted to marry into us. We were on the point of intermingling—assimilation. Both sides deluded themselves. It seemed that we were brothers, body and soul. We on our side were prepared for it, and to show how delighted we were with the match we started aping them in every way, with everything—dress, speech, behavior, manners in the house and outside. With our festivals. With our names—Abraham became Anton; Jeremiah, Jerzy; Getzel, Maxim. The women followed suit. Hannan became Gertrude; Esther, Isabel; and Dvoshe, Cleopatra! Everyone tried to outdo the other. All wanted to show that "I am not I."

What came of it? Nothing! Worse than that! It finished up with rows and scandals. What can we do if we are not really equal sides? We can't impose friendship by force. It won't work!

These are the three main reasons why they hate us, always and everywhere. They hate us because we are strangers and because we want to eat. They hate us because we are a nation without a land and without an ideal. They hate us because we do not have equal links with the nations. We only push the cart from behind, leaping and jumping and grimacing all the time to attract attention. In one word they hate us and hunt us more and more as time goes on, more and more brutally. I hope I'm wrong.

B. Because as we go on things keep getting worse, and things are becoming so dangerous that it cannot possibly continue as in the past. When they reminded us of our faults and revived all the old accusations against us, we responded by finding excuses, trying to justify ourselves, to show that we are not as bad as they made out. You will see that we are right if you give us a little more time, a little more freedom to speak. "Give us a chance to educate ourselves, give us education, and you will see that we are an entirely different people."

Now, when we see plainly that being on the defensive will not help, that self-vindication gets us nowhere, that since we are a nation like all other nations, that we will never mix and mingle with other nations, and that we are hated everywhere in the whole world, we must look for some other way to assure our existence; we must find our own remedy. Our help is in ourselves alone.

C. What is our help, what is our remedy? Our wise men have long pondered this question, have written a great deal about it, our scholars, our providers and protectors—and they have found only one way—Jews must have an ideal. And the ideal must be a land. In a word, Jews must have a land, their own land.

Only sixteen years ago a great man, Dr. Pinsker, published a little pamphlet with the name "Auto-Emancipation." It caused a stir in the Jewish world. "To end our troubles," Dr. Pinsker said, "we must have a land. But not to wait for someone to give us the land. We must find a land ourselves, a piece of earth, a corner, that is our own, no matter where it is, so long as it is ours."

Does a Jew realize what lies in these few simple words—"a piece of earth, a corner that is our own"? Does a Jew feel how necessary and how advantageous it is for each and every one of us, and for the whole community, for us all? Does a Jew ever think what we would have looked like among the nations of the world if we had a piece of land somewhere, our own small corner—that we would be no longer paupers, wandering gypsies, outcast and unwanted!

Dr. Pinsker had given a lot of thought to the subject, and he had concluded that only a land of our own can bring us salvation. He laid the first stone of that great structure which our people created afterwards. For he was followed by other Jewish writers who discussed and considered the matter. It started a search over the world for a land where we could settle Jews who had got stuck like a bone in the throat in the countries where they lived. One said Palestine. Another Argentina. A third Brazil. Some thought Africa would be the place. Others plumped for Cyprus. Back of beyond! God knows where! There is an apt saying—a big world, but no room to sit down. None of the other nations came out to welcome us, to say Sholom Aleichem, were in no hurry to invite us in, but on the contrary fought over us like those seven towns when a synagogue cantor applied for a job, each wanting some other town to take him on. The conclusion was reached that if Jews want to live as a nation, there is no other way but to go there, to the ancient Holy Land of our forefathers, the land of the patriarchs. We were shown with all the necessary evidence that every other way was wrong, was false, that the Jewish People are too much divided already, split up, scattered, and dispersed. What we need is a merkaz, a center.

The question, "Wohin?" ("Where to?") ceased to be a question. Disappeared from the agenda. The organization "Chovevei Zion" was formed then, and it still exists. Though it is true that when the emigration started, more Jews went and still go to America, the heart of each immigrant lies over there, in the land of our Fathers. Palestine, Eretz Israel, Zion—those words are heard often among our people, everywhere, even in distant, free America. We already have in Palestine a good many fine colonies that Baron Edmond de Rothschild founded. We also have our own colonies there, where our brothers distinguish themselves with their work.

But time has shown that the colonizing of Palestine is proceeding too slowly. The number of Jewish people grows and their poverty grows more. Jews need, most of all, a land of their own, where they can go and settle openly, not having to sneak in as in the past. These are the words of Herzl, who convened the first Jewish Congress held in Basel.

Indeed, Dr. Herzl did nothing new by using these words. He said almost the same thing that Dr. Pinsker had said sixteen or seventeen years before. The difference was that Pinsker spoke in general terms, that Jews must have a country, and Herzl came out openly before the whole world with the demand that Jews must have a country, their own land, and pointed straight at Palestine. Dr. Pinsker poured out his bitter heart quietly, reasonably, without fuss or clamor. While Herzl demanded publicly, to the whole world, a ready-made Jewish state. I refer to Herzl's *Judenstadt,* which made a stir, not only among Jews, but also among other people.

"A Jewish state," Herzl said, "is necessary not only for us, but for the whole world. For it is the only way to get rid of the unhappy Jewish Question . . . Of course, as long as the idea of a Jewish state, a Jewish land remains the idea of one or a few people, it will be no more than a very fine idea, and that's that. But as soon as it becomes the idea of the whole People, it will not be difficult to carry it into effect."

"The Jewish People," Dr. Herzl proceeded, "cannot and must not be destroyed. We will not be destroyed because our enemies will not allow it. We will not be destroyed, and this is proved by our nearly two thousand years of suffering, and we are still here. We must not be destroyed, because that is not desirable. Some leaves may fall off, but the tree remains. And that we should not be destroyed, we must have a land. Our own land . . . Time now," says Herzl, "for us to reveal our mission to the world, for all we will do in our new land will be to the good not only of our people, but of everyone, all mankind."

"Palestine or Argentina?" Herzl asks, and this is how he answers his own question. "The Jewish people will say thanks for every piece of land that will be given them, to settle there freely, to develop their powers and their energies and abilities. The difference between Argentina and Palestine is that the Holy Land, Zion, is bound up with our ancient history. The very name Eretz Israel is enough to attract the love of the Jewish people."

Herzl went on to present his plan—how Jews should make their land purchases in Eretz Israel, and how in time a Jewish state would develop there, of course, with the consent of the sultan and of all the European powers.

It would take a whole book to reproduce the plan in its entirety. Yet everybody will understand that building a grand edifice like that is no easy matter. It is a work not for a year or even ten years. As the saying goes, "Things don't work as fast as we talk." Jews must first of all understand the idea properly, grow accustomed to it, get done with the question we posed before, "Why do Jews need a land of their own?"

"That means we must see to it that all Jews should feel and understand how necessary and useful it is. We must see to it that this idea should be the ideal of the entire People. We must see to it that our wives and sisters should understand it, so that our children will be brought up under our national flag, so that our children should be Jewish children, who will not be ashamed of their People . . . Jews must return to the Jewish People before they return to the Jewish land."

Professor Schapira had this to say at the Basel Congress: "If our ancestors had contributed each year the shekel from the time we lost our state, we could by now have enough funds to buy the whole of Eretz Israel."

I think this is a mistake. With this amount of money we could have bought half of the whole world. Does it mean that because our parents didn't do it, we mustn't do it either? What a great legacy we would leave our children and our children's children. They will inherit this holy ideal from us, the ideal that will go with us, a heritage from generation to generation. A land, our own land— that will be the ideal among all Jews the world over. Our children, or our grandchildren may live to see it. We ourselves perhaps, too.

Messianic Times
A Zionist Novel

1
Messiah in the Synagogue

Not bees swarming round a hive, humming and buzzing, flying to and fro, scintillating, dazzling ones eyes. Not ants attacking a patch of earth, crowding one on the other, in heaps, covered over completely. Nor were these crows who had come flying into the wood, cawing all at once, scrambling one on top of the other, cra-cra like a broken-winded rattle dinning at your ears. No, these were some of our little Jews, may they multiply, gathered on a Sabbath day after the kugel in summertime, in the old synagogue in the old Jew Street, in the old Jewish town Mazepevke. The synagogue, oh that old Mazepevke synagogue! To what shall I compare it? It's called a holy place, but that isn't true. How can such a place be holy, when you drink brandy there, every morning but Saturday, the Sabbath day, accompanying it with some cake or a bagel or home-baked biscuits? They call it a place of worship. But that isn't true either. How can such a place be a seat of Torah when people discuss their business there, talk politics, and anything else you can think of? I would call it a Jewish Bourse or a Jewish club. Only it isn't a Bourse, and it isn't a club. It is a kind of hospital, where a few sick old Jews, some of them cripples, stay. That's where they groan and, poor souls, die. It's all these things combined, all of them together—a house of worship, and a bit of a tavern, too, a Bourse and a club, and something of a hospital as well.

Why not? Where else should honest Jews go to get a drink of brandy and a bite when you have Yorzeit for your father or your mother? Where else should poor old sick Jews stay, when Mazepevke has no Old People's Home? Go, go out into the open street and die there? Where and when then can Jews hear the news and tell stories and jokes if not on the Sabbath day after the kugel? If all the week long you must carry the yoke, weighed down with worries about earning your living? This is the one place where the Jew in Mazepevke feels free, can say what he wants to say and what he has in his mind. Where he is not afraid of anyone. Where he can give his enemies the finger?

On this Sabbath day with which we are concerned the old synagogue was besieged from outside and packed full inside with so many Jews, bless them, as had never been seen before in Mazepevke. On that Sabbath there was hardly a Jew who had dared to take his afternoon nap. Everybody came to the synagogue after the midday meal to listen to an address which the shamas had announced to be delivered just before Mincha. The smell of radish and onion and other such smells from the Sabbath table made themselves very much felt, as soon as you came in at the door. It was impossible to push your way in from outside, certainly not to the best seats by the east wall, where the elite, the notables of Mazepevke, the rich men, the cream of Mazepevke had their places. There wasn't room for a pin to drop. And to make matters worse they were all trying to push their way in one direction, everybody to the top. Nice to be near the rich.

The synagogue is agog. In turmoil. A rush and a roar. A tumult. Everybody talking at once. Jews in their Sabbath-day gaberdines leaning against the stands. More Jews hanging on to their backs, and still more Jews on the backs of the others. And because everybody is talking all at once it is impossible to know what anyone is saying. But since every Jew has sharp ears, he can, while himself speaking, hear what the others say. One begins, another ends, the third hasn't heard properly and comes barging in with a silly question which has no bearing on the subject, something quite irrelevant. Somebody else at the side chips in with a remark that turns the whole thing upside down, the questioner contradicts him and repeats the same thing over again. Next a new voice chimes in with a wild compromise suggestion, so wild that it makes your hair stand on end. Here is another one who doesn't understand what is being asked, and there somebody else who hasn't heard the answer. So both argue with each other, not knowing what it's all about, till suddenly someone else bursts in, interfering. Because if he may put his spoke in when I speak, I may put my spoke in when he speaks.

"Hush! Quiet please! We're going to read something out to you!" That's Shamai, the shammas, banging the table three times, and immediately after Yossel Moishe Yossis mounts the Bimah. A strange young man with a pale face and intent black eyes, one of the Mazepevke Maskils. He would never have been allowed to speak in the old synagogue from the Bimah to such a big assembly of Jews, but for his father, Reb Moishe Yossis, a Jew with Torah, and a man of wealth besides. One of the top Jews in the town.

"Rabosei!" he begins with a quivering voice, his hands shaking and his face white as a wall—"Rabosei, I have news for you, something that has not happened to our People since the temple was destroyed. I am sure this news will make you happy. It will give you joy!"

Hearing the word "news" the Jews assembled there opened mouth and ears. For news, something new, is always welcome, especially news that he said would give them joy.

As Yossel Moishe Yossis went on speaking he gained confidence, his voice grew firm, rose louder. His cheeks flushed and his eyes shone like burning coals. He told his listeners that there had been a congress of Zionists held in Basel. He spoke with passion, using high-sounding words—nationalism, Zionism, anti-Semitism. He spoke of our history, our ideal, and again history, history! Words that 99 percent of the people in the synagogue did not understand. And he kept calling out again and again, Dr. Herzl, Dr. Nordau, Dr. Mandelstamm, and more such names of doctors unknown in Mazepevke. And over and over again, Zionism.

"Every Jew," said Yossel Moishe Yossis, "as soon as he hears the word Zion, should throw away everything, drawn to the land that flows with milk and honey, the land where we once had our Temple, our Kohanim, our priests, the Levites, our prophets, our kings, our army, and our generals, the land where every stone is stained with the blood of our heroes, who fought for our freedom over the centuries, the land where there are the graves of our patriarchs, the land that sits weeping and lamenting like a young maiden forsaken by her lover. And you hear, you Jews hear (so he concluded his speech) you hear how the land calls to you, our ancient mother, and you are silent, you see, you Jews, how she weeps, our old distressed forgotten Zion, and you do not come forward to wipe away her tears. You know that your help is near, and that it depends on you, on you alone, and you pretend not to see and hear. 'By the waters of Babylon, there we sat down and wept, when we remembered you, Zion!' We can now repeat the same words, but to a different tune. By the waters of Babylon we sat down and rejoiced when we remembered you, Zion! Over there in Basel delegates came together from all over the world and agreed that we are a nation, a People, a living People, with our own history and our own language and our own ideal. There in Basel we talked about the bitter plight of our brothers everywhere, in all countries, and we found only one way to save our poor Jewish people—'Raise the banner to Zion!'"

And much more Yossel Moishe Yossis said, with passion, with enthusiasm, with fire, repeating every now and again the word Zion, rebuking the people who wait for miracles, for signs and wonders, for Messiah to come on a white horse. He quoted passages from the Talmud, from Midrash, that Messiah will not come otherwise than if you are not first prepared to go to Zion. He showed with proofs that Messiah is in ourselves, that these are messianic times, for everybody talks of Zion now, everywhere in the world, even in distant America. Everywhere you hear nothing but Zion, Zion, Zion.

When Yossel Moishe Yossis descended from the Bimah, the sweat was pouring down his face, and the people in the gathering, most of whom understood little of his discourse except the words Temple, Zion, Messiah, broke again into a medley of talk and argument, like at the start. Jews talk, Jews argue, one says this, the other says that, each goes his way, and each is sure his road is the right one, and the other man's road is bosh. It was like a fairground. The noise rose to heaven. You couldn't make out the drift of what people were saying. You could only catch an isolated word here and there—Messiah, Zion, Basel, Eretz Israel, Dr. Herzl, Stamboul, Golus, Temple, messianic times. All together, mixed-up, a jumble of words, and a mishmash of voices, high-pitched and low, soft and gruff, squeaky, shrill, hoarse—like a hundred unoiled cart-wheels all at once, accompanied by a choir of croaking frogs.

Only there, up by the east wall, on both sides of the Ark of the Law, where the "Golden Banner" hidden from sight by the stands, in the corner has its place, where the rabbi, Reb Joshua Heshel has his seat, nodding, half-asleep, you can distinguish hearing a full sentence here and there, because people don't interrupt so much. This is where the rich men sit, and say what you will, one has more respect for the rich. Even if he talks nonsense, one listens.

"Children! Babes in arms!" says a voice on the east side. "Scalawags who carry things on the Sabbath! They talk of Messiah!"

"And they bring you proof in the Talmud and in Midrash," adds another, in support. A rich Jew, with a broad girdle and a big paunch. "If I were in Moishe Yossis's place, and my son gave us such a piece of impudence, I'd show him who Messiah is!"

"You're right! Absolutely right! Sure as I'm alive!" This from a red-headed man, a poor Jew, anxious to be in the good books of Mr. Moneybags. "Like a bolt from the blue, suddenly, in the midst of everything—Messiah!"

"They are right though," says another man, breaking in, but with a milder tone, so as not to offend the rich man. "If you consider it, why indeed shouldn't Messiah come? Isn't it time? Aren't Jews suffering enough? Did you listen to that list of names Yossel Moishe Yossis called out—some doctor whom the Jewish sufferings drove to do something about it? And talking between ourselves—don't we suffer enough for Messiah to come!"

"All right! Why not?" someone else also at the east wall wants to know. A fine type of Jew, Reb Yenkel. "What do we lose by it? Would to God Messiah really came at last! May we live to see it! There's only one thing I want to know—why just now, why must we go to Eretz Israel today? And what has it to do with Yossel Moishe Yossis?"

"Yes, what sort of a boss is Yossel Moishe Yossis?" the red-haired man butts in again, his eyes fixed on Mr. Moneybags, as if to say—"You see how I back you up! Every word you say! You won't forget it, will you? When I come to ask you a favor?"

"True!" says a Jew in the corner, trying to use soft conciliatory words, "the question is, only why now, why today? That is the question! Yet the answer is the question over again. For if Messiah does not come, the question will still be there—why today? And coming back to it, I can't see what harm it can do anyone that youngsters start talking about Zion!"

"On the contrary!" says Reb Yenkel, "I like it! It's only annoying that Jews should delude themselves with things that haven't been and won't be!"

"There's nothing to it!" the red-headed Jew again interferes. "It's only a fairy tale! Never was and never can be!"

"I don't see why," the Jew in the corner takes him up. And another rich Jew at the east wall breaks in, with "Let's not fool ourselves. What? Eretz Israel? From whom? The Turk? Who? Doctors who haven't a penny to their name? I mean, really, truly. As regards—"

"Troublemakers! Wreckers! Don't pay what they owe! Borrow and don't repay!"

This interjection from a moneylender, "They've given us another holiday, they have, so as to get out of paying their debts on time! You can't trust them!"

"So they walk straight up! They stand erect!" that's the red-headed Jew again, getting his word in and thinking to himself that his stomach isn't rumbling just for fun."

"Think they're doing us good, they do," says a smug, very self-satisfied Jew, with a broken nose and blackened teeth. "All they need is to have the police after them!"

"Sure to get to the police!" says the red-headed Jew, thinking in the same breath that the moneylender was hand in glove with the police and would probably inform them himself.

The Jew in the corner, still trying to be conciliatory, suggests: "Supposing we do go to Eretz Israel. The police here would be our last worry! What could they do to us? What power would they have over us?"

"What pull have you got here, eh?" the Jew with the blackened teeth is demanding. "Think the police will be frightened by your Doctor Shmerzl?"

"That's Jewish power for you!" interjects a young man at the east wall, with a silk capote and a velvet cap. "A Jew has power only in the synagogue. As soon as he goes outside and runs into the police he has no power. He backs away and cowers in a corner!"

"Or he takes to his heels and makes off as fast as he can!" This from another young man, who keeps blinking his eyes and opening his mouth all the time as though he was catching flies. The Jews at the east wall all burst out laughing, most of all the red-headed Jew, who opens his mouth and reveals all his teeth still intact.

"What do you say to all this noise here?" asks another of the east wall people, a melancholy-looking man with a pale weepy face and a squint.

"They're having some argument about Messiah," explains a fat tubby little man with a strange, outlandish sort of beard, growing in curious fashion on the broad side. "They've opened the Book of Daniel, looking for the End of Days, calculating on the fingers of their hand when Messiah is to come."

"You're wrong!" says the young man in the silk capote. "What they're doing is arguing about the Jewish State. They can't agree about dividing up fair shares."

"What they're worrying about," says the young man catching flies, "is Shlomo the Melamed, who insists that he must be the police chief in Eretz Israel. Berl Stutterer says he is not fit to be anything but an ordinary policeman."

That makes everyone round the east wall laugh out loud. And laughing loudest of all the red-headed Jew. He throws back his head, opens his mouth wide, and goes into a fit of laughing, coughing, and choking. The fly-catching young man lets off a few more witticisms and an epigram or two and has his audience splitting their sides, hugging each other, chortling, guffawing, shouting, screaming, making an uproar. Everybody shouting down everybody else, explaining one Bible text and another, expounding, interpreting, one this way, the other that way, each going his separate road, each convinced that his road is the only right road, and the next man's is just muck.

"Quiet, please! Keep quiet!" That's another voice from the east wall, where everybody takes up the cry, "Be quiet! Hush! Quiet, please!" Hands banging on the lecterns. "Do keep quiet! Please be quiet!" The whole congregation joins in, everybody crying, "Quiet please!"

"Time for Mincha, and then we can go home for the third meal," someone at the east wall calls out, looking through the window and motioning to the rabbi. And the rabbi, a poor, sick, frail old man, with a yellow face and red-rimmed eyes, nods to the shammas, who pushes his way forward, bangs the stand three times, and starts Mincha. "Jews, say Ashrei Uvo L'Zion!" ("And a Redeemer shall come to Zion") He means to start at that point, because a good many there had no doubt already bolted down the preliminary prayers before they had come from home, and those who hadn't would gabble them off quickly and catch up. In this matter of catching up the Mazepevkeites are past masters. They do everything by "catching up," like "catching up with one's prayers," "catching up with one's meals," "catching up with one's sleep," and "catching on," (looking into someone else's affairs), "catching up with," (capturing a seat at the east wall), "catching in," (getting into a business deal), and "May the devil catch up with them!" meaning the Mazepevkeites' devil catch them!

2
Messiah in the Beth Hamedrash

At the time the rich men of Mazepevke sat, each at his own table, over the third meal, singing Sabbath table hymns, each in his fashion, each hymn lovelier than the other, the poor folk, alas, and the middle-class tradesmen were in the Beth Hamedrash, feeding on a different kind of meal, not so much for the body as for the soul, such dishes that you never tire of, and which never upset your stomach. "Like a ripe fruit early in summer, while you still hold it in your hand you swallow it," so now they swallow each word that comes from the mouth of Reb Israel. He wears a satin capote. His grey hair is wavy. And his big black eyes shine from under his high forehead. He sits at a long table with a heavy tome in front of him, explaining, expounding. About thirty or forty people standing around him, people of various groups—Hasidim, Misnagdim, scholars, idlers, craftsmen, and plain ordinary Jews. Reb Israel himself is a learned Jew, but begging your pardon, without a penny to his name. Nobody knows what he lives on. They say that he feeds on the joy he has from sitting in the Beth Hamedrash every evening before Mincha, teaching, elucidating. Or perhaps his struggle to live keeps him alive, fasting every Monday and Thursday, and other days beside. But how a Jew lives in Mazepevke? One lives, thank God! And as long as one lives one hopes. Especially a Jew like Reb Israel, who most certainly hopes. True, Reb Israel has been hoping for years, without any change for the better. In fact, things have got worse with him. There is an explanation, of course. The Golus—the Jewish exile. Waiting for Messiah. The Golus goes on and on. As for Messiah? Don't we say every day in our prayers, in Ani ma'amin, the Principles of the Faith, "I believe with a perfect faith in the coming of the Messiah, and though he tarry I wait daily for his coming." Reb Israel is sure the Messiah will come. Without a doubt. Very soon. All this talk now in the synagogue about Messiah. Something big going on in the world. Only one thing Reb Israel can't understand. What have those snotty noses got to do with it? Who told them to interfere? Yet Reb Israel is not the kind of man to affront anyone, to offer even a youngster the slightest humiliation. Let the young men repent, let them reform. Let them engage in the coming of Messiah. Isn't their concern with his coming proof that he is near, is on his way? As for the youngsters—it is only the beginning. The real thing will come later!

The real thing will come "Losid Lovu," in the future, when Messiah is here. Reb Israel chants the words from the book, shaking to and fro with great fervor, and his eyes and the eyes of all his hearers are burning flames. When Messiah comes the Jews will bring an action against the Almighty. Look, they will say, look how many things we did for you. We sanctified your Name on the sea, we sang songs of praise, we received your Torah with gladness, when no other people would accept it. We keep your Commandments with pain and anguish, how many edicts and discriminatory laws were issued against us, yet we hold on. We say our prayers every day. We sing and praise you, and you have delivered us into the hands of Esau. Compare—the king had taken a dislike to a matron and had her driven from the palace. So she went and covered her face and stood under a pillar, where the king who had driven from the palace was passing. "Lord King," she called to him. "Is this right? Is it proper?" And a voice will descend from Heaven and will say, "Happy Israel! Fortunate are you, Israel! You are a dear child, God's firstborn child, his beloved! Happy Israel! Fortunate are you, Jews! All your sorrow, all your torment, all your poverty that you have suffered till now has passed. The wicked will have a bitter end. But you will be placed happily and will live in contentment, for all the wealth of the world, all its greatness, is now yours. These are your seven years!"

The people in the Beth Hamedrash are proud hearing this, that they are so acceptable to God. It gives them more pleasure than when they were told earlier this day about Zion. "O, that it was true what they say in town, that Messiah is coming, any moment now. This is high time!"

They had all the signs and indications. First of all, the Book of Daniel. And now, this talk of Zion everywhere. Even the unbelievers are all talking about it. Only Reb Israel, stiff-necked, with his eyes fixed on the page he is reading, doesn't look up. He reads on steadily as before.

"Losid Lovu," when Messiah comes, and the nations will hear that God, Blessed be he, has lifted up the fortunes of the Jews and has brought them into Eretz Israel, then they will shake and tremble, suffer pangs like the birth pangs of a woman in labor. Then God, Blessed be he, will address them: "Fools, unbelievers! How many lords have lorded over you, and my children were not angry. Now when my child lords it, you storm and rage. Then all the nations will bring gifts to King Messiah. And when they come to him, Messiah will say:

"Are there none of my Jews among you! Be so good and bring them here to me. But with dignity and not with dishonor."

Then they will bring the Jews from all over the world. And the old people who can't walk, they will carry them on their backs. And when they have all come to Jerusalem the Shechina will come to meet them, and Jerusalem will be the chief city of all lands. As the Midrash says: "Jerusalem will be a lamp for all the nations of the world. And all will go towards its brightness. Many nations will become proselytes of their own free will, will lay tephilin, make fringes and fix mezuzas to their doors. In that day the seven thousand Jews who live in Eretz Israel will rise out of their graves and will become new beings, a kind of spirit, almost without substance, nothing at all. They will hover in the air and fly like angels. Each Jew will be a hundred ells tall. The streets of Jerusalem will be full of diamonds and other gems, and everyone will take as many as his heart desires. All the bare trees will grow fruit, the earth will bring forth bread and silk garments. Wheat will be as tall as a date tree. By their own friction they will produce flour. Each grape in the vineyard will be the size of a barrel of thirty quarts of wine. A stream will flow out from the Temple, whose waters will cure and heal. The dumb will speak. Barren women will bear children. And we will become transfigured, with a fine face and with fine bearing."

When Jews hear any talk of a feast, they immediately imagine Leviathan and the Great Ox. And the very poor ones with their stomachs rumbling keep moving nearer to Reb Israel, who is reading all this aloud. "God, Blessed be he," he proceeds, "gives a feast for the Tzadikim—Leviathan and the Great Ox. Three angels will serve, Gabriel the shochet, Raphael the baker, and Michael the cup-bearer. These three who once ate at Abraham's table will now return that hospitality."

"How," Reb Israel reads on, "will Gabriel slaughter? He will put the Leviathan with the Great Ox and set them one against the other. The Great Ox will lift the Leviathan between his horns and tear him to pieces. And the Leviathan will pick up the Great Ox between his fins and crush him. The Tzadikim will stare in wonder at such a shechita. And they will ask: 'How come! We have read it differently in your Torah, how to carry out shechita.' Then God, Blessed be he, will answer: 'There will be a new Torah which I shall hand down. Eat heartily!' And the Tzadikim will say to God, Blessed be he, 'They will perhaps deduct from us in the higher world for what we ate in the lower world.' And God, Blessed be he, will say: 'Have no fear! There will be no deduction. Eat heartily!'

"So the Tzadikim go to wash before eating, each under his own canopy of gold set with brilliants and shining like the stars. And sixty angels stand at the head of each Tzadik, saying: 'Go and eat! Eat heartily! And drink the wine, drink it down! This is the wine that was prepared for you from the days of Creation!'"

The poor folk listening love the story of the Leviathan and the Great Ox. They imagine that they can smell the good food, gefilte fish, and roast. They swallow their spittle, and their stomachs rumble as though someone was driving wheels over them. Reb Israel himself wouldn't have refused a piece of fish, had it been there. Never mind! If it isn't there you must beat the Tempter and go on with your reading. We've waited so long, we'll wait a little longer.

"After the feast," Reb Israel reads on, "the cup of wine will be passed to Abraham, our father, to lead the saying of grace. He will decline the honor. 'Not me! From my loins came Ishmael!' They will then ask Isaac. He too will decline: 'I fathered Esau.' They will then ask Jacob. And Jacob also will say, 'No, I took two sisters for wives.' Moses refused as well: 'I was not worthy to enter Eretz Israel.' Next it was the turn of King David. And his answer will be: 'It is from me that Messiah will descend. I will say grace!' Then he will take the cup, which holds two hundred and twenty-one quarts, and he will say grace. After that King David will take his fiddle with eight strings and play. And the Tzadikim, who will shine like the sun and the moon and the stars will dance. And God, Blessed be he, will sit at the head, and they will all point their fingers at him and say: 'This is our God, in whom we placed our trust. Let us rejoice with our God!' And they will all rejoice, and they will sing a new tune. And they will go for a walk with God in Gan Eden, in Paradise, among all the trees."

The idea of a walk with God is enchanting to Reb Israel's listeners. And Reb Israel goes on reading:

"Over there, in Gan Eden, there are two gates of precious stones and their name is Chad-Chad, and seated on them are six times a hundred thousand angels, whose clearness is clear as the heavens. When a Tzadik enters, they immediately strip him of his garments and replace them with eight robes of woolen purple, with two crowns of gold with diamonds and pearls, and they put in his hands eight myrtles that smell with the fragrance of fine herbs. So arrayed he enters into Gan Eden, in which there are three hundred and ten worlds. And God, Blessed be he, sits among the poor folk and explains to them the Torah. There, in Gan Eden, they see all the treasures of gold and silver and brilliants, and the precious vessels of the Temple that the Levites had hidden, with a solemn oath not to reveal their secret place till Messiah comes, till all Jews will be delivered from the Golus and will have entered Eretz Israel, in God's good time, speedily. And these are the treasures: precious stones, thirty-six thousand; diamonds, the same number; gold, twice a hundred thousand hundredweight; silver, a hundred and twenty times ten thousand hundredweight; copper vessels and fire pans and other vessels of fine copper; iron, without number and without weight; gold armor and gold tables of refined gold; and thousands and thousands. And more diamonds, with more precious stones, a thousand times a thousand and three times a hundred thousand and seventy thousand."

"Oh dear!" A thousand times a thousand and three times a hundred thousand with seventy thousand! That's what the poor folk listening think to themselves, their heads whirling with all this talk of so much gold and silver and gems lying waiting for them to take. If only one could get hold of just one little diamond now, one small lump of gold, say a hundred and twenty pounds in weight, to have now, for the present! But there! It won't be long now, not so long as it's been till now. For according to what people are saying Messiah is on his way. "Oh, dear God! Oh, God Almighty!" they sigh.

"By now the fiddles that King David has made of cremona wood, overlaid with gold, a thousand fiddles and seven thousand cymbals, of pure silver, with bells, good bells, and many other instruments, countless, without end. These are all the instruments that lie hidden waiting for the time when Messiah comes. Then all Jews will gather from all the four corners of the earth and will go to Eretz Israel with song. Would that it were the will of the Holy One, Blessed be he, that we should all live to see it and be privileged to behold it with our own eyes, soon, speedily, in our own life time. Say Kaddish!"

One said Kaddish, and the whole gathering responded "Amen! Let His Great Name be blessed!" And they remain standing, voiceless, as if bewitched, as though they had just returned from some far-off distant land or had just wakened from a sweet dream. Almost as though still enjoying the fragrance of the sweet herbs that grow in Gan Eden. Almost as though they still had shimmering before their eyes the glitter of the gold and the diamonds and gems that lie about there. Strange—these Jews have this Sabbath day heard two kinds of different readings, one before Mincha, a story about an event that had just occurred, a gathering in the town of Basel, a congress to which Jews had come from all the corners of the earth; they had looked for ways and means to help our poor suffering people, and they had found there is only one remedy, a land, a piece of land that is our own, and this land is Zion, the only land where Jews should buy land, quite plainly and simply with money and work, the land worked with our hands in the usual way, not waiting for miracles till Messiah comes, but to bring down Messiah ourselves. This story went in one ear and out the other, leaving everyone with a different interpretation, each as he wishes and wants it. The other, after Mincha, had told a story of the time to come, what would happen in the future, something outside the normal course of events, full of miracles. And this story went deep, very deep into their bones.

Where, Lord God, have you another People like your People Israel?!

3
Messiah Among Jewish Children

The Sabbath day is ended. The sun has already set. Almost night, but no star yet to be seen in heaven. In the Mazepevke Beth Hamedrash Jews keep looking out of the windows, wanting to start evening prayers, but because of the dust all round the Beth Hamedrash they can't see the world. That's what the boys in cheder have done. It's these young imps with their games who have brought down this darkness. Summer evenings Jewish children are busy playing, throwing sand at each other and getting sand into each other's eyes, heaping an old Jew with sand from head to foot. He stops, wipes his eyes, coughs, spits, and shouts with this toothless mouth: "Scamps! Young rascals! Wild animals! Because of you Messiah doesn't come! You wait till he's here! You'll catch it! You and your father and mother! Bastards!"

But the young rascals only laugh at him and scoop up more sand to fling at him, and the sand hits a couple of drovers passing with their cattle and sheep and pigs. The Jewish children cheer, hailing it as another blow against Esau. And they start a singsong:

> Here you come with your sheep and cows.
> Messiah will come soon to us Jewish boys!

Esau doesn't seem to like this kind of reception and makes a rush at Jacob with his drover's stick. "Dirty Jews!" Esau shouts. "A curse on your mother's mother!"

Jewish children know that Esau, stick in hand, can render a better account of himself than Jacob can with words alone, and they fall back on the old Jewish trick—pick up your legs and go! Quick as you can! They hide in the synagogue forecourt, well out of sight, silent as mice. Till they see there's no one about, and then they come out of their hiding place, first one, then another, and they form up again in front, outside the Beth Hamedrash, and go back to their game, scooping up handfulls of sand and dust from the ground and flinging them high up in the air, like Moses when he brought the Sixth Plague on the Egyptians.

"You know what!" cried one of the boys, Mottel Split-Lip, "let's play Exodus! I'll be Pharoah! And Moishe Petele and Blind Arke will be Moses and Aaron. Little Yossel will be Joseph, and Yenkel, the carpenter's boy Jacob."

"Do me a favor!" said Berl Puchlek, a boy with fat cheeks and red lips. "How do Jacob and Joseph come into the Exodus? Why not bring in Terah too and Adam as well? It would liven things up a bit!"

That raises a laugh among the boys, and Mottel Split-Lip steps back embarrassed.

"I've got a better idea," says Fishel, a boy with flaming red hair and freckles all over his face. "Let's have a new game—Messiah! My mother said this morning that Messiah is on his way!"

"Right!" all the boys agreed. "Let's play Messiah!"

And immediately they start a quarrel over allocating the parts. Who is to play Moses, and who the Prophet Elijah, who King David, and who the Saints, who the wicked, and who Gog and Magog.

"Let David Clubfoot be King David!" says one boy. "It fits him. His name is David!"

"Nice king he'd make with a clubfoot!" one of the boys objects.

"I'd make a better King David!" says Medi Loshak. A lanky ten year-old, with a head like a horse. Which was why he had the nickname Loshak, which means young horse.

"And I'll be the Prophet Ali!" That's Ali, the repair tailor's boy, pleading with the rest for a part. He's a very poor and sad little boy.

"All right!" says Pinni, who is an only child in a rich family. "You be the Prophet Ali. Always wearing a torn capote."

"And I'll be the Messiah!" says Big Nissel.

"No, Nissel! You'll make a better Gog-Magog!" says Little Nissel.

"Why Gog-Magog?"

"Because that's what you are! A Gog-Magog."

That brings a burst of laughter from the rest. Only except one boy wanting to know, "Who is Gog-Magog? What's Gog-Magog?"

Nobody knows. Nobody can explain the meaning of Gog-Magog. Some of them had heard one of the men in the synagogue say Gog-Mogog—"Messiah is coming! To take the Jew out of Golus. To bring them to Eretz Israel. After a great war with Gog-Magog."

"I know now," cries Kopul, Leib Aaron's boy. "I know! Gog-Magog is a Turk. If it's a war, it's a Turk!"

"Kopul's head isn't a head. It's a baking tin!" says Feitel, a boy from a poor home, but with lots of spirit. He makes the others laugh. And the talk goes back to the Messiah, to Eretz Israel, to the resurrection of the dead.

"Resurrection of the dead!" says Getzel, the widow's son, a little fellow with big black thoughtful eyes. "If it's resurrection of the dead I'll soon be seeing my father, may he rest in peace!"

"Where is your father?" asks Hershel, the shochet's son, very earnestly.

"What do you mean where? Here in the graveyard, like all Jews!"

"Then," Hershel goes on, speaking like a grown-up, "then it will take a long time for his bones to roll all the way from here to Eretz Israel, because it is in Eretz Israel that his bones will rise up on Resurrection Day. So will all our ancestors who lie here, outside Eretz Israel, and will have to roll all the way to Eretz Israel."

At the mention of the word Resurrection the Jewish children stop laughing, look up to Heaven, up to the moon shining down with a smiling face and to the stars twinkling, each star the soul of a human person, and they stand still as if under a spell. An end to their childish game. They are thinking hard. For each of them has a portion in this cemetery, each has someone near buried here, a father, a mother, a grandfather or a grandmother, a brother or a sister, a neighbor, a friend—and they will all before long roll under the ground from here to Eretz Israel, to rise up at the Resurrection. What joy, they think, it will be after so many years in the ground! They will fall on each other's neck and hug and kiss and shed tears. "Father! Mother! Brother! Sister! My dear ones! What have you been doing all this time. Tell us about things in Eretz Israel!"

That's how Jewish children imagine these things with their childish imagination. And they hope with all their heart that Messiah should come soon. First of all they would be rid of cheder—no more Rebbe, no more prayerbook, no more cane. Jewish children would be free to enjoy themselves, would have a jolly time, going idly all day through the streets, with pockets bulging with dates and carobs, apples and pomegranates, bathing three times a day in a river of olive oil and honey, and climbing up all the high peaks of Carmel and Lebanon.

Suddenly angry shouts from the Beth Hamedrash. Jews coming out. "Have you said your evening prayers! Louts! Hooligans! Rogues! You wait! Tomorrow in cheder you'll get what's coming to you!"

And our happy venturesome, aspiring youngsters fall immediately right down from the heights on to the everyday ground of the synagogue forecourt, with the worshipers gathering round them for the Blessing of the New Moon, dancing towards her with the words: "As I dance towards you and cannot reach you, so shall my enemies fail to reach me." Then they greet each other, saying three times, "Sholom Aleichem," and they call it a good omen, "If God wishes it will be a good week, an auspicious week, that Messiah may come!"

Quietly, thoughtfully, Jews make their way home, hearts full of something both happy and sad. On one side Messiah, with Leviathan, Great Ox, gold and silver and diamonds and brilliants, and great honor and prestige from all the nations over the world. On the other side troubles and troubles and troubles. Jews blackened and defamed, persecuted and oppressed, even where we think everything is already good and fine. On one side news from Zion, about buying it from the Turk, working the land of Eretz Israel. Sure! Why not? But where do we get the small change? Heaven above, where do we get the cash? How do we manage to live to see the day when Messiah will come? Heaven help us, Lord God! How do we live to see it, Father in Heaven, dear Father, sweet Faithful God?

Quietly, thoughtfully, Jewish children go along, expelled from Gan Eden, driven out of Paradise. Not all together, but separately, in ones, and in their hearts they are both happy and sad. On one side Messiah, high mountains, Eretz Israel, dates, apples, carobs. On the other side the cheder, the Rebbe, the cane. They stare up at the moon and ask her, quietly, each of them in his heart: "Tell me, moon, whose reflection are you? Tell me, moon, when will we get rid of the Rebbe? When will Messiah come? Heaven help us! When will he come, when will Messiah come, dear God, Messiah, the son of David!

Quietly, thoughtfully, Jewish children going home from the synagogue forecourt, on this beautiful bright warm summer's night, and none of them has even a moment's thought to spare for nature, the night-blanket that has covered all space, speckled with sparkling brilliants, to listen to the nightingale far away in the Monastirski Park, preparing for tonight's concert, to enjoy the fragrance that the wind has brought here, a rare, delightful smell of green grass and fresh hay newly cut. What has all this to do with Jewish children? What do Jewish children in Mazepevke know about rolling in the grass, on the fresh hay, and watching at the same time those tiny creatures running around on God's earth, the beetle with its green capote out for a stroll, thoughtful like a dignified householder, with folded wings, and so on to the tiniest ant that has managed to climb up to the top of a blade of grass and is showing off there with its acrobatics. When have Jewish children seen little lambs, black and white, snug in some deep valley or high up on a mountain, nibbling at the grass or lying still with their legs under them and their heads on one another, like small children? Where have Jewish children seen a field of golden corn, swaying wherever the wind tells them? As for being in the field oneself, helping oneself cut corn, binding the sheaves, bronzed by the sun, and returning at night, singing. Jewish children, cheder boys, have learned in the Bible that once there was a time when Jews had the custom of bringing the first ears of corn to the Temple as an offering. But that was a long time ago, when Jews had their own fields and their own land, Eretz Israel. Though what good does it do you now that once upon a time there was all this? There was a time once when Jews had all these good things—a Temple, a king, a priest, a prophet, and also fighters, heroes, like Samson and King David, whom the whole world feared. What do you get out of it now, that we had all this once and haven't now?

Whenever did Jewish children hear of gymnastics, which includes acrobatics, swimming, climbing, jumping, dancing? God forbid! How could such things fit in with Jewish children? How would it look! Jewish children, poor mites, have to go to cheder, the narrow, cramped cheder, far away from the fields and the sun and the bright world. Jewish children have to go in fear of the Rebbe, must tremble before his cane. Jewish children whenever they come up against nature, some summer's night, have a little chat with the moon: "Tell me, moon, whose reflection are you? Do you perhaps know when Messiah will come? Dear God, when will he come, Messiah, the son of David!

4
Messiah Among the Hasidim

"Elijah the Prophet, Elijah the Tishbite, Elijah the Gileadite." This is the song Reb Simcha Perlzweig, a wealthy Jew and a Hasid of the Makarevke Rebbe, is singing with his very fine voice, this Saturday night before the third Sabbath meal, his eyes turned piously upward, snapping his fingers to the rhythm, and the company of Hasidim with him joining in at all the right places, clapping their hands in accompaniment. "Speedily, speedily, he will rebuild the Temple speedily, with Messiah, the son of David."

Reb Simcha has a third Sabbath meal feast every Saturday night for years past. It's no burden on him. He is, thank God, in good health. With a shining face and red cheeks. Always in a good mood. He won't let anything upset him. He hates worrying. "For what tomorrow may bear, God will take care."

Even if it sometimes happens, at one of the fairs he goes to, that things don't turn out right, even if it so happens that he can't pay up (which happens with Reb Simcha every three or four years) it doesn't dishearten him. He has a good way of straightening things out. He doesn't default, God forbid! He closes down an account at one of the fairs, puts things straight, pays part in cash, spreads the rest over several years, and whatever real money there is he puts into a safe place, an orphan's inheritance, or a young girl's dowry, and it finds its way to Reb Simcha. He is a good sort, a companionable man, with special relationships with everybody separately, the first among the first everywhere, president in every society. Any deputation, any arbitration, any decision to be made, and it goes to Reb Simcha as the adjudicator. As for the rebbe—there Reb Simcha is most at home. Among the Hasidim he is "our Reb Simcha," and no one dare say a bad word about him. It wouldn't be safe! And his wife, Ittelle, is highly respected in the town, almost herself a rebbetzin. The way she says the prayers, aloud, so that the other women can follow. How she weeps over her devotions! Scoffers have invented a legend that she puts on tephilin, and they call her "Reb Ittelle."

Reb Simcha and Reb Ittelle have one daughter, an only child, Pearl, beautiful as the sun in summer, gladdening the heart of the most incorrigible moaner. With sky blue eyes and the sweetest of smiles. And because Pearl is an only child, there is nothing her parents find too costly for her, the loveliest dress, the latest fashion—anything for Pearl! The best teacher in town! The best piano, for Pearl! Pearl's beauty, Pearl's intelligence, Pearl's letter writing, her piano playing! The whole town knows about it! And not only in Mazepevke, in her home town; her fame has spread to all the towns round about, the whole region, among the Makarevke Hasidim, with whom Reb Simcha is "our Reb Simcha" and his wife Ittelle is "our Reb Ittelle."

"That's our Pearl!" "Our Pearl!" Everyone who knows Pearl, and also those who don't, has a match for her. Proposals from everywhere, all over the world! But what can you say to this? She won't hear of it!

"Time! Plenty of time! Time for Pearl to get married!"

"Time!" Reb Simcha agrees. "Just bring me the right bridegroom!"

"May God, Blessed be he, give us more years," says Ittelle, "and there will be a marriage, a grand marriage, in God's good time. God himself will send her the right match. May we live to see it soon, Amen, Selah!"

"Play us something lively, Pearl!" says Reb Simcha in the course of the third Sabbath meal. And Pearl, though she is otherwise engaged—locked in her own room, writing a letter—puts it all aside, goes to the piano, and plays a lively, jolly piece, with everybody joining in, clapping their hands to the rhythm.

> The Rebbe said we must merry be,
> Drinking wine plentifully,
> Till the bright day dawns happily!

"You can have Israel's fiddle and all the musicians for her one little finger!" says Reb Eli, a little Hasid with a big grey beard, and red-rimmed eyes.

"Blessed hands," the others chime in, clapping hands in time to the music.

"If she were a boy, I would kiss every inch of her," Reb Eli continues, with his eyes on Pearl's lovely white fingers, gliding over the ivories to Reb Eli's intense delight.

"A fine girl! What a dear child!" everybody agrees, chiming in and clapping hands.

> The Rebbe said we must merry be,
> Drinking wine plentifully,
> Till the bright day dawns happily!

"Why don't you say something, Reb Simcha?" says Reb Eli. "Aren't you doing anything about a match for your daughter?"

"Who has a mind these days for marriages?" says Reb Getzel, a Jew with a scrawny beard, laughing, with all the rest joining in the laughter. "Not now, when any moment Messiah will be here!"

"Yes," Reb Simcha agrees. "What do you all make of this story about Messiah's coming? Everybody is talking about it! Who are all these doctors that Yossel Moishe Yossis had on his list?"

"Heretics! Unbelievers! Scoundrels!" Eli answers, without taking his eyes off Pearl. He had noticed that when her father mentioned Yossel Moishe Yossis she had started, looked round, and then back to her piano.

"True!" says Reb Shloime, a man with a high forehead, flabby cheeks, and a pointed little beard making his face look like an inverted Magen David. "True! Heretics, unbelievers, scoundrels! Only the heretics have such power in them to destroy everything!"

"All right! What then?" Reb Eli asks, addressing himself to Reb Shloime, with his eyes still on Pearl.

"So what do you want us to believe?" another man intervenes, "that they will find their way to the Turk with the red fez and buy Eretz Israel from him?"

"Buy? Why buy! Take it by force!" someone says, thinking to make a joke of it.

"Take it by force and kick out Ishmael!" another one joins in, bursting with laughter, and all the rest laughing with him. Except Reb Eli. Reb Eli is furious, as though someone had spoiled a deal he had made at the fair.

"I would take such youngsters like Yossel Moishe Yossis, lay them down in the middle of the Beth Hamedrash, and count fifty-five lashes, to draw blood!" So says Reb Eli, with his little red-rimmed eyes on Pearl, wondering why she had suddenly stopped playing.

"Play, Pearl!" Reb Eli turns to her. "Play something jolly! Something Jewish! Send them to hell, all those rascals! Let them bang their heads against the wall, together with the Turk! I can't listen to rogues like that who desecrate the Sabbath, carrying things, talking about Messiah, and crying Eretz Israel!"

"It isn't called Eretz Israel any more," says Reb Getzel. "They call it Palestine now!" And again everybody laughs.

"Let it be Eretz Israel! Let it be Palestine, so long as it's true!" says Reb Simcha, very thoughtfully, thinking to himself—"I wish it was true! It would save me a lot of headache before every fair, taking from one and paying another. The whole world would straighten out! A kosher pot with a kosher spoon! Who'd bother then about a bill of exchange? Who'd lodge a protest? What's mine is yours, what's yours is mine! And that's that!"

"Why so thoughtful, Reb Simcha?" one of the men asks him.

"I'm thinking," says Reb Simcha, "how all this has grown up suddenly."

"It's grown from someone named Dr. Herzl," Reb Shloime suggests.

"Herzl Shmerzl," says Reb Eli angrily. "Some ruffians think up a lot of stuff and nonsense, and you have to repeat their stupidities! Pah! You should be ashamed of yourself!"

"But there was this Yossel Moishe Yossis reading out a story from Basel that this Dr. Herzl had just arrived there from Stamboul."

"What have I to do with Basel? Or with Stamboul?" Reb Eli interrupts him. "Scamps! Ruffians! Idlers! Do nothings! Tell you all sorts of fairy tales, and you swallow them!"

"They say that the Zfir"—Reb Shloime tries to get a word in.

"The Zfir, no less!" Reb Eli continues his attack. "The real holy Shrine!"

"No! That's not what I said! I said—"

"I know what you said! I know what you want to say. I know what you want to say before you said it! But it's rubbish, muck, just muck! Nothing at all! Rubbish from start to end. Take my advice, Reb Simcha, and fetch up a quart bucket of wine out of your cellar, your Koveshamer wine!"

"That's right! Koveshamer wine!" comes from clammering voices all-around. "Reb Eli is right! Koveshamer wine! Fetch up the Koveshamer wine!"

Everybody now joins in the cry, shouting and singing and clapping hands to Pearl's playing at the piano.

> The Rebbe said we must merry be,
> Drinking wine plentifully,
> Till the bright day dawns happily!

Pearl keeps playing, but her mind is elsewhere. She would rather have gone to her own room and finished writing the letter she had left off in the middle. A very important letter, written to—she wouldn't like to say to whom she was writing this letter. It would be embarrassing. Not the right company for Reb Simcha and Reb Ittelle and for all this crowd. That "our Pearl" should do such a thing! But since there are worse things in the world, which shouldn't be done and yet are done, we'll tell tales out of school, we'll reveal the contents of the letters that Yossel Moishe Yossis wrote to Pearl, and that Pearl wrote to Yossel Moishe Yossis. It had been long agreed between them—their sworn secret—

that they were engaged, that they would marry. No Adam's son knew anything about it. Except Feierstein, the teacher, the only person privy to their secret, their witness and their letter carrier. On guard, Jews of Mazepevke, on guard against Feierstein, the teacher! Feierstein was the first to discover that Yossel Moishe Yossis was in love with Pearl and Pearl was in love with Yossel. They had both confided their secret to him. In front of him they had both sworn eternal troth. Through his arranging they had met several times, lovers' meetings, and through him letters passed to and fro, day after day. On your guard, Mazepevke Jews! That teacher Feierstein is betraying you, dealing you a death blow!

From Pearl Perlzweig to Yossel Moishe Yossis—

"My dear true precious Joseph,

Thank you, dear Joseph, thank you for you dear sweet words in your precious letter, and for the books you sent me, and for all the other news that our true only friend Feierstein has passed on to me. I thank you for not forgetting me, dear Joseph, even at this time when there are so many more important things, at this time when you have so much work to do, when you are occupied with the sacred idea of Zion. May God give you strength and patience to carry all the difficulties in your way, to overcome all the troubles, with God's help, that our holy plan should be realized. Then we shall have our minds free to think of ourselves. Oh, how high, how lofty and beautiful are the words you write to me: 'First let us live to see the happiness of our People, and after that we shall think of our own happiness.' Yes, you are right, my dear, you are right! One thing I can promise you, Joseph—all that you tell me to do I will do! Whereever you tell me to go I will go! For as you know, I am yours entirely, body and soul, yours to eternity! Only death can part us! Oh, how much pleasure I had from the books you sent me! Especially the flaming fiery speech by Dr. Max Nordau! It shows that our God lives! There are still among us great, noble, sincere people who are prepared to sacrifice themselves for the People of Israel! I am fully convinced that a few more men like Max Nordau, Dr. Herzl, Dr. Mandelstamm, and Messiah will come! I am fully convinced, dear Joseph, that your name will one day be included together with the names of these great men! No one knows you as I do! No one understands you as I do! No one feels what is in your heart as I do, when you speak of our poor suffering people, and of our holy precious land Zion! Oh, Zion! How sweet is that word! How beautiful that name! How happy I would consider myself if I could be a sacrifice offered up for my People and my country, if I could in any way be of use to my sisters in Zion! Dear Joseph, you say we are unfortunate because we live in a backwoods place like Mazepevke, a seat of black ignorance and fanaticism. I say we women are doubly unfortunate. You have found a few young people like yourself with whom you can discusss these things. I am alone! With no one else, without a soul to say a word to. If not for you, dear Joseph, I don't think I could stay here another day! If you had been in our house on Saturday night during the third meal and heard the things the people there said about Zion, about Messiah, it would have made your gall rise! I had to laugh and cry, both. Laugh because our elders can utter such absolute rubbish. And cry because sincere Jews, watching out for Messiah and praying to God every day to lead them back to Jerusalem, now when we come to them and tell them to go to Zion, they laugh and jeer, scoff at us, refuse to listen, make nothing of our effort, because we want to bring Messiah down before his time!

"But however low the men in our circle stand, their womenfolk stand lower. I must tell you, dear Joseph, your beautiful thought-laden speech in the old synagogue was a wasted effort. They didn't understand you. I asked my mother and some of the other women as well, to tell me what you had said. None of them knew. All they said was that you had spoken well. I asked them, 'What did he say?' 'He spoke well!' That's all I could get out of them. 'What did he say!' 'I've no idea! I coudn't make it out! You can't make out the words in the old synagogue!' They came with nothing and went with nothing. There was a lot of talk about Messiah! Messiah was coming! Would soon be here. Farfetched tales, cock and bull stories! That's all they got out of your speech. My dear Joseph, you don't know how ignorant our women in the small towns are! They are miles away from our ideal of Zion! Much further away than Zion is from us! No doubt our great men who care for our People will do everything possible to open the eyes of our People, men and women, that they should see the road that leads to salvation, so that they will all understand that happiness lies in their own hands, that our true hope is the Holy Land, Zion!

"Only one thing I beg of you—in God's Name, don't lose courage. Don't give up your work for the Jewish People! Would that I could be as useful among the Jewish women, my sisters, as you are among your brothers. Then I would indeed count myself fortunate!

"Oh, why can't I be at the meeting now with you! Write to me, my dear, write to me often, since it is not possible to see you. I go in fear of Jewish tongues. I am afraid of my parents. That they should not find out about our love and end our happiness. But if you decide, dear Joseph, that we should see each other, I am ready any moment! Write to me only where and when. For I am yours entirely, completely, forever! Your Pearl."

5
Messiah Among the Chovevei Zion and the Zionists

Dr. Herzl surely did not work as hard in Basel at the congress as Yossel Moishe Yossis worked here in Mazepevke this Saturday night at the big meeting of the Chovevei Zion held in Yossel Moishe Yossis's home. At this meeting he was himself the shammas, the secretary and the president. It hadn't been easy to get his father's consent to use the big salon for the meeting.

"I can see, Yossel," his father had said banteringly, "I can see that you and your pals have taken it upon yourselves in real earnest to bring down Messiah.

What will happen when he comes with all my contracts and my mortgages and my outstanding loans and all my other business affairs?"

"When we are working for the good of the People as a whole, one man's affairs don't count," Yossel answered.

"So you really want to make a pauper of me! A bankrupt! Think it over, Yossel! Pity your father! Postpone the whole thing for at least six months, till I can wind up my affairs. After that you and your Chovevei Zion friends can bring down Messiah and lead us, empty-handed, to Eretz Israel."

"That's the trouble with you!" said Yossel, flaring up. "You're always putting things off with a joke. Think of our people, how we are placed, what is going on in the world! Listen to what educated people say! You can't bear that! One good day in your affairs is more important to you than the life of our people, who drown in a sea of troubles, crying for help!"

"And you, with your friends, will help our people?"

"Happy the generation whose great men, whose elders follow the lesser, the young!"

"I know!" rejoined his father. "I know you can quote Hebrew to make your point. Not for nothing I nearly ruined myself to give you a good education. But take care you don't go too far and have people laugh at me because of my son who is a philosopher. Not a good recommendation for a marriage settlement."

"Don't worry about that! I won't go too far. And it won't hurt my marriage prospects."

Moishe Yossis couldn't make out how his son came to be so firm in what he said, so sure of himself. He had always been such a quiet, shy young man. Never raised his voice. "Must be those books he reads day and night," he thinks to himself. "Or not so much the books as that teacher Feierstein! No, we must get the boy married! The sooner the better!"

And Moishe Yossis opened the door of his study, leaving it ajar, so that he could look into the big salon and see the young people who were assembling there and listen to their conversation. He recalled that he had also been a young man and had friends of his own age. But it had been a different world then. Other ideas. Other discussions. Not like now. Boys had played games. None of them had wanted to sit and study. Their ideas had been about a beautiful bride and a fat dowry and big business. Not now! That wasn't what the young people were thinking now—they talked about the People, about Zion and colonies in Zion and about Messiah and the messianic times! Moishe Yossis looked through the half-open door into the salon and saw his son Yossel running around, busy, placing chairs, greeting new arrivals, all the young Chovevei Zion.

Moishe Yossis listened to their conversation, what these people were saying, everybody talking at the same time. For after all, young Jews are also Jews. And Jews tend to do all the talking themselves, not listening to what the other man is saying.

"Quiet! A little more quiet, please!" That's Yossel pleading with them.

"We've got important decisions to make. Should we elect members first or should we first talk about Zionism, and then elect members?"

"Elect members first," said Hershel Leib Aaron's.

"Talk about Zionism first!" said Yenkel David Moishe's.

"Why not elect members first?" said Mottel Chaim Berz's.

"Because members are not needed so urgently," said Itzel Abraham Simcha's.

"It's the other way round—very much needed," said Abraham Koppel Manasseh's.

"Then let's get on with the elections! Now!" said Yudel Leiser Wolf's.

"You tell me first why we need members," said Mendel Ben Zion's.

"So what have we decided?" Yossel Moishe Yossis wanted to know.

"First we elect members and then we talk Zionism," several voices all at once.

"First talk Zionism and then have the elections," several other voices.

"If you don't mind," said the rabbi's son Naphtali, who has decided to call himself Pantelman. A nice young man with a red shirt and a big mop of hair. Studying to be a pharmacist. Speaks half Yiddish, half Russian.

"I find the whole controversy pointless. To begin with, I don't hold with the whole idea, with the whole movement of the present-day Zionists. I mean to say, they can do our people a lot of harm. Much more than the anti-Semites. I'll prove it to you if you want me to. Like twice two. If you will let me say what I think. I know that you will denounce me, call me an assimilator. But everybody has a right to his opinion. The difference is that one says it openly, and the other is ashamed to say so. I'm not sure which is the more honest. I am generally the kind of man who doesn't stop to choose his words, especially on such a question, which affects our people. You want to heal us with a new remedy, Zionism. Now will you first tell me what is the aim of Zionism? You want to establish a state in Palestine. So the first thing is, you must get the consent of the Turkish sultan and of all the states in Europe. But let me assume that your representatives succeed. First of all, I want to ask you not to interrupt me. Where was I? All right! Let me assume that we have obtained full permission from all the states, and everything is as right as right can be, excellent! We are still left with the question—first of all, is our people ready to go to Palestine? What will we do in Palestine? Farm work you say. But first of all, have we lost the ability to do farm work? So many centuries—wandering from one country to another. All these nations hate us. Call us exploiters, parasites. We have lost all respect for our people. For our history. For our religion. We have lost our national awareness. We have become totally bankrupt. You will say the next generation will be more able than we are. In the first place, has our youth been trained already in the spirit of the nineteenth century, at a time when all the nations are making progress and will soon abandon nationalism? There will be no difference then between religions. All nations, including our nation, will enjoy complete solidarity. We will no longer need any help from your Zionism.

And if you persist and force on us your idea of nationalism and Zionism you will only, in the first place, incite people to hate us more than ever, at a time when there is already so much hate against us. Instead of being useful to us you will only harm us. You will bring about retrogression, hold back the tide of progress for another century. And all our work will go for nothing. All our effort in education. As for the Jewish state, Dr. Herzl's dream, I can assure you it is a fantasy. Not worth talking about. For in the first place, the Turkish sultan will not allow Jews to settle in his country. And the other European states to say nothing of the Catholics, will be against us. They'll present us with a pogrom that we'll remember till Messiah comes! And the land itself, in the first place, is in ruins, waste. So that I can't think what our poor brethren can do there for a living. Where will they get, in the first place, all the bread needed to feed themselves and their families? Where will they get it from? Who will defend them when the wild Arabs attack them? Therefore, I say, let your defenders, in the first place, Dr. Herzl, Dr. Nordau, Dr. Mandelstamm, and the rest of your defenders devote their attention rather to the plight of our luckless brethren here on the spot, who suffer poverty, hunger, and cold, lost in dark ignorance and fanaticism. They need, in the first place, bread and a kind word. Then you would receive, in the first place, thanks from our entire Jewish People."

This speech by Naphtali Pantelman fell on the Chovevei Zion youngsters like a bucket of cold water. They had all come to the meeting feeling very warm over the news of the Zionist Congress in Basel. They all still had the taste of Dr. Max Nordau's great speech there on their tongue. And now suddenly they had gotten this cold douche. It had destroyed the whole idea which was the basis of Zionism and of Zion. And where? Here, at the meeting where the Chovevei Zion had assembled to discuss Zionism. Who had brought this Pantelman here? Who had asked him to come? All eyes turned on Yossel Moishe Yossis. Who realized that it was his fault, for having asked Pantelman to come to the meeting, a person who did not fit in. It was for him now to make up for his mistake. He would have to be answered, his arguments refuted. And he, Yossel, was the only one there who could answer him.

So Yossel Moishe Yossis stood up, his eyes blazing, his hands trembling (and his father behind the door saw it and heard it all).

"Friends," Yossel began, "the world says you must never hear one side only. You have heard till now, and you have read till now only about Zion. Now you have heard a few words against Zion. I think you should find it pleasing to hear such complaints. Every idea has its followers and its opponents. Our Zionism too has its opponents. It shows you that our idea is no empty notion. Your opponents, the anti-Zionists, are scared. As you heard, they tremble lest we should bring harm, God forbid, to our people, by telling our brothers that we are a nation like all nations, that we have, besides world history, also our own Jewish history, that besides the other literatures in which Jews also play a part, we have our own Jewish literature, that besides the other patriotisms, we have our own Jewish patriotism, that we are devoted to the countries where we live, love them and are loyal to them, we also love and long for our own Jewish land Zion which is tied and bound up with our Jewish history, with our faith, with our whole existence. Tell me, where have you seen a Jew to whom the word Zion is not close to his heart? Show me a Jew who does not believe in Messiah, each according to his own understanding? The name alone, Messiah or Goel, 'the Redeemer' is, I think, so noble to every one of us that not wanting Messiah, not believing in Messiah seems mad, for who does not want to be saved, to be redeemed? Who does not want to be free, to be liberated? Whether our people is ready to be redeemed is, I think, a superfluous question. You will not ask a sick man if he wants to be sent home from the hospital. Nor will you ask a prisoner if he would like to be set free. Whether our people are able to till the ground in the new Jewish land, that too is a superfluous question. A nation which consists of 90 percent paupers, the poorest of the poor, would gladly till the ground even with their bare hands. A people that does not know how to survive from day to day, you don't ask such a people if they can or want to work. When you listen to such complaints as we have heard here now, you might suppose that till now Jews had sat with folded arms, eating from a well-laden table, without any idea of what it means to work. All the nations, they tell us, hate us. True! But not because we do nothing and know nothing. Because we do everything, catch hold of everything we can, turn on this side and that, and know a great deal, too much! We have lost, they say, belief in ourselves and in our nation, in our faith. True! That, indeed, is what we mean. We want to give back to our people the national feeling, our lost faith, the oldest of all the faiths. Not the faith in the rebbe with his signs and wonders, but our pure, clear faith, the holy Jewish faith, the belief and the hope in Messiah, in better times.

"Our opponents, the anti-Zionists, laugh at us, scoff at our hopes. They call them false hopes. They tell us to have different hopes, to look to a time when our people and all the nations of the world will be equal, as Isaiah foretold, when the wolf will lie down with the lamb. And when we tell our people that we can live happily on our own soil, on our own land, working our ground with honest toil, they cry it is imagination, a chimera, stuff and nonsense. And they scare us with pogroms from the Arabs. They don't seem to be aware that the Arabs are more our friends than the educated Europeans, who boast of their learning and their humanity and behave to us much worse than the 'wild Arabs,' worse than the ignorant Turks. Our opponents, the anti-Zionists, slander our land. They say it is desolate and neglected. And how will the Jews, they ask, find bread there to eat. Of course, if Jews come to Eretz Israel to write sacred works and live on Chalukah as till now, if they sit on their backsides and do not exert themselves, then, of course, they starve. But we are taking our brothers to cultivate the Land of Israel, to plough and sow and reap, to build and trade. When we do that it will be as the prophet says, 'When the Lord has comforted Zion, He has comforted all her waste places. And made her wilderness like Eden, and her desert like the garden of the Lord.' The only question that remains is whether it is possible, if there is enough land in Eretz

Israel, if the climate is congenial. To that question I can only say, 'Go there! Make the effort. Study the geography and the history. A land that once could support a population of six million, a land that was once famed throughout the East as flowing with milk and honey, such a land need not fear that her children will go hungry. If only we might live to see the day, if only we want to go there, the sooner and the more of us the better. Our opponents, the anti-Zionists, say that our impoverished brothers who are dying of hunger and are lost in darkness and ignorance need no sweet hopes but bread and a kind word. And what do we want? What is our aim? Our aim is bread, giving our people dignity, and the ground on which to grow their own bread, in our own land. That is what we want to do, to plant in the hearts of Jewish children, as Dr. Herzl said, light, and the civilization of Europe. We want to be the middlemen between Europe and Asia. Our mission has not changed—'For out of Zion shall go forth Learning and the Word of God from Jerusalem'"

"Bravo, Yossel! Bravo! Bravo!" The whole gathering broke into applause. So much clapping and cheering that Yossel's father, Moishe Yossis too, who had seen the whole thing from behind the door, listening to his son, couldn't hold back. He rose from his place and strode into the salon, clapping with the rest. Father and son exchanged looks. There were tears in Yossel's eyes, tears of joy, happy tears. One thought was in their minds—messianic days. And both thought of the passage in Malachi: "And He shall turn the heart of the fathers to the children, and the heart of the children to their fathers."

They sat late, our young folk, the Maskilim of Mazepevke. The cock had long since crowed at midnight, and our Mazepevke Zionists still sat talking, arguing, enrolling members, making plans how to help their poor brethren with bread, with money, with education, trying to find ways how to lead the Jewish people to Eretz Israel, founding organizations everywhere, collecting money, opening banks, making calculations how to use the money, buying land, establishing colonies, planting vineyards, building houses and roads, opening schools, establishing universities in all the big cities of Eretz Israel, building railways, providing postal and telephone communication, developing trade with the entire world, providing for the possibility of a war between the nations and the urgent need to defend Eretz Israel.

The Zionists in Mazeppevke sat up that night a whole state, a Jewish state. And when they at last rose to go, it was already dawn. One by one the stars faded. On one side of the sky there was a bright strip. Old Jews with skullcaps showed themselves to the world, standing by their front doors and staring wonderingly at our young folk out in the street so early, and still eagerly talking among themselves, sometimes at the top of their voices, and all together, like at a fair. Half-dressed women and girls, driving the goats to the fields and muttering to themselves: "Must be very late! We'll never catch up! Far behind!"

A peasant woman in a big shawl sat high up in the farm cart, on top of the potatoes and onions, staring at the young people in the street, who shout and throw their arms about. What brought all these young people out so early? Something must have happened! Thieves! Must be thieves about! "Hold him!" she called down from the cart. "Hold him!" "Don't let him go! The dirty Jew!"

The night has long gone. It is already bright day. one corner of the sky is bright. The sun is rising. And soon the Mazepevke market will be setting itself out, speaking with a thousand voices, calling the customers. Jewish men will soon be out to turn an honest groshen. Jewish women will be out bargain hunting. Mazepevke will be fully awake and astir. And our Zionists are still in the street, by Moishe Yossis's house, still talking, arguing, shouting. The air is so good, the wind so fresh, and the discussion so much to their liking that they don't want to stop and go home. After the wrangling, the bickering, the quarreling the Chovevei Zion and the Zionists had come to an understanding and made peace, shalom. And out of that shalom had grown affection, love such as never before, and they were all good friends, comrades. Even Naphtali, the rabbi's son, Pantelman as he calls himself now, was becoming more gentle, more understanding.

"I don't, in the first place," he said, "change my opinions. As soon as I see you agree in principle with my opinion, I must, in the first place, join your circle. I discovered from your talk that the idea of Zionism, is, in the first place, a philanthropic idea, and Zion is the only salvation for our people."

To Our Sisters in Zion

A Few Words to the Jewish Daughters

> In Mind Of
> My Dear Little Daughters
> Esther, Sarah, Naomi and Miriam,
> A Gift and a Reminder from Father
> The Author.

Dear Sisters! Jewish Daughters!

Don't take me badly, dear Sisters. I want to talk to you for a while in Yiddish. Your pardon a hundred times, Jewish Daughters. I want to address a few words to you in the tongue of our great-grandmother, the language of our people. I beg your pardon, in Jargon.

Jargon? Pah! First of all, who today understands Yiddish? And secondly, is Jargon a language, too? A language lifted from the Teitch Chumash and the Ze'ena Urena. Pah! "It reeks of tcholent!"

But forgive me, that isn't the story. In the first place, everybody understands Jargon. Let's have a bet on it, that not a single one of you will walk out of here because she doesn't understand me. And secondly, be sure of this—Jargon is a language used by over five million people of our nation. I don't say that Jargon is a holy tongue, and that we must all speak Jargon. Our Jewish holy tongue is Hebrew, Loshen Kodesh, and each of us may speak in what tongue he can.

You'll ask me why I must make excuses to you for speaking Yiddish. Will a Russian, say, or a German, or a Frenchman make excuses for himself when he speaks Russian with Russians, or German with Germans, or French with Frenchmen? Surely, it seems funny, mad, that Jews should be ashamed of talking Yiddish!

And the reason is our names, Jewish names. Aren't we ashamed of them, don't we keep changing our Jewish names everywhere for alien non-Jewish names? In what way, tell me, is Anna better than Chanah? Or Elishevah worse than Elizabeth? Why do we call our daughters Bertha, not Batya? Serafima, not Shifra? Liza, not Leah? Clara, not Chaya?

Is it the Jewish nose? Aren't we ashamed of our Jewish noses, our Jewish appearance, don't we keep making a song and dance of it when a Russian pays us the compliment of saying—"You don't look a bit like a Jew! Not the Jewish type!"

No small matter to be flattered like that! But try it the other way around. Tell a Russian that he doesn't look like a Russian. Not a bit like a Christian! He'll look at you in amazement. What d'you mean I don't look like a Russian? I don't look like a Christian?

I'm not speaking now of somebody who goes into ecstasies if he gets accepted into Christian society, travels along with them for a few stations on the road, and with God's help has not been recognized as a Jew, has been passed as a fellow human being, talked to as such, admitted into the company, and as usual, has descended to telling jokes, including jokes about Jews, Berka, Moshka, Sarka, Hershka—"Going to Berditchev? Ha! Ha! Ha!" Everybody laughs at this bit of humor, and he, with the rest, laughing like the others, though he doesn't see the joke, though in his heart, it hurts, deep down inside him, hurting like a fire, but he must laugh with the rest, because if he doesn't join in they may, heaven forbid, hit on the truth, that he is a Jew!

Where does it originate, where does it come from, this difference between us Jews and the non-Jews? It's a weighty question! What is behind it, the reason, that no nation is ashamed of its language, on the contrary, is proud of it, its names, its type, and we Jews are ashamed of our language, changing our Jewish names, burying them deep down underground, together with our Jewish noses?

How often do you hear Poles speaking Polish in the street, or in the theater, or Belgians speaking their language, or Russians speaking Russian and Turks, Turkish, just as though they were at home?

You'll say it is because we are a lower breed, an inferior lot in the eyes of most people, because a Jewish name is sure to raise a laugh, because a Jewish nose looks funny. But do you know the real reason for the low opinion people have about us? It's because we know so little about ourselves, as individuals or as a nation, about our history, which is full of miracles, full of heroes, full of blood, and full of tears.

> Why am I weeping, do you know?
> It's because of a book I'm reading.
> It tells the story how long ago
> There was a nation all others leading,
> A great nation, whose heroes laid our enemies low.
> We had cities and broad fields under the plough,
> And cattle and sheep enough and enow.

Do you know who wrote this song? Our Jewish poet, our folksinger Frug, written indeed in our poor Yiddish folk tongue Jargon.

> You had many heroes in your time.
> To them in fear you kept returning.
> Many nations from the Jews
> Acquired their knowledge and their learning.

Do you know what book he means? Our Bible, the book that is older than all other books, our Chumash, our ancient Jewish history. But what do Jewish daughters know of Jewish history? Let's not fool ourselves! Let's think it over. Who among our womenfolk studied Chumash, Pasuk [Prophets and Writings], Midrash, or ever saw Jewish history? The pious women of the old world who look into the Teitch Chumash on a Sabbath afternoon, who read the Ze'en Urena, they know something at least of the history of the Jewish People. True enough, they don't all understand what they read in the Teitch Chumash, in the Ze'ena Urena, which are indeed a little old-fashioned for our day. Not everyone understands the words of the holy prayers, which were written in German-like inflated style. There is little these women know of the history of the Jewish people. Yet they know more than our "ladies" do. I mean those who "with respect beg to inform that they suffer from nerves." They read novels, travel to the spas, take the "cure"—what do these ladies know of Yiddishkeit, Jewish history, anything outside "nerves," novels, social calls, concerts, dining out, card games? Even the educated Jewish daughters, those who have been through high school, what do they know of our Jewish history beyond the page and a half Sloveisky included in his *Universal History?* In those one and a half pages he gives us very ably the whole history of the Jewish people! Jewish daughters learn these one and a half pages off by heart, and they are perfectly content to have only a page and a half to deal with, thank God! That's as much as they need, and more than they want.

But what if we have a whole treasure house of writings? A vast literature, an immense library of material, and quite a number of books on the subject? The Jewish daughters don't know that, and don't want to know that. Jewish mamselles, the educated ones I mean, who have studied at high school and have learned the general history of the Romans, the Greeks, and the other nations. They know a lot of delightful stories about world-famous women. Like, for example, the Egyptian Queen Cleopatra, and the French girl Joan of Arc, the Polish Queen Jadwiga, the Queen of Scotland Mary Stuart, Marie Antoinette, Maria Theresa. Jewish mamselles who went to high school know all about these women and about lots of others. But what do they know of our famous Jewish women, in our own Jewish history? What do our mamselles know about Deborah, the wife of Lapidus, who was a prophet and a poet, and who judged Israel at that time and waged war against the Kenites? Or about Jephtah's daughter, who made her father carry out his vow to make her an offering for the army of Israel against Ammon? Or Hannah, the wife of Elkanah, the mother of Samuel? Or King Saul's daughter, Michal, who at the risk of her life saved her husband David? Or Hulda, the Prophetess, the wife of Shallum, through whom King Josiah cleaned out the Temple and destroyed the vessels of the idols? Or Judith, who slew Holofernes, and saved Israel? Or Queen Esther? What do our mamselles know? They know we have a day called Fast of Esther and a festive day called Purim, when we eat pie and other good things. Our pious wives who go to synagogue to hear the reading of the Megillah, the Book of Esther, weep over the fate of Queen Vashti, when she is commanded to appear before King

Ahasuerus. As for our "ladies," who are, "with respect to report themselves subject to nerves," read novels, travel to spas, take the "cure," and play cards, how can they lower themselves to go to the reading of the Megilla? How does it fit them to read a Jewish book, and to make matters worse, a book written in Jargon?

Much they know, our women, our ladies, our mamselles about the famous women whose stories are told in Talmud and in Midrash, those lovely tales which Jewish daughters ought to know. Like the story of Rachel, the wife of the great Rabbi Akiba. It was in Jerusalem—so the Midrash tells us—that there lived a wealthy man named Kalva Sabua. He had much land, and sheep and cattle, and he had a shepherd, named Akiba. He also had a daughter named Rachel. And as these things happen they loved each other and had made a pact to marry. Kalva Sabua didn't like the idea of his daughter marrying an ignorant shepherd, and he swore that his daughter would not inherit even a thread from all his possessions. Rachel, his daughter, grieved because of this. She spoke about it to Akiba, and she persuaded him to go away to study. He went to a Yeshiva, and he stayed there for twelve years, winning renown as a scholar, and returned with a following of twelve thousand pupils.

Rachel had waited for him all this time. "How much longer will you wait?" they asked her. "For my part," she answered, "he may stay away another twelve years studying." When this was told to Akiba, he dropped everything and went back to the Yeshiva to continue his studies. At the end of the time, when he did return, the great and famous Rabbi Akiba, with a following of twenty thousand pupils, the whole town turned out to welcome him. And among the welcoming crowds was also Rachel, who fell to his feet and kissed his feet. His pupils wanted to move her out of the way, but Rabbi Akiba stopped them. "This woman," he said, "is my beloved. She waited twenty-four years for me. All I know and all you know is hers. We have her to thank for it." How do you, dear sisters, like this Jewish love story?

Or take Beruriah, the wife of Rabbi Meir. In one day two of their sons died, while he was in the Beth Hamedrash studying. Because it was the Sabbath, she held back the news of their death, not to disturb his Sabbath peace and joy. At the Sabbath end she revealed it to him in a fable: "What is the law when someone left a pledge with me, and after a time came to ask for it back? Should I return it or not?" "Of course, you must return it!" said Rabbi Meir. So she uncovered the dead bodies, and said: "This is the pledge that God left with us for a time, and now He demands it back. We must not grieve. The Lord gave, the Lord has taken away."

You can find many such delightful stories about famous Jewish women. If you knew as much about Jewish history and Jewish literature as you know about the history and the literature of all other nations, if you knew Jewish history and Jewish literature you would meet a lot of names of world-famous Jewish women, like these: the Jewish Queen Alexandra, Queen Mariamne, the wife of Herod, the learned Yalta, the wife of Rabbi Nachman, the wife of Rabbi Joseph

Ibn Nagdala, Minister of Granada, Rachel, the learned daughter of Rashi, Rabbi Yahuda Halevi's poetess daughter, Miriam Shapiro, who became the head of a Yeshiva, Dina Wahl, Famina del Medigo, Rachel Morpurgo, the pious Gitel, Yenta Volender, Betty Rabinowitch, Miriam Mossesohn, Amalia Epstein, and many, ever so many more, whom you would meet in our history and our literature. But who among our sisters has read Graetz's *History of the Jews,* or Dubnov's *History of the Jewish People,* or the *History of Jewish Literature* by Karpeles, *Jewish Women* by Kayserling, and much, much more, books and booklets of our own literature in various languages?

Jewish daughters, educated daughters, have all read Shakespeare, Goethe, Schiller, Pushkin, Lermontov, Gogol, Turgenev, Tolstoy. But who has read our own Jewish writers, Judah Halevi, Ibn Gabirol, Levinson, Mapu, Ginsburg, Smolenskin, Gordon, Abramowitch, and all the rest, our own Jewish literature? I am not saying, God forbid, that none of you have ever read a Jewish book. Certainly some of you are well acquainted with our history and our literature, more perhaps than many of our menfolk. I am only saying that the bulk of our sisters are so trained that they don't know that, besides the foreign sources, we have also our own sources. They don't know that they are the daughters of a people, poor indeed, and wandering homeless, but still a people with our own wonderful history, our own sacred language, and our own national tongue, a rich literature of our own, and our own land, with our endless ideal—Zion. And the task of reminding you of all this has been undertaken now by the movement called Zionism. To remind you is the task, as you know, from the Jewish Congress that was held in Basel, where it was agreed that, in order to exist in the world, we must awaken, restore, freshen the old ideal of our people, the holy idea of Zion. That is the task now assumed by the Zionists. There in Basel, where the most outstanding Jews from all parts of the world met and reached the conclusion that to save ourselves from our long ordeal of dragging ourselves round the world for nearly eighteen centuries, from one country to another, to be liberated from all our troubles and humiliations, we need our own bit of land, our own small corner in the world, a land of our own, and this land is the ancient, neglected, forgotten land of our Fathers, that belonged to us four thousand years ago, where we had our Temple, our kings, our Cohanim and our Levites, our judges and our prophets, the land where at every step we tread on the footprints of our ancestors, where every stone is stained with the blood of our heroes, the warriors who battled for our honor and our liberty over many hundreds of years, the land that sits desolate and in mourning, like a woman forsaken by her husband, who still waits for his return, if not today then tomorrow. He will come back, will lift away the black veil covering her eyes, kiss away her tears, comfort her after the long absence. And the name of that man is Zion.

"But before the Jews return to the Jewish land, the Jews must first return to the Jewish nation." That is what Herzl, the president of the Zionists, said at that congress in Basel. The sense and meaning of these words is that Jews must first learn to know themselves, to know Jewish history, Jewish language, Jewish literature, the Jewish ideal. It means that Jews should be Jews, that our daughters should be Jewish daughters, our children, Jewish children. And since our children are in your hands, and their education, their upbringing, their happiness depends on you, we must, dear Sisters, come to you and tell you what the Germara says: Rabbi Akiba, whom we spoke about before, said, "In the merit of the noble, virtuous women our parents were liberated from Egypt." Because they influenced the education of the children, and inspired their husbands. That shows us that then too our women played no small part in the affairs of our nation, in the beautiful, wonderful history of the Exodus from Egypt, which was not just over and ended. Not so quickly or so easily as we imagine, and as we tell the story to our children at Passover, year by year, from the Hagadah, at the Seder table.

It would be shameful and against ordinary simple decency if our women would now, in the present bitter plight of our people, stand aside, afar off, now when our entire people is beginning to understand that our help lies in ourselves, that our only remedy is a land, our own land, and that this land is the only land for us, Zion.

It would be shameful and against ordinary decency if you would fail to understand how useful and how necessary your help is to us, in our present great task, for the holy idea of Zion.

It would be shameful and against ordinary decency if you would not take upon yourselves the task of educating our children in the spirit of this lofty holy idea, for our children—our children who are our future heroes, the warriors of Israel, the workers and builders of the Judenstaat, the Jewish state, Zion.

To educate and train our children in the spirit of our Folk—that for the present is the only thing, Jewish Daughters, that your brothers, the Zionists, ask of you. And so that you should best achieve this, you must first yourselves become convinced of it, make yourselves properly acquainted with our people, and so that you become yourselves convinced of it and make yourselves properly acquainted with our people, you must, in general, first acquaint yourselves with our history, with our language (Hebrew), with our literature. And when you have gotten to know our history, our language, and our literature, only then will you realize what you are, and you will stop being ashamed of a Jewish word, of your Jewish name, and your Jewish type. Then you will see that it is no disgrace that you understand Jargon, that Rachel is no worse a name than Margaret, and that a Jewish nose is no more than a nose. You will then be Jewish daughters, our sisters in Zion.

So that's it—learn Jewish history, Jewish language, Jewish literature. Learn it yourselves and teach it to your children, your young brothers, and above all, to the poor, the lonely, the naked, the hungry, the thirsty, of whom our sages say: Be careful with poor children, for from them comes learning, talent, genius, great minds. From these poor lonely, hungry, thirsty. This is for the present your job. What you have to do in this matter of Zion.

Surely Zionism is no easy task. And the word Judenstaat is easier to say than to achieve. It is a labor for years. Meanwhile, what is important is that the idea is to penetrate among our people, through and through, small and big, poor and rich, men and women. Noble, wise women could and should impress it on their menfolk. Noble, wise women could and should impress it on their brothers. Noble, wise women could and should impress it on their children.

To what extent our women are idealized among our People, and are loved by all, even God himself, we can see from the way the Midrash relates the story that follows: "When the Temple was destroyed and Jews were scattered and driven into exile, the Patriarchs, Abraham, Isaac and Jacob, and all the other tzadikim came to God and pleaded for mercy for the People of Israel. It didn't help. Till Mother Rachel came weeping over the bitter fate of her children. Then God, bless His Name, took pity on Israel. And God said: 'For your sake, because of you, Rachel, I shall bring Israel back to his own land'.

If you will read our history and our literature, you will find many places there which show what a role women played at all times in our history. Is it possible that at this time, when our people is in such a plight, our women should not come to help? Is it possible that now, when our people is beginning to rise from sleep and is looking round to see where it is, where it finds itself, lifting its eyes toward Zion, that our sisters should stand aloof, not be the first for Zion? No, it is not possible! It can't be possible! For our daughters are Jewish daughters, and our sisters are Jewish sisters, our sisters. Remember, Jewish Daughters, and inscribe the words for yourselves, and you will receive the gratitude of your poor brothers. You will receive the thanks of your own children. You will receive the thanks of our poor People!

1898

The Red Little Jews

A Pure Invention

The first Encounter of the Little Red Jews with One of Ours, the Good News He Brought Them, and How He Was Uplifted on a Hurrah[6]

Once on a Sabbath in those hot summer Sabbaths, while the Red boys and girls were parading in couples along the Dry Road, the main street of the town of the red Little Jews, something happened that started a tumult, a turmoil, a rumpus, great excitement among all the red Little Jews, first in the Dry Road, and then all over the town. What was it about? They had spotted a man, somehow strange, quite crazy, mad, not at all a Red. Nobody like it had ever been seen there before. Nobody could possibly have imagined such a thing— that a Jew should not have red hair, a miscreation, a monster. Everybody stopped to look. God's wonders! They pointed their fingers at him, looked at each other, and asked each other,

"Who is this? What is it? Where did it come from? What's it doing here? A monstrosity! Ha-Ha!"

The monstrosity, so it happens, was quite a good-looking man, already advanced in years, with a high broad forehead, long hair and a long beard, a handsome, clear, smiling face and kind eyes always smiling. He seemed not to have noticed what a sensation he had caused in the street. He walked steadily on like one who belonged here, his hands behind his back, head up, eyes on the Dry Road, with its painted walls, and humming a tune to himself, under his breath, as though he was in no way involved in the bother. And all the time the street was getting more crowded, more excited.

"Ha-Ha! Funny creature, isn't he? What can it be? And what is he doing here? Strange creature! Ha-Ha!"

To cut the story short, it was decided to approach the strange visitor and ask him who he was, what he was, where he came from, and what he was doing here. But as no one wanted to be first, one urged the other to make the approach. Each one suggested the other man.

"You go and start a conversation with him."

---

6. The Legends of the Ten Tribes, supposedly transported to the other side of the legendary River Sambatyon, where they are still said to live. According to the legend they are all red-headed.

"Why me? Why not you?"

"Just to put the question to him."

"Look, you go up to him. I'll do the talking."

"No, you go up to him, and I'll do the talking."

"No, I'll do the talking."

"You go up to him, and I'll follow you and I'll speak."

And that's how they stood and argued for a long time, till they confronted the strange intruder on all sides. He saw that he could not go any farther, neither forward nor back. So he stopped, and he addressed the whole crowd in a loud voice. And as he spoke his eyes flashed fire like two burning coals.

"Good Sabbath to you, my dear Brothers and Sisters. I see that you find me very surprising. You want to know who I am, what I am, where I come from, and what I am doing here. Let me introduce myself to you. I am your brother, a true blood brother, one of your ten million brothers living on the other side of the River Sambatyon, and it is quite possible that you don't know even a tenth part of what we know about you. I count myself fortunate that it has fallen to me to bring you the good news that we think a great deal about you, we do a lot for you, we want to take you, all the red Little Jews out of this foreign land, to which you were driven three and a half thousand years ago. We want to settle you in our own land."

"Ha-Ha-Ha! Eretz Israel, of course!" Several hundred voices burst out laughing aloud, like a dozen cannon shooting all at once. "He's speaking strange words. He's crossed the Sambatyon. He wants to take us out to Eretz Israel. He's an Israeli Jew! Hurrah, Eretz Israel Jew!"

"Hurrah!" several hundred voices chimed in, and the street was flooded with people. All laughing, holding their sides with laughing, crying as if with one breath "Eretz Israel Jew! Hurrah!"

The stranger, whose friendly message had got him this warm reception from the red Little Jews, stood there, puzzled and confused. He had no idea what was going on. He took to his heels and started to move backwards, with the whole crowd, boys and girls and elders following him, laughing, whistling, and shouting, "Hurrah!" and calling him "the Eretz Israel Jew!" "Look at him! You mustn't miss him! The Eretz Israel Jew!"

The poor man had a hard job twisting and turning, trying to break through, to evade the crowd, before he managed to find refuge in the Red Inn, where he had already booked in. He locked the door of his room. But that didn't mean that the red Little Jews went away. A bigger crowd joined them. The street outside the inn was thick with them, shouting and sniggering and jeering, bursting their sides with laughing: "Eretz Israel Jew! Hurrah!"

Luckily it was the Sabbath, or the crowd would have had the whole inn building smashed up, rack and ruin. Nobody wanted to move away, to go home. Till the innkeeper, a strong, burly fellow, a Red also, stuck his red head out of a window and screamed down to them:

"Red bastards! Idlers! Loafers! What do you want! There's a guest staying here, a man like all other men, only he isn't a Red. Why all this fuss about him? What do you think you're doing! Away with you! Go home and leave the man alone!"

Only then the crowd at last dispersed, each to his home. The red Little Jews like it when something is said to them with good taste.

ii
A Meeting of the Red Little Jews. The Stranger Delivers a Speech. The Red Little Jews Have No Time and Keep Interrupting Him.

Saturday night, immediately after Sabbath end, after Havdala, the stranger had the representatives of the town summoned to the inn, all the prominent people, the rabbis, the scholars, the rich men, the Maskilim, the learned and educated, as well as some of the artisans, some of the common folk. He told them he had something most important to say to them, something affecting the whole community, a very necessary matter, which would vitally concern them.

That made a stir in the town, caused a commotion. "Some foreign visitor, just arrived from abroad, one of the Black Jews, had arrived from the other side of the River Sambatyon, says he is an Eretz Israel Jew, and wants to bring us the news. We really should go and hear what he has to say."

The red Little Jews didn't hang back. They all came to the meeting, young and old, all classes of people, not so much for the matter itself as because everybody was curious about the stranger, the Eretz Israel Jew, and wanted to hear what he had to say. Very soon the Red Inn was packed tight with red Little Jews. A terrible crush. Pushing and shoving! Danger to life! Everyone trying to get nearer the top, to hear better. The walls ran sweat. People stood on top of each other. And still more came. Till the Red Inn keeper had an idea. He locked the doors. And let off a string of swear words at the crowd, those who had gotten inside. That done, the stranger stood up, and people started clapping and crying, "Hush! Quiet please! Be quiet!" Then came a blowing of noses, as though people hadn't blown their noses for years past. Then somebody coughed, and a lot of others followed. An epidemic of coughing.

"What's all this coughing about!" the rich man at the top table wanted to know in a very angry voice. "Couldn't you get done with your coughing at home, before you came here? The cheek of these paupers! Can't find anywhere else to cough!"

At that everyone fell absolutely silent. Nobody made a sound. The red Little Jews like licking the boots of a rich man. If a rich many says stop coughing, you stop!

"Now listen, Rabosei, hear me out, dear beloved Brothers!" That was how the stranger started his speech. And his eyes burned like fire. "Your native brothers, the red Little Jews, who live here ever so long, did not receive me today with any particular friendship, not like a welcome guest. They looked at me as if I was mad, and they mock-hurrahed me. They didn't understand what I was saying. Don't think, God forbid, that I hold it up against them, that I feel hurt and feel less towards you because of it. I only feel sorry for it, my Brothers, because it shows me how gross your people here are still, how low you are. But since you have come here, the responsible representatives, the glory of the town,—I see here rabbis and scholars, men of wealth and good name, Maskilim, men of learning, fine, good people—I take it that you will understand me. First of all, you should know, my Brothers, what hardship and suffering I encountered before I found my way to you, my dear red Little Jews. For you hid yourselves away from us. Forgive me, God knows where you are. In order to reach you one must go through deserts, through wildernesses, over hills and deep valleys, through woods and forests. And then the crossing of the River Sambatyon! It's easy to speak the word Sambatyon. But the journey was very hard. I knew it would be hard to find you, that it would take much time and effort before I could reach you, but I persevered. For if I had abandoned the journey to you, my Brothers, I would have been much better off than I am now. It would have been better for me, and certainly for my children. But my heart drew me to you, my Brothers. So I decided to come here. I denied myself the honors and the prestige I had where I lived. It would have been better for me and for all of us had I stayed where I was. Instead I said goodbye to my life of happiness in this world and set out to be a sacrifice for you. I wanted to meet you, red Little Jews! I wanted to bring you greetings from your ten million brothers who live on the other side of the Sambatyon, your blood brothers who, together with you, serve one God and come from the same stock, the children of Abraham, Isaac, and Jacob.

"I wanted very much to see you, to see what is going on among you, and to pass on the good news about you, and to tell you that we have you in mind, that we are concerned about you, and we are doing things now which will, in God's good time, bring its reward for you."

"What's he saying? Why is he going on so long? Shut up! I want to hear what he's saying!"

"Why can't you be quiet? I want to hear what he's saying."

That was some of the red Little Jews calling out, all of them together, getting tired of the whole thing. And the guest was still going on. "If you understand me, my Brothers, we want to take you out of here. You have been here long enough, cut off from us. Time to stand up, time to wash and to cleanse your garments, and to be like all decent folk. We want to take you out of here, as your fathers were taken out of Egypt, and to settle you in our own land, the land of our Fathers, the land that God swore to Abraham, that he and his seed would inherit it forever, the land where we once had our Temple, where we had our priests, the Cohanim and Levites, where we had our king, our prophets, and Eretz Israel was the Holy Land, from where came the Divine Light, our Torah that has illuminated the whole world. We have given everyone the light of the Torah. Why do you stare at me? Why are you silent when I speak to you? I am calling to you, red Little Jews, rabbis and scholars, Hasidim, Jews with Tallis Kotons, with long gaberdines, with beards and ear-locks. You know what Eretz Israel means—our Eretz Israel! Jerusalem! You repeat the prayer every time you say grace—"Jerusalem, Thy city and Zion, the place of Thy Glory." And the constant refrain, "Next year in Jerusalem!"

"That's in our prayers!" called several pious red Little Jews. "That's what we are Jews for! To say our prayers. To serve God!"

"Prayers and serving God," the stranger cried. "That's the whole trouble! That you pray and don't know what you pray. You speak and don't know what you speak. You are sick and don't know what is wrong with you. You walk around in a trance! You're asleep!"

"Cut it short!" the red Little Jews cried. They have no time. "Cut it short! Get to the point! We've had enough exhortation!"

"You want me to cut it short? You don't like exhortation? You don't like hearing the truth! You've fallen into a trance, I tell you. You're asleep! I have come to waken you, to scream into your ears, 'Wake up! It's time, Brothers! Nearly two thousand years you have been lying around here in the mud and the muck. You feel warm here, and you think there's nothing better, nothing sweeter. Wake up! Look round you! Consider how you are placed. You are in danger! In terrible danger! You weaken day by day. You are sinking deeper in the mud.'"

"What's the point?" the red Little Jews cried. "Tell us, what is the point!"

"You want to know the point? You've no time to wait for it! You're just the same as our own people, where I come from. The same people and the same character. We went through the same experience with them, your ten million brothers on the other side of the River Sambatyon. The very same! Only we caught ourselves in time. We saw that we were in danger, were going to be swallowed up alive. Or we would be left to swallow ourselves up. We were given warnings, beatings, blows. We came to believe that the world is a great sea and the people are fish. We came to realize that all the sweet songs our prophets and our sweet singer over long years sang to us were indeed lovely songs, but only songs, about a time that was coming, when the Messiah would arrive. We came to see that our help lies only in our own hands. If we did not help ourselves no one would help us. We realized that if we want to live, we must be like the others, equals, on the same level, the same level as we were once before. Once. We acquainted ourselves with our own history and our own language, and we saw that we had no reason to be ashamed of the name Jew, that we were a nation like all other nations, only we lack a land, a land of our own. So we raised a bitter cry before the whole world: 'Land! Land! Give us a land!' We began to meet, all in one place, to consult ourselves about one thing. And we decided that first we must wash ourselves clean and wash our children clean, educate ourselves, become men, prepare ourselves and our people as a whole for the great task before us. We started holding meetings, congresses, collecting money, creating a fund."

"We don't want your schools! No schools!" Suddenly several hundred red Little Jews shouted, all of them together.

iii
The Stranger Rises From the Table, and the Red Little Jews Start Talking All Together, All at Once, They Argue, Dispute, Wrangle, Bicker, Clash. They Shout to be Heard Above the Clamor and Then Go Peaceably Home.

Those red Little Jews—as long as they keep quiet they're all right. But when they start talking they can't stop. They go on talking for all they're worth. They let their tongues run away with them. They wave their arms about, they gesticulate, shout, storm, bellow, growl, make a noise like crows croaking in the forest. They can't shut up. No human being can stop them. The stranger kept begging them to let him finish what he was saying. People clapped their hands, banged on the table, called, "Quiet please!" It didn't help. They took no notice even of the rich men at the top when they called for order. In the end the stranger had to break off his speech in the middle, get down from the table, and hear how the red Little Jews try to explain what he had been saying, interpret his words, each in his own way, according to his own understanding.

"He wants schools! We don't want schools! He comes from the other side of the river! Keeps talking to us about Eretz Israel! What do you make of him, the way he talks? Got too much to say for himself! That's the trouble! If it's about Eretz Israel, let me say a word. I know something about Eretz Israel! Shut up, you! If you don't stop talking, I'll clout you! You're mad! That's what's the matter with you! Keep quiet! There's still a lot to discuss. It needs a lot of money!"

"You see! I knew they'd be wanting money from us."

"I knew they'd be after our pockets. Let's get out of here!"

Some of the rich men at the top hearing this start to move out.

"Where were you last night?" one asks another.

"Playing cards. We played till the first minyan. Till morning prayers!"

"Who lost? Come along, tell us!"

"Don't ask! It was a massacre. When we had to uncover our cards everything went black before our eyes. Come now, let's go! The night doesn't stand still!"

"Heretics! Unbelievers! Vandals!" That was the rabbi and the religious leaders trying to shout down the tumult. They had all collected in a corner and were protesting against the whole Eretz Israel idea. "Rogues! Rascals! Criminals! Breakers of the law! They want to take us out of here to Eretz Israel! Want to bring down Messiah! Why do you keep quiet? Hear, O Israel!"

More than all others it was the scholars, the learned men among the red Little Jews, who were against the idea, the intellectuals, the thinkers, the brain twisters, the philosophers, the linguists, the grammarians, the politicians. They wanted to know in the name of reason, in the name of history, in the name of political understanding, in the name of humanity, how was such a thing possible, how was it ever heard of, to take a nation of red Little Jews who have been sitting for two thousand years quietly on this side of the River Sambatyon, interfering with nobody, molesting nobody, treading on nobody's toes, and say to them: "Get yourselves together, red Little Jews, pack your things and go over to the other side of the River Sambatyon and settle there in some desolate tract among the wild Turks! What will all the other nations say? Who ever heard of such a thing? Show us where in all history such a thing has ever happened! When in all history had there been such a thing? That's point one. Point two— It's a smack in the face for civilization! A shame and a disgrace! The whole world is agog to see the sun shine, brightening every corner. All the countries of the world will become one country; and peoples, one people; all languages, one language. All men will be one man!"

"There you go! Mazel tov! What do you mean, all men becoming one man?"

This query was put by a young man with spectacles, a scholar too. "Though all peoples becoming one people," he added, "that's understandable."

"Not so fast!" said another scholar, with a big bald patch on his head. "Let's consider this again! What do we mean by a people? What's the meaning of the word? What's the origin?"

"A people is what we call a nation," explained the young man with the spectacles. "And we write the word nation with an *n*, not with a *c*, not 'nacion.' Just nation. Now do you understand?"

"We ought," said another scholar, with very thick eyebrows, "we ought to write a book specially about it. Most necessary!"

"A lecture!" interjected another young scholar, feeling very happy because he had brought in this high-sounding word. "A lecture!"

"What makes you so happy about the word lecture?" said the spectacled young scholar, envying him the use of the word. "A book is not a lecture. They're two different things. A book is research. And a lecture is just a lecture."

"It's all the same!" cried the other young scholar, a little angrily. "There's no difference!"

"They're like day and night!" the other insisted.

"Don't take it badly! There's no difference!"

"What do you mean, don't take it badly!" speaking this time in German. "There's a big difference between the two!"

"That'll do for now!" one of the Maskilim intervened. "Have you ever heard of such a thing on which two scholars can find themselves in agreement? If one says day, the other says night. You'd better try to work out a way of establishing unity between ourselves, forming a united body of the red Little Jews, so that we do something more important than splitting hairs, with your philosophy and your research, and your lectures."

It was after midnight already and the red Little Jews were still talking, arguing, wrangling, bickering, shouting, storming all together, gesticulating, waving their arms about. "Idlers! Rogues! They want to bring down Messiah!" And the rabbis were screaming, "Heretics! Unbelievers!"

The thinkers, the brainy ones, the philosophers had not stopped arguing and quibbling all the time. They demanded evidence, wanted clear proof, immediately, now, at once, on the spot, how would it come about that a whole nation would be taken across to the other side of the River Sambatyon and settled in Eretz Israel. It somehow didn't sound right! "Let's consider it," they said, "in the light of the history of all other nations!"

"All the other nations is something different!" Another learned man observed. "And the red Little Jews is also something different."

"It's all the same! All one!" the other one shouted back.

"Like day and night!"

"There's no difference between them at all!"

"I beg your pardon!"

"We must put an end to this!" said the Maskilim. "We must try to do something for the good of our people. Your quibbling and hair-splitting won't fill their stomachs. If you don't like the idea of Eretz Israel suggest something else. The people are waiting. They're waiting for you. And you argue and quibble, your philosophy and your politics!"

But now nobody was listening. Everybody wanted to talk. Nobody would listen. They go on talking and talking till almost everybody gives up and goes home. And on their way home they pour out wise sayings and make fun of the others, scoff at them, pooh-poohing what they had said. Especially the stranger who had come over the River Sambatyon, and the Red Inn keeper and the rabbis, and the learned thinkers, the Maskilim, and the new Red Eretz Israel Society of the little Jews. They belittled everybody, all the red Little Jews and the whole world.

Lunatics

i
The Traveler Discovers a New Land. The Red Little Jews Hear a Lot of
Stories That Excite Them. One Sets Out on a Journey There. Returns and
Publishes His Description. Expects It to Make His Fortune.

For many, many years the red Little Jews thought they were at the end of the
world. On one side the River Sambatyon, on the other the wilderness, and in
the middle the red Little Jews. That's it! The lot! What more do you want?

There had been talk about a notion that there was some sort of a country on
the other side of the Sambatyon. But even if that was true, it was a matter of
doubt whether there were any Jews there.

Though come to think of it, there must be Jews there. How could there be a
country without Jews? And secondly, where had the Ten Tribes gotten to? Then
suddenly a rumor went around that a traveler—no idea who and from where—
had said he had himself been there, over there. Yes, but how had he crossed
the Sambatyon, when everybody knows that all the week long it throws up
stones, only except on the Sabbath day? That opens a question!

The traveler's tale was that he had been there, and he had with his own eyes
seen the Jews there, had spoken with them. They are, he said, in no way like
our Jews. To begin with, they all have black hair. And in the second place, they
are quite a different kind of Jews. They pride themselves on their good manners, and they all live happily together. Couldn't be happier! For example—
they all earn pots of money. No poor people there! Everything dirt cheap. Next
to nothing! Gold lies about in the streets!

"Did you hear what he said?" one asked the other, with a nudge.

"Rubbish! The things people say! Just talk! Fine words!"

"Take, for instance, what he said about gold in the streets. Is that just talk?"

"Gold in the streets? Why doesn't somebody pick it up?"

"That's silly! You talk like a donkey! If somebody picked it up, there wouldn't
be any gold lying in the streets."

The red Little Jews, who are by nature given to exaggeration, as soon as they
heard the word gold wouldn't listen to any more. They started building up in
their imagination whole mountains of gold and silver and diamonds and other
gems and all good things. "Now that's a country where you can live well,

spending the few years left to you!" That's what they said, one to the other, with a heavy sigh. "You don't have to work hard there, struggle and strain, rack your brains how to get enough for the Sabbath table. You go out in the market and choose whatever your heart desires. You want gold? Take it! Silver? Take it! Just like that! You've got two hands, haven't you? Take!"

There were, of course, disbelievers, who threw cold water on the whole story. Argued against it.

"The things people say! Donkeys! Dolts! Idiots! Somebody pitches them a yarn, pure imagination! Invention! The snows of yesteryear! Moonshine! A cow jumped over the moon and laid an egg!"

"But we heard it ourselves. A traveler was here, and he spoke to the Jews here. He gave us proof—all the Jews there have black hair!"

"Did you say proof? As much proof as to say your aunt's got a nose! Spit in his face, that traveler! Ask him how he crossed the Sambatyon, when we know it throws up stones all the week round!"

"But you see—"

In short, the gold and the silver on the other side of the Sambatyon started a whole tumult among the red Little Jews. No joke! Many of them took it seriously, dreamed about it day and night, couldn't lie still in bed, tossed from side to side, groaned and moaned, and kept thinking all the time, "Lord God! It isn't hard for you to carry me across, even if only for one day!"

The pious ones, the believers repeated it in their prayers. "Our Father, our King! Dear, sweet Father in Heaven! For your great Name's sake, for the sake of our forefathers who trusted in you, show us now your kindness and mercy, work a miracle for us, for you can!"

What miracle did they want? That God should take them across to that other land? Or that God should bring that land over here? They were not sure which they wanted. Actually, all they wanted was the gold and silver there. Better, more just, they thought, to have the gold and silver in their pockets than to let it lie around in the streets. But to pick yourself up and go there yourself— nobody liked that idea! To begin with, go where? Get up and just go, without knowing where? And then, what are you going to do about the Sambatyon? How can you swim across a river which keeps throwing stones at you? The world hasn't gone mad! If people say stones, it's stones!

About two years before, round this time, something like this had happened. One of the red Little Jews, a greedy little Jew, not one of the religious ones, whose name was Moshe, almost the only man with this name, not a nickname, went out one fine morning, with his stick, to the market place, and he didn't come back. He disappeared! No one knew where he'd gotten to! They searched for him in every corner. In every mouse-hole. Every cellar. Every garret. Every loft. They looked for him even outside the town, on the other side of the mill. Behind the bathhouse. At the river's edge. No sign of him. Lost, as though under the water. He had left at home a young wife and children, orphaned, without a bit of bread. Everybody pitied them. Where had the man gotten to! A grown man isn't a pin! Rabbis sent letters to all the other towns, giving all the details—his name is Moshe. He's a Red. Medium height. Which means not tall, nor short. And two other things—he talks in his sleep. And he doesn't eat cheese. They sent these details to all the Yiddish newspapers. They put up big posters. They even promised that anyone giving information which would lead to finding the lost man would be sure of bliss in the next world. Even that didn't help. Till one day that lost man turned up, a whole year after, carrying his stick. You can imagine the joy of his wife and children, when they got up one morning, looked round—and, He's here!

Of course, he got his first reception from his wife. She played him a dance as he deserved. When she finished, he got Sholom Aleichem greetings from all over the place, from relatives, from neighbors, and from just acquaintances.

"So you're back! Sholom Aleichem! And where did you spring from? What's the news out there? What's the price of corn?"

"All right! Laugh at me!" he turned on them. "If you knew where I've been, where I've just come from, and what I've seen, you'd sing a different tune!"

"Oh? Let's hear what you have to say! From the other side of the Sambat-yon?"

"That's right! As though you'd been there yourselves! What a country!"

"You're telling us the truth? No kidding!"

"May I live so sure! And you as well. I'm telling the absolute truth."

"Then why do you keep your mouth shut?"

"What do you want me to do, shout?"

It didn't take half an hour, and the whole town knew that Moshe, the lost one, had returned. He had come from that happy land where gold and silver lie around in the streets, and he was telling stories that could drive you mad.

People dropped everything they were doing, shears and pressing iron, bag and baggage, and ran to see the man who had come back. They went to him like to a wonder rabbi. He was no longer a joke. He was envied and praised and marveled at, after making all that distant journey, alone, by himself. They begged him to tell them the whole story, what and how and when, everything. At once. Was it really true about the gold?

The crowd grew bigger every minute. More people arrived, and all wanted him to tell them the whole story over again, from beginning to end. How and what and when. He was on the point of repeating the whole story, when his wife turned up.

"Do you know," she said to her husband, "do you know why all these people have come to see you? What brought them here? They want your news! So they can wait! You'll tell them afterwards! I waited longer!"

That was her way of telling them to clear out!

Now the red Little Jews, who consider themselves very grand and high and mighty people, and who are very sensitive about the respect due to them, are not so sensitive when it's something they want to be in on, a bit of news they want to know more about. So they stuck their dignity in their pockets and went on clamoring for Moshe's story, the whole story. Moshe got the message. It was clear to him that today he was the top man in the town. And he decided to make the most of it, to stretch it out, keep them on tenterhooks, prolong his hour of triumph.

"What shall I tell you, brothers? What a place it is! What Jews they are! Since God has been dealing with Jews, he hasn't created Jews like these! They are a strange kind of being, such as you don't see the like of here! It's something, I tell you!"

"Cut the cackle! Get on with the story! What do they do there? How do they live? Tell us that!"

"I don't know what to tell you first. If I told you everything, you would have to sit here with me for at least three whole days. Did I say three? Thirty is more like it! Thirty days and thirty nights! If we wrote it out, it would make a big book. From floor to ceiling! Wait, I've got an idea! I'm a clever fellow, I am!"

"Yes, you're a very clever chap! But the story, tell us the story! About those Jews on the other side of the Sambatyon!"

"Why should I tell all of you the story separately, always beginning with Ma Tovu? I can put it all down on paper, and you can all read it. It would be a book. And everyone could read it. From beginning to end. What you can put down with pen on paper you can never tell by word of mouth. Don't you think it's a brain wave of mine! Only don't rush me! Leave me to sit down and write it out!"

"Good idea! And when will it be ready? In the spring, round Purim time?"

"God forbid! Not so long! Writing and printing, having the whole thing ready, not more than two months. Three at most!"

"You talk like the wise man in the Passover Hagadah! You must be mad, out of your mind!" the red Little Jews screamed at him, as though he was a hired man of theirs, a community servant. "Did you say months? Which of us is able to wait for months! We're only human beings! What do we do if you go and die in the middle of it, before you've written it all out?"

"Please yourself!" his wife now stood up for him. "My husband doesn't owe you anything. He didn't engage himself to be a story teller for you! Suppose he'd lost his tongue and couldn't say a word? Off with you! Go home and leave us alone!"

The crowd saw there was nothing they could do, so they broke up and dispersed. And Moshe kept his word. He bought paper and ink and a whole lot of pens, and he sat down to write out the whole account of his journey as a serial story, which he named, "The Lucky Land or a Place for Lunatics." When he had finished writing it he asked the printer to print a lot of copies, at his own cost (I am afraid a few thousand copies). His reasoning was: In this town alone there are, good luck to them, about twenty thousand red Little Jews. Say only one in ten buys the book, and you've already got two thousand copies. What about the other towns? There are over a million red Little Jews, bless 'em! A few thousand copies wouldn't meet the demand. There would have to be reprints. And more reprints. I'd make a pretty penny out of it!

As it happened, publication was considerably delayed. It took more than two months, more than three and four, more than six months. What had happened? The printer had found himself short of type and had to stop work till he got new type. Our author was in trouble all round. On one side there was his wife, going at him all the time. "What sort of work is this?" she wanted to know. "Turned publisher suddenly! What sort of a job is that? You must be off your rocker!"

Then there were the red Little Jews, clamoring for a book. "Where is it? How much longer will it take? Give us the book!" And the printer, who had been as sweet as honey, suddenly put demands. "Money! I want my money!" He explained that he had to keep going to the pawnshop to borrow money. He had to pay his way. All that printing work he'd done! Till God worked a miracle, and the book was out.

Everybody made a rush for it. Moshe's home was besieged. Everybody wanted a copy. Moshe's wife saw what was happening and took command.

"You don't know how to deal with such things. You know that you're a fool. And as God has sent us a bit of luck like this, let's make the most of it. Let me handle it! You're not charging them enough. They'll pay whatever I ask. As long as you keep out of it!"

It didn't take long, only a couple of hours, and the number of would-be buyers had dwindled to next to nothing. And then nothing. Nothing and no-body! The red Little Jews lost all interest. "What's the fuss about! We know the whole story now!" And indeed they did. Those who had bought the book had told the others what was in it. Man to man. Word of mouth. Without a tele-phone! So why spend money to buy the book?

That was number one. Number two was disappointment with the story itself. "Nothing to it!" they said. "Cloud cuckoo land! No gold, no silver! Funny sort of Jews there! They're all mad! Wasn't worth waiting all this time to find out!"

"The whole story is a lie! He invented the lot! Out of his own head!"

"He had a dream about crossing the Sambatyon!"

"Pah! Pitching us a yarn like that!"

The upshot was that nobody wanted to look at the book. Some who had bought it brought it back and demanded their money back. They actually offered it to him for half price. "You keep half and give us back the other half!" What could be more fair than that! There was one man who flung the book back at him, through the window, like a dead cat. It got the whole town laughing, splitting their sides!

You can imagine how the poor author felt. And the kind of life his wife led him because of it. And the printer, who was ruined by this business. The red Jews laughed at Moshe, made fun of him, made him feel small. They gave him a new name—"Moshe, maker of books." He became an object of contempt.

One of the booklets fell by a miracle into our hands, and we read it from A to Z and found it not at all as bad as the red Little Jews thought. As evidence we reprint it here, word for word, and ask our readers if any of them finds something odd there, or in places exaggerated, overdone, or begging your pardon, plain silly, stupid. Don't blame us. Blame the author. He won't hear it, so it won't hurt him.

ii
His Arrival in the Town. First Encounter. The Synagogue. They Put a Hat on His Head. Fight for the Privilege of Having Him As Their Sabbath Guest.

"I arrived in the land of the lunatics," his book of travels begins, "on Friday, just before dusk, time for lighting the Sabbath candles. And as I was in a hurry because of the Sabbath, I had no time to look round the town, with its fine, broad, clean, paved streets, and the tall, bright, imposing houses. I flew like an arrow from the bow. All the time my mind was bobbing and throbbing, agitated by one thought—where will I go to usher in the Sabbath? Where will I land in this foreign country? To whom shall I turn without a recommendation? My first thought was, synagogue! Let me just get to a synagogue!"

"Among Jews! That was my thought." That will put everything right! I won't be lost!

I stopped the first Jew I saw and asked him:

"Tell me, Brother, where's the synagogue round here?"

This Jew—but first I must describe the kind of Jew he was—tall, black hair, black beard, head held high, very self-important, dressed all in black and with a shiny black topper on his head.

"Don't get me wrong, Brother," I said to him. "If you are, I beg your pardon, a Jew, here's my hand. Sholom Aleichem!"

"Aleichem Sholom!" he replied, pressing my hand warmly. "What can I do for you?"

"Is there a synagogue round here?"

"Come with me," he said. "I'll come with you! Where do you spring from?"

"All the way from the other side of the Sambatyon. From the back of beyond!"

"I see, the red Little Jews! I am very, very happy to meet you! You're a stranger here, eh, a visitor? Perhaps I may ask you to be my Sabbath guest?"

"Delighted! I was looking for a synagogue, thinking the shammas would beg someone to take me as a Sabbath guest."

"Beg someone?" he laughed. "No need to beg here! We are only too glad when God sends us a guest."

"With us," I told him, "the custom is quite different. With us the shammas won't let the congregation leave till the poor people have been fixed up for the Sabbath."

"Really?" and he pulled a face, as though I had said our people walk with their heads down and their feet up in the air.

"No offense meant," I went on. "Who's yahrzeit is it? Your father's or your mother's?"

"Why do you ask? What put that question in your mind? What makes you think I've got yahrzeit now?"

"Because you're going to synagogue."

"I'm going to synagogue to daven. The Friday night service."

"I know it's Friday night." That's why I'm asking you! Because where I come from, a fine gentleman, begging your pardon, like you, goes to synagogue very seldom on a Friday night."

"Really? And what do they do all day on the Sabbath?"

"Play cards! Poker. Solitaire. Rummy. Whist. Don't you play cards here?"

"No! We've given up cards here. We have better things to do! Look, that's our synagogue."

I looked. There in front of me stood a fine, tall building with lots of white marble and a kind of bright dazzling light flooding it from the top down.

"Is this what they call a synagogue?" I muttered to myself, thinking of our big synagogue, which has been standing ever so long bent almost in two, like the worshippers inside when they fall Korim at prayers. It's been propped up for years with big beams, shored up. And young scamps climb up the beams to get on the roof. And the walls are bare, naked, and nibbled at by the goats, who use them for their droppings. You can smell it ever so far off.

We were greeted at the entrance by a tall men with gold buttons, who bowed to us, and opened the door wide, as if to say, "Welcome! Glad to see you!"

Inside I stood and gaped. The whole interior, from top to bottom, was dipped in a golden light. Light shimmering on every side. A man with a topper on his head and a long robe with buttons and a Magen David pinned on came quietly up to me and motioned to me to follow him.

"I've been told about you," he said. "People have seen you. Would you mind coming with me for a moment?"

"And who," I said, "may you be? But first I must give you Sholom Aleichem!"

"Aleichem Sholom," he responded. "I am the shammas of this synagogue!"

"Fine shammas you are! All dressed up, with a Magen David, just like our shammas, I don't think! He wears a threadbare caftan, broken down high boots, and his nose is stuffed with snuff."

"Where are you taking me?" I asked him. "Can you find me a place where I can deposit this parcel I've got?"

"Please come with me!" And he took me into another brightly lit room, with white marble walls. And with washbasins. He put a piece of soap in my hand, with a clean towel, and told me to wash.

"What sort of madness is this!" I thought to myself. "I understand washing my hands. That's what we've got a barrel of water in our synagogue for. But washbasins—beyond me!

"And who told you about me?" I asked the shammas.

"Mr. Schneider."

"What Schneider?"

"The gentleman you came with."

"So he's a schneider (a tailor). A worker. An artisan. Then what's all the fuss about! His head stuck up in the air as though he was goodness knows what!"

"He is the gabbai of this synagogue!"

"I see! So this is the tailor's synagogue!"

"No! It's not the tailor's synagogue. It's a Jewish synagogue!"

"I know it's a Jewish synagogue, not a goyish one! But how does it come about that you have a tailor as your gabbai? Couldn't you find anyone better? How do we say it—"For want of a better a herring counts as fish?""

"Isn't a tailor a Jew?" And he opened a cupboard and fetched out a shining black topper for me to wear in place of my travel cap.

"Mad!" I said. "I must be out of my mind! What's this idea of dressing me up suddenly like a comedian?"

"But you must wear a cylinder!" he smiled at me. "In our synagogue everyone wears a cylinder. No one can come in without it!"

"I suppose there are lunatics everywhere," I said. "But here everybody seems to be mad. It's Sodom! Wild creatures! Savages!"

"You must wear the cylinder!" he insisted, speaking like one who says, "Do as we tell you, and it will be all right. If you don't, clear out!"

Meanwhile it was getting late. Any minute and it will be the Sabbath. What is one to do? Go and look for another synagogue? It would be the same story over again! If I've gotten among a lot of lunatics, I can't do anything! So I put on the cylinder, and as I passed the glass door I caught a reflection of myself; I could hardly keep myself from laughing. "How do I look?" I asked the shammas. "How do you like this chap with a chimney pot on!"

The shammas didn't answer. He conducted me to a seat of honor and handed me a small prayer book. I stood up to look round, to see in what sort of a world I found myself. Fine, soft plush seats. Carpets on the floor. Nowhere to spit. Everybody dressed in their Sabbath best. Like a wedding. Everybody wearing cylinders. Everybody silent. What sort of people are these!

I motioned to the shammas, and he comes over to me. "Tell me, please, where is East? Mizrach?"

"Mizrach," he repeated, pointing, "that's Mizrach!"

"I know where Mizrach is. The direction. What I'm asking is, where do the bigwigs sit? The moneybags, the magnates, the plutocrats! The flowers of your community!"

"All the same!" he answered.

"All the same? You mean anyone can sit anywhere he likes? No order! Just a scramble! Wherever he wants, there he sits?"

"Lunatics!" I said to myself, laughing inwardly. "If we were to tell one of our rich men to sit somewhere not at the East wall, the heavens would open! A year ago we had a terrible to-do over something like that. There was a seat at the East wall put up for auction. Israel, the butcher, bought it. Wasn't there a row over it! "What!" the rich men cried. "Are we going to let a butcher sit at the East wall! No! We won't have it!" And they got together and bought the seat over the head of the butcher, even if they had to pay more for it. Even if there was no one going to sit there. They'd rather see it empty. No butcher at the East wall!

Suddenly I heard from above a burst of song, a mish-mash of voices such as I had never heard in all my life. A flow of sweet singing, deep voices and still deeper voices, high voices and still higher voices. And all of them flowing together, merging, sweet as olive oil over every limb. I could swear I heard a violin. I heard a flute. A trumpet. And a violoncello. A whole orchestra. Then, as from out of the ground, some scarecrow with a white hat on and a Tallis, rose. Their chazan, their cantor? I asked myself. He made funny motions, bending and bowing this way and that, and singing, "Ma Tovu," "How goodly are Thy tents!"

"There you are!" I told myself. "On Friday night Ma Tovu! What about 'L'Adonai Ki Tov'?" "Give thanks to the Lord, for He is good!" And where is Mincha? Lunatics!"

Immediately after the chazan two or three other men appeared at his side. Wearing cylinders. One of them was my Schneider. Seems these were the heads of the community. Then there was a functionary with a four-cornered black hat and a white collar. They all took their seats at the top, facing each other. And the chazan started the service. He jumped from Ma Tovu straight to Lechu Nerannena, "Come, let us exult before the Lord!" And what do you say to a jump like that?"

When I heard this, that we were already at the Inauguration of the Sabbath, I took up the Lechu Nerannena, with a voice and to a tune I am accustomed to. Now, I thought, the whole congregation would start to daven, to pray. Not a bit of it! Nobody said a word. The chazan began, and the choir finished it. And the worshippers looked into their prayer books, silent. Scared that they might be caught repeating a word of Hebrew.

When we got to Lecha Dodi (Come, friend, to meet the Sabbath bride) the chazan, now by himself, without the choir, handed us a Mizmor shir Leyom Hashabos, A Song for the Sabbath, and indeed, he did it in real Jewish style, in plain Jewish pronunciation. He just let himself go. He outdid David Moshe and Moshe Yossis, even the great Hirsh-Baer!

Then he turned to face the congregation. Imagine a chazan without a sign of a beard, dolled up like a young girl. No Adam's apple, no scarf round his neck, and no drop of sweat! After that the shammas with the Magen David brought him a gold goblet of wine, and the chazan said Kiddush, the Sanctification, "Remember the Sabbath to keep it holy." He said it well, and in a good loud voice. But I couldn't help laughing. First time I heard Kiddush in a synagogue! (Kiddush is properly said in the home, with the Sabbath meal.)

After the Kiddush there was more singing, and the congregation dispersed, silently, without saying, "Good Sabbath!" They pressed one another's hand, and said, "Next year in Jerusalem!" And they left, one by one, without a word, but with friendly smiles for each other. No pushing, no shoving—strange Jews!

The shammas went up to the man with the four-cornered hat and the white collar, and said something to him. Then he came over to me, followed by the three heads, the big chiefs, including my Schneider.

"Our rabbi," the shammas told me very quietly.

"Some rabbi," I thought to myself. "This decides questions of ritual law!"

"Sholom Aleichem!" the rabbi greeted me, pressing my hand. And the other two after him.

"Aleichem Sholom!" I responded.

"What is your name?" the rabbi asked me in Hebrew.

"Why Hebrew?" I asked him. "Is it because you don't use the common tongue on the Sabbath? My name is Moshe. Where I come from we have three Moshes. One who is tall, and we call him the Little Moshe. Another is short, and we call him Big Moshe. I am just Moshe."

"I have heard," the rabbi went on, "that you come from a far country, the land where the red Little Jews live. How are they there, our poor little brethren?"

"How would you expect them to be?" I asked. "The one with the pelf does well for himself. And the one who hasn't the sponduliks lying around might as well be buried deep underground. Especially, forgive me, since the panic started lately. Things got real bad. People ran wherever their feet took them. No one knew where the other had gotten to. Take me, for instance. I've landed up here, don't ask me how! I couldn't tell you! We had committees at first supposed to look after us. But it all ended up in thin air."

I talked and talked. I told them everything that goes on among us. And the two heads and the rabbi and the shammas stood and watched me like a sort of rare animal one sees only once in a lifetime. Every time I mentioned the red Little Jews, the way they suffer, poor things, they all sighed, commiserating with them. It really hurt them.

"I think," the rabbi said to me with a friendly smile, "you must be dead tired after your journey. And you must be hungry."

"You're dead right!"

"We'll have time to continue our talk later. You'll come with me. I am inviting you to stay with us for the Sabbath."

"Excuse me, Doctor," said Schneider, "the man's mine! I asked him first, on our way to the synagogue."

"Sorry," said the rabbi.

"When," said I, "is a poor man out of luck? When he's got two wedding feasts to go to, in one day."

The rabbi, the two synagogue heads, and the shammas laughed. But I could see that they all envied my Schneider that he had got me first. Lucky man!

"Strange Jews! Mad!" I thought to myself, walking with my Schneider to his home for the Sabbath. "They have no East wall. No Mizrach. Anyone can sit on top. Rich and poor alike! A doctor with them is a rabbi. A Schneider is the head of their synagogue. And a shammas wears a topper. To them a poor man is a welcome guest. A Jew to them is a precious jewel. They fight over a Jew. To get one. Absolutely mad! Lunatics!"

Coming into Schneider's home, I was immediately aware of a strange brightness, a happiness, a feeling of at-homeness, which is impossible to describe. We were welcomed in by Schneider's wife, who was dressed like a lady. Not with pearls, like a rich woman in our parts, but nicely dressed, neat and tidy. And at her side two young girls, Schneider's daughters. Pretty girls, with black hair, and black flaming eyes.

"God has sent us a guest," Schneider told them happily. "I've brought you a Jew, one of our distant brothers. We call them the red Little Jews."

"Sholom Aleichem!" all the three women greeted me; they shook my hand just like the men do with us.

"Aleichem Sholom!" I responded. "The first time in my life, begging your pardon, that I have had to exchange Sholom with women!"

The two Schneider daughters started talking to each other in a kind of strange language that I could swear was our holy language, Hebrew. Only they spoke so fast that I couldn't understand a word. Schneider nodded to his wife, and she asked me into the dining room, where the table was already laid, and she invited me to take a seat.

"Forgive me," I said. "My seat won't run away. But I'm a Jew who is used to making Kiddush myself, not taking it from your very fine-sounding Chazan, who already made Kiddush in the synagogue for all Jews."

"Oh!" they all cried out, and they brought me a silver goblet and a bottle of wine, and they stood to hear me make Kiddush. When I had finished, I told my host, "Good wine, this! Long time I haven't tasted wine as good!"

"It's our wine!" Schneider said very gratified.

"What did you say? You keep a wine shop as well? I can well believe that Schneidering (tailoring) isn't enough for living in the style you do."

"No! I didn't mean that. What I meant was, it's Jewish wine!"

"Of course! I didn't expect you to give me goyish wine!"

"No! What we meant was that it's Jewish wine from our own Jewish vineyards in Eretz Israel!"

"Your Eretz Israel? I don't understand! Eretz Israel belongs to the Turk!"

"It's ours! Eretz Israel is ours!" Schneider repeated, his eyes shining. "Eretz Israel is ours! Was and will be ours!"

"Amen!" I said. "I hope so! Our people too say 'Next year in Jerusalem!' But first let's have Messiah come, and then we'll all, in God's good time, go to Eretz

Israel! Meanwhile we've still got the Turk there running things! And we are the same old bunglers we always were! Looking for the day before yesterday!"

I could see that Schneider was struggling hard to give me his answer. But Mrs. Schneider stopped him. "Leave the discussion for after! Let our guest wash. He must be starving!"

"She's no fool!" I thought to myself, "even if she's a Schneider's wife!"

"You're absolutely right! May the whole year be as right as you are!"

After we had washed, we sat down to table. The friendship and hospitality these people showed me was such that I felt immediately at home with them. Only one thing puzzled me—the Schneider daughters were speaking to each other in a language very similar to our holy tongue, Hebrew.

"Don't mind me," I interrupted them, "but one who asks doesn't lose his way. What language are your daughters speaking?"

"Hebrew! Our language! Don't you know it?"

"No wonder that I know it. I caught a few words here and there. What I'm surprised at is that your daughters know Hebrew. How does that happen?"

"What's the surprise?" And the two girls started hurling questions at me in Hebrew.

"We were taught several languages when we went to cheder. Hebrew was the first language we learned."

"I'm sorry," I addressed Mr. Schneider, my host. "I keep hearing such impossible things here! What sort of a cheder have you got here where girls learn languages, and Hebrew first of all!"

"It's the word, cheder, that puzzles you," Mrs. Schneider explained. "We call it cheder. But in fact they are schools, Jewish schools, Jewish high schools. Seminaries."

"Jewish seminaries? Jewish high schools? You're joking! You're pulling my leg! You've got a poor innocent Jew here, and you're making fun of him!"

"God forbid! We wouldn't dream of such a thing! Making a fool of a visitor, a guest! We'll show you our Jewish high schools and our Jewish gardens and gardeners, our Jewish aid funds and our Jewish bank, and our—"

"Jewish bank?" I nearly jumped out of my chair. "Do you mean a real bank, where you get money? Then those people are right who say you have gold and silver lying in the streets!"

"In the streets? No!" They were anxious to put me right, all four of them together. "There is no gold and no silver lying about in our streets. But we don't need it. Thank God, we have all we require!"

"Excuse me for asking. The shammas at the synagogue told me that you are a Schneider. You're a tailor? A workman?"

He repeated, "A tailor?" "Yes, my father was a tailor. And all my brothers were tailors. We are well-known for our work here."

"And a living? Do you make a living out of it?"

"Yes, thank God! I have this house, and I have two other houses."

"Own them?"

"Yes, I own them."

"Not mortgaged?"

"No!"

"And you still do tailoring, with the needle?"

"Yes, I've worked in my time. I still work. I will go on working!"

"Then I don't understand you. I don't understand what sort of man you are. You own three houses, clear—no mortgages, and you still go on stitching with needle and thread. That seems to me, forgive me for saying so, good and mad! One other thing I want to ask you," I went on, "I don't see a single servant in your house. People of your station in life, how do you do it?"

This time Mrs. Schneider, my hostess, answered. "Our servants," she said, "are free on Sabbaths and festivals. As the Torah says!"

"Torah?" I repeated. "You know the Torah, it seems, better than I do. I read the Portion of the Torah every Friday, and I don't remember anything in the Torah about servants being free on the Sabbath!"

"But it's written in the Torah!" said one of the two daughters, and she passed me a small Bible and pointed to a passage in Deuteronomy in the week's Portion—"Observe the Sabbath day to keep it holy. In it thou shalt not do any work, thou, nor thy son, nor thy daughter, nor thy manservant, nor thy maidservant."

"Well then," I said, "if we have to keep everything that's in the Torah! I still don't understand—if you let your servants go free, who prepares and serves?"

"My children do! They have been trained. They can do everything in the kitchen. They cook and bake, wash and iron. These challas—my elder daughter baked them!"

"I see! Now since your daughter is such a capable person, she deserves a tip-top husband. May I perhaps find a good match for her in my parts?"

That made the elder girl laugh. "Thank you, kind sir, but I'm already engaged."

"A good young man?"

She went red in the face and passed me a photograph of a young man in uniform with epaulettes.

"A general?" I asked.

"An engineer, in Eretz Israel," Mr. Schneider informed me, looking very pleased with himself. "He works on the railway we are building in Eretz Israel, in our country."

"What is your connection with Eretz Israel?" I asked him.

"We go to Eretz Israel every summer," he told me. "Those are—"

"Yes, I know," I went on. "That's the Wailing Wall there. And that's Mother Rachel's Grave, and that's the Cave of Machpelah. They say the goats eat carobs there, and old Jews go to die there."

That made Mr. Schneider laugh. And the others joined in.

"Seems," he said, "that you have really come from the back of beyond. "You have no idea what is going on in Eretz Isarael. What you were saying was long ago, long ago!"

"What do you mean long ago? What about today?"

"Today," he answered, "we have, thank God, several hundred agricultural colonies in Eretz Israel, whole villages of our own, vineyard and wine cellars, all sorts of businesses, factories, ships and railways, all our own!"

"Tut-tut!" I turned to him. "One inch more and you'll have built a paper bridge (the legend that Messiah will come over a bridge of paper). We'd do better to use our finger bowls and say grace. I'll tell you the truth—my head is in a whirl after all you've been telling me. I must go and lie down."

After we had said grace, they took me into another room, beautifully clean, where the best of everything had been prepared for me for the night. As soon a my head touched the pillow, I was asleep.

All night I dreamed mad dreams, jumbled, deranged—Eretz Israel Jews with Turkish shawls, girls with toppers on their heads, speaking Hebrew, and I myself a general with epaulettes, leading the red Little Jews over a paper bridge. I ran, and the red Little Jews ran after me. Then suddenly I felt the bridge collapse under me. Any moment and, God forbid, we'll all be in the sea. I cried, out, "Hear, O Israel!" and I woke! Bright day! Time to go to synagogue.

iv
He Wakes from Sleep. A Black-haired Man. Sabbath Tea. They Go Together to the Synagogue. More Wonders.

Where am I? That was my first thought when I woke from my sleep and started looking around to see where in the world I was. How clean and neat and tidy everything is here! Give a rouble a piece for a bedbug—there aren't any! Where do I wash my hands? Over there, just against my bed. There's a white washbasin with a tap. How that tap spurts on every side! Enough to have a bath!

Bang! Bang! Bang!

"Head against the wall!" I said, as I opened the door. A big, burly black-haired fellow stood there, in his Sabbath best. "How did you sleep?" he asked me.

"Who wants to know?" I retorted. "And who may you be?"

"I work here. I work for Mr. Schneider. He told me to look after you when you wake up, and if you want to go to synagogue, I am to take you there."

"So!" I said. "So you work for Mr. Schneider! Tell me, what Yom Tov is today, what festival, that you're all dressed up like that?"

"Mr. Schneider is a good man. I like working for him. I've got my two hands, and I'm not short of anything. I have nobody to worry about. No wife, no children. Only my old blind father, who lives with me!"

"All right, have a good time! How much does Mr. Schneider pay you per week? Not to speak of business on the Sabbath. . . ."

"Fifty," he said. "And I have a small share in the business, on top of that."

"Give me the full figure! How much in all?"

"I told you. Fifty roubles a week. And a percentage of the business on top."

"Fifty roubles a week!" I cried out. "Dear oh dear! With us if a young man like you earns three roubles a week, we start arranging a marriage for him. I'll tell you the truth, I'm beginning to be sorry because my father didn't make me a tailor."

"Then what sort of workman are you?"

"Me? I'm not a workman. My father wasn't a workman. And my children won't be workmen." I'm a Jew. That's what I am."

"I mean what do you do? What do you do for a living?"

"What do I do for a living? Anything God sends my way. We live on air."

"What do you mean on air?"

"I mean, one goes round the market place with one's stick, and one wonders, will God send me this or that, something or other. God provides!"

"And you do nothing?"

"What do you mean, nothing? We do all we can!"

"And what can you do?"

"I'll tell you what I can do! But you tell me, my dear, what do you do with all the money you earn, and why don't you get married?"

"I've told you. I've got an old father to look after."

"So what? That doesn't mean anything. It doesn't mean you can't get married."

"Honor thy father!" he said, baring his teeth. "Honor thy father is no small matter. My father, may he live many more years, is spending his old age with me. He lives like a lord. Works all day in the garden. He is better than a man who can see."

"Your garden? How did you get a garden?"

"From my father. I got the house and the garden from my father."

"In that case," I said, "you really should give him honor. He deserves it. I'd love to go with you, please God, tomorrow to look at your house and garden and to see your blind father working in the garden."

"Fine! I'm inviting you now. It will be a red letter day for me. And for my father."

"What was your father before? Also a tailor?"

"No! He was a gardener all his life."

"A gardener! What sort of a living is that! Can you live on it?"

"It's a living, like everything else. My father is a very good gardener. Especially planting trees. It's his life. He managed to save a little money too, and he bought the house with a bit of land; he turned it into a beautiful garden. He knows each tree, each plant. Blind as he is! He never goes farther than the garden. It's been his life for years. Except for his dream of going to Eretz Israel. Then he went blind."

"Did you ever!" I said to myself. "The idea! A Jew who loves plants and flowers and trees. And wants to go to Eretz Israel!"

"Would you like a drink?" the young man turned the conversation. "Tea, coffee, or chocolate?"

"No, thank you!" I said. "I'll do without the tea and the coffee and the chocolate. On the Sabbath I make my own tea from the water on the hob. You haven't a samovar, by any chance, with boiling water, the way we have it on the Sabbath?"

"No, God forbid! We have no samovar here, not even on weekdays."

"Then where do you get your boiling hot water from on the Sabbath?"

"From the tap. I'll show you; come with me."

And he took me to the kitchen. Clean, neat, tidy. You could see your reflection everywhere.

"This," he said, "is the cold water tap. And that is the hot water tap. It gives us all the hot water we need."

"And the third tap?" I asked.

"That's the electricity switch."

"What's it do?"

"It gives heat and light. Want to see?" And he reached out to the switch.

"Not on the Sabbath," I cried. "You don't play with fire on the Sabbath! Come, let's go to the synagogue. Must be getting quite late."

"If you wait for a moment, I'll tell you what they're up to."

And going over to the wall, he lifted a receiver and spoke to the wall. He called a number. And immediately: "Is that the synagogue? The shammas? Yes, would you be good enough to tell me where you're up to in the prayers? Thank you!" And to me he said: "Let's go! They're about to take out the Torah."

I stood and stared at him. "The wall told you that?"

"It was the shammas who told me!"

"What shammas? There's no shammas here!"

"That was the shammas on the telephone."

"Telephone? What's that?"

"You don't know what a telephone is? A machine through which you can speak ever such a distance."

"How can you speak over a distance?"

"I'll show you. You tell them a number, and a bell rings at that number, and you can talk to whomever you wish. And when you've finished, you hang up the receiver, and we are disconnected."

"And what's it for?"

"What's it for? To communicate. Like the telegraph. You know about the telegraph, of course?"

"Sure!" I said. "The telegraph. I know all about that. A child knows about a telegraph!"

"Well, the telephone is the same as the telegraph. Wires here and wires there. Only with one you tap and with the other you speak."

"So that's all! And I though it was goodness knows what! Come, let's go to the synagogue."

Going to the synagogue with my young companion, I saw the town for the first time. What a beautiful town! The paved streets. So clean and tidy. The tall, bright buildings and the green trees everywhere. I never imagined anything so spick and span. "I wish," I said to myself, "we were half as clean inside as they are outside. But where," I reflected, "where is their gold and silver supposed to be lying about in the streets?"

"Are you looking for anything?" my companion asked me.

"Yesterday," I said.

"Hopeless," he rejoined. "You'll never find yesterday!"

"Thank you for your assurance," I replied. "I had no idea that you're a thinker as well!"

"I'm no thinker. But I do have some idea of things. And I read."

"So you're still studying? You just said you're a working man. When do you do your studying?"

"In the evening. We meet every evening, workmen, drivers, gardeners. We all meet in the synagogue, and we read and write and do arithmetic. And athletics too."

"And what sort of a customer is athletics?"

"Running and jumping, gymnastics. And dancing. We dance from childhood. We teach dancing in all the Jewish schools. Even in the cheder."

"Madness!" I said. "Dancing and jumping! Do you know what is missing?"

"What?" he asked.

"Going," I said. "Going to synagogue with your head down and your legs in the air!"

v

The Rabbi's Sermon. Academies in Eretz Israel. The Red Little Jews. Yikum Purkon with an Organ. A New Madman.

We arrived in the synagogue when they had already finished the Reading from the Torah. The rabbi stood on the Bimah, with his white collar and his four-cornered hat. He was preaching his sermon. The congregation all wore shiny black toppers, with little scarves round their necks, like the one the shammas now offered me.

"What's this little scarf for?" I asked him.

"It's a Tallis," he said, very seriously.

"Some Tallis!" I said, hardly keeping myself from laughing. "It's childish! What can he be telling them in his sermon?" I asked myself. "What rebuke can he address to them? That they shouldn't carry things on the Sabbath? Not look up to the women's gallery? And what women! Like princesses! In silks and jewels, and lovely hats with feathers!"

I listened to the rabbi's discourse. I tried to follow him, to catch a word, a whole sentence, to see how he translated the text, how he brought in an epigram or a wise saying, a fable or a parable. But nothing of the sort! He just stood there, talking about side issues, about education, about academies in Eretz Israel.

"Academies in Eretz Israel," I though to myself. "They don't know what to think up next. I know about homes for the aged and hospitals. But academies! Mad! Lunatics!"

"Academies," the rabbi went on talking, "academies are more important to us than bread. Because bread is only a means to live. Academies, that is life itself!" And he enforced his argument with a text, "It is a tree of life to them that grasp it." "Education!" he cried, "Learning! Light! Knowledge! Let us fulfil the words 'Out of Zion shall go forth the Law!'"

I thought that would be the end of his sermon, so I called out at the top of my voice, "Yihu Purkon min Shemayh!" (The passage recited after the Reading from the Torah—"May salvation come from Heaven"). Just the way I was used to at home.

I saw the whole congregation turning their heads to look at me, like taking a look at a bear. But the rabbi droned on, all about side issues, the state of the Jews generally, and about our red Little Jews in particular. He started telling a story from the "Arabian Nights." How there are on the other side of the Sambatyon (meaning us) a body of Jews called the red Little Jews (as though we didn't know). How many, he told us, we couldn't say. But according to calculations they are estimated at five to seven million, perhaps even eight million. (Mud in his eye! Stones in his heart! He doesn't even say Kein Ayin Hora—no evil eye!) Because they increase and multiply very nicely (may they go on increasing). But, he went on, "their life is no life because they are poor, because they starve, have no crust of bread to eat, going to bits. He painted a grim picture of the way we live. And the whole congregation hung on his words. Every now and then someone in the congregation heaved a big sigh or groaned. And up in the gallery I could see the women dabbing their eyes with their white handkerchiefs. So that people should think they were weeping.

"What good, kind people you are," I said to myself, sighing and groaning over our sad plight. But what use are your sighs and groans? What can we do with your tears? If you are really concerned about us, help us in some other way! Get together, have a collection, and send us a few roubles!"

So I lent my ear to the rabbi, to hear what more he had to say. What text he would choose to finish his sermon. And I suddenly reminded myself that it was the Sabbath, when we mustn't carry or think of money.

"We are in duty bound to release our poor, unfortunate brethren," he continued, "from those unhappy lands, to settle them on the soil, in our Holy Land. (Did we ever ask them to? What's all this talk about the Holy Land? Would be better to help us where we are!) Two thousand years, he said, they have been waiting for us to come to them, (I never heard of it) to help them to liberate them from their long, black, and bitter Exile. ("And a Saviour shall come unto Zion!") And with this, he concluded his sermon. He was followed immediately by a burst of singing from above, "Amen!"

I could swear I heard a violin and a flute and a trumpet and a violoncello.

"You have music on the Sabbath, with musicians?" I asked the shammas.

"No, they're not musicians. It's our organ."

"Organ?" I asked. "What instrument is an organ?"

"The Levites used to play the organ in the Temple."

"It must have been beautiful in the Temple," I told myself. "The Temple and the High Priests! The organ playing. The Levites singing. And on the altar a fire offering. A sweet smell rising from the sacrifice."

Then in the midst of my meditations I was jerked back to the present day by the chazan with the clean-shaven chin opening his mouth to sing Mi-Sheberach (Blessing on this holy congregation, together with all other congregations), and as it happens in our Jewish way, as our Hirsh-Baer does it, he let himself go. You could tell he enjoyed it. So much relish, so much zest. He reveled in it. His voice did not ring out so loudly with the words, "Wine for Kiddush and Havdalah." I got the impression that he was waving them aside, out of the way. But he rose to the heights when he came to, "Who give bread for the wayfarers and charity for the poor." He trilled and boomed and warbled. And he repeated twenty or thirty times the one word La'ani'im (to the poor). Then still on La'ani'im his voice dropped, low, hushed, quiet, till you could hardly hear him, so faint, so quiet, so low. Then suddenly he rose again to the top of his voice, loud, sonorous, clamant. "For those who devote themselves in full faith to the wants of the congregation."

"We know," I thought to myself, "What it means to devote yourself to the wants of the congregation. Where I come from one man, Reb Frenkel, built a home for himself on the wants of the congregation. He married off his children on it. It gives you a good living devoting yourself to the wants of the congregation. If you have a bit of luck!"

"And send blessing and prosperity," the chazan concluded, "upon the work of their hands." This brought another burst of singing from above, with the organ joining in. And that was Musaf starting, I said to myself.

"Good Lord!" I was thinking in my mind, "how does one get a couple of red Little Jews out here! For them to see the things I see! They'll never believe me when I get home!"

The next thing was standing up for the Musaf Amidah. Of course, nobody said a word. Nobody prayed. All this was left to the chazan and the organ. The congregation just stood. Like rigid poles. Not a man among them shook and swayed. Nothing!

I did what I had to do. I stood. And inadvertently I stepped on somebody's toes, somebody standing immediately behind me. He moved away and banged against another standing behind his back. His topper flew off. It fell against a third man, and it started a rumpus. With everybody turning to look at me as if I were some strange animal.

Filing out of the synagogue, I heard my host, Mr. Schneider, call, "Good Sabbath" to me. "I am sorry," he informed me, "but I've had to surrender you to a great friend of mine for now." And so saying he handed me over to a thickset man with a paunch and with podgy hands.

"Sholom Aleichem!" he greeted me, putting his pudgy hand in mine.

"Aleichem Sholom!" I responded. "And what is your name?"

"Isaac," he said, peering into my eyes, with a look as though I was taking him home as my Sabbath guest, not the other way round.

"Isaac?" I repeated. "Isaac isn't enough by itself. May I know who you are, what you are, and what you do?"

"I live here. And I am a carpenter."

"A carpenter?" I echoed. "A workman?"

"A workman," he agreed, but with an air as though he was boasting that he was a rabbi, or a shochet, a kosher meat license holder, or a registered town advocate.

"This place," I remarked, "enjoys a rich harvest of workmen. So I have noticed."

"And what," he said, "is your work?"

"I'm not a carpenter."

"What are you?"

"I'm a Jew!"

"I know that! I mean what do you do? What is your occupation?"

"What I do?" and for a joke I said, "I write books, seforim."

"Really?" bowing to me slightly. "So you're a writer? A very fine profession, a very distinguished profession. I know somebody, a relative of mine, in fact, who is also a writer."

"What sort of a writer is he? Novelettes for girls? Or does he write petitions and official applications?"

My carpenter puffed out his cheeks and laughed fit to burst. "You're a real joker!" he cried.

"And you're a chump, a clot, a nobody! A dullard, a clown!"

Hearing these words from me the carpenter roared with laughing, held his sides. He laughed so much that I began to fear for his sanity.

Seeing my alarmed look, he pulled himself together and stopped laughing.

"Excuse me," he said. "I couldn't stop laughing! I laugh terribly. Once I'm started off, I can't stop. My wife reads funny books to me. And I laugh and laugh. My wife's an educated woman! She'll love meeting you. When she hears that you're a writer, author! My wife has a high regard for authors. It's a fine thing if God gives you the talent, and you can become an author!"

What's he authoring me about! I thought to myself. I have put my foot in it this time! That other fellow, the Schneider, is a strange chap. But he is a human being, a normal person. This carpenter is just a fool. No! He's a lunatic! As I'm a Jew, he's mad!

vi
The Synagogue in the Carpenter's House. Joining the Army. Stories about Messiah. Jewish Papers and Periodicals. Oneg Shabbat.

"My wife!" the carpenter introduced me at his home. "And this," he went on, "is our Sabbath guest. From the other side of the Sambatyon."

The wife looked a real lady. The explanation about who I was seemed to please her. As though someone had brought her news that she had won the big lottery prize. She couldn't make up her mind where to seat me. She bombarded me with words, wanted to discover everything about me immediately, at once. About our life over there. What we do. Was it true what people here write about the red Little Jews, that we are all still barbarians, savages.

"Savages?" I said. "They're as well bred as your Jews here any day! Maybe cleverer! Only one thing they're short of, lunatics. We have no mad people!"

"What do you mean by that?" she wanted to know. She had read several descriptions, she said, about my people. According to the writers we were all still living in the Dark Ages.

"It's dark everywhere when you put out the light," I said.

"Sweetheart," the carpenter interrupted his wife, "did you think you could get the better of him? You've found the wrong man for that! He's a writer, this fellow, and an author among the red Little Jews."

I thought Mrs. Carpenter was going to drop when she heard these words. She raised her eyebrows and shot a lot of new questions at me—who was I? What was my true name, and what books had I written?

All my bad dreams on that carpenter's head for what he let me in for! A nice mess he'd gotten me into! Tell her what books I've written, when the fact is that I've never written a book in my life! Luckily at this point the carpenter butted in with a question of his own. "Sweetheart, why do you keep our guest waiting? He wants to eat. Leave the books till after! There'll be plenty of time later!"

So we sat down to table.

I have already seen big parties in my life, weddings and circumcisions, but I'd never seen a banquet like this in the carpenter's house before. I won't speak of the various dishes and the wines they served. A royal banquet! A meal fit for a king! They had everything! Enough for a dozen more guests. And the gaiety, the jollification, the joy, and the happiness at that table! There were several well-built sturdy youngsters, ten young handsome fellows, sitting round the table. And a few small children. All complying with the injunction to eat heartily. They had healthy appetites. Ate for all they were worth.

"Who are these youngsters?" I asked my host when he had finished saying Kiddush. (Their Eretz Israel wine was so potent that after drinking the first glass, you let your tongue run away with you; you're drunk!)

"My assistants, my apprentices!"

"They're certainly good trenchermen! They'll make fine soldiers!"

"That's what they're going to be, in God's good time! The only trouble is, they may not pass the test. That's what I'm afraid of!"

"Afraid? I think you ought to be glad if they're not accepted!"

"Why?"

"Why? You ask that seriously? What's the good thing about being a soldier?"

"What's the good thing about being a human being?" That was one of the young men calling across to me.

"You hold your tongue!" I responded. "You're not a grown man yet! Don't you interfere when older people talk!"

The young men looked at each other and smiled. The carpenter bit his lip and motioned to them, as though to say—"You'll never catch him out!"

"What's the great excitement of God helping you to grow up and be a soldier? My brain won't take it in!"

"Let me explain," said Mrs. Carpenter. "To begin with, army training is a good thing in itself. A sign that you are able and fit, that you're sound and healthy. And a man. Secondly, it's a good thing to be a soldier. You can get promotions and win medals. And thirdly, we must have our own soldiers, our own army in Eretz Israel. What does a people look like if it hasn't a land of its own and its own army?"

"What?" I asked, "what do we want an army for? Are you going to fight, are you going to war against somebody?"

"We don't want to go to war. But we must be prepared. No state can exist without soldiers, without an army."

"And where is your state?" I asked.

"Eretz Israel!"

"Do you really expect Messiah to come soon? Seriously!"

"Messiah has come already!" they all chorused together.

"Mazel tov!" said I. "Congratulations! When did he arrive?"

"From the moment," they told me, again all of them together, "from the moment when we all, without exception, adopted the idea of Yishuv Eretz Israel. That moment Messiah arrived!"

"How did he arrive?" I persisted. "On a white horse? And where is the Prophet Elijah? And where is the war of Gog and Magog? And where is the loud blast of the shofar? The last trumpet? And the earthquake? And all the other signs of the coming of Messiah? Be careful! Be careful that you're not having your leg pulled. Some hoaxer! Make him show you his papers, his credentials, black on white!"

I don't know where I got so much talk in me from! I opened my mouth, and the words tumbled out, a spate of words. I never thought I was so garrulous, had so much talk in me. And the whole gathering there, at the table, sat silent, looked at each other and wondered how one man had so much to say. That I wasn't just an ordinary little Jew. They came to realize that this was some Jew. A man who knew his onions, knew what was what. They exchanged glances, and then, all of them together, turned to me with a query—

"Wouldn't you like to lie down for a bit? A rest after the meal? Don't be ashamed to say so."

"What is there to be ashamed of?" I asked. "And what about all of you? Don't you have a nap on the Sabbath after your meal?"

"No!" they answered.

"Then what do you do?"

"Go for a walk, go to our Folk Library."

"Where?"

"Our Folk Library."

"To do what? Read Psalms? Study Mishna?"

"See what news there is in the Jewish world."

"News? You can hear the news in the synagogue. Talking between Mincha and Maariv."

"Who goes to the synagogue to hear news? A synagogue isn't a club!"

"What saintly people you are! God with tzitzes! Tell me now—you get together every Sabbath after the meal in your, what did you call it?"

"Folk Library."

"And what do you do in your Folk Library? Not to compare the two, like Gentiles in the pub. You read newspapers, periodicals, books. Trivial things!"

"We read newspapers and periodicals."

"You must have a lot of papers there. Everyone of you reading a paper—why, you would have to have a hundred papers!"

"Several hundred!"

"Who needs so many papers? Who reads all that stuff!"

"All of us! We all do. We couldn't live without papers and periodicals and books."

"Yes, I understand," I said. "How can a carpenter live without his paper? And then there are the women! Don't the women read? The Teitch Chumash, I suppose."

"They read the same things we read. There's no difference, men or women."

"No difference between men and women? Then you really are what we mustn't utter with our lips. So I'll leave you now and lie down to have my Sabbath snooze, and you go to your Jewish papers and periodicals and books."

"That's a real pleasure," I said to myself. "It's a worldwide custom, on the Sabbath day, after the big meal, to lie down and sleep it off. Seems to me there is no greater enjoyment possible. And these people here get together, the whole lot, and read newspapers and periodicals and books. A nice way of spending your time! They've got their brains upside down! Like their idea that Messiah has come! They don't sing Z'miros, and they uphold Eretz Israel. Look like princes, eat and drink, and they love work. And they say men and women are all the same to them! Mad people! And a mad country!"

I dropped into one of the soft couches and fell asleep.

vii
A Meeting of Madmen. More about Academies in Eretz Israel. A Letter from Rothschild. He Is Turned Down. The Red Little Jew Can't Take It.

Saturday night. After Havdala. Finished saying the invocations to Elijah, as the forerunner of the Messiah.

"Where has your husband flown to so soon?" I asked his wife. No foolish woman, by the way. "Gone to a Mlave Malke?"

"To a meeting," she answered. "I shall be going there too. You can come with me if you'd like to."

"Do women here go to meetings as well?"

"Why not? Aren't women human too?"

A pointless question. Go and find an answer to it!

Instead I asked, "What meeting is it? What's it about? The meat tax? The rabbi's salary? A roof for the old Beth Hamedrash? I know something about Jewish meetings!"

"No!" she said. "It's a meeting about Eretz Israel."

"Eretz Israel again! Why have you got yourselves fixed on Eretz Israel? Nothing else on your minds?"

"Eretz Israel means a great deal to us," she answered, with great emphasis. "Eretz Israel is of great concern to us. Very much on our minds. We have everything—money, people, health, education. We're short of only one thing. To be equal with all other nations. A land. When we have a land, we shall be a nation. Eretz Israel is the Jewish land. The People of Israel are the Jewish nation!"

"Listen to that!" I thought to myself. "She can say it even in Hebrew! I'd like some of our people to see me going on Saturday alone through the streets with another man's wife, talking about strange things, and in Hebrew at that. They'd think I'd gone mad!" Then aloud, "Where is the meeting?"

"In the rabbi's house."

We came to a big house and entered a large, brightly-lighted salon. Several long tables with tablecloths, a lot of chairs, and ever so many people, men and women, girls and boys. On top a very old, very grey man, ringing a bell. A meeting with a bell—the first time I've seen such a thing. And speeches! Everybody spoke separately, not like us, all at the same time, all together. Nobody interrupts. Every speaker is allowed to have his say to the end. The rabbi himself (some rabbi!) when he wants to say something, asks the old man's permission first. Imagine a rabbi in our parts asking anyone's permission to speak!

And the things they spoke about! Wild, mad things! Difficult to know what they want. One stands up to ask a question. Why is this year different from every other year? Every year, he says, they take from him so much and so much money. This year they didn't take as much, not half as much. Did you ever hear such a complaint?

Another man stands up. Another complaint. Why isn't he given some welfare work to do? Someone else was doing this and that, and he, poor man, had to sit and pray to God to send him someone to help, to do some good! You can see how that poor man suffers! They won't let him help people!

A third man rises and reads out a list of the things done till now, what could have been done, and what is still to do. "Done?" said this smart-aleck, "Till now we've done nothing! A few hundred agricultural colonies in Eretz Israel is nothing. We should have had more than a thousand by now! And if we have about two hundred million pounds sterling in our National Bank, it should by now have been at least two billion! Judging by the huge donations and the enormous bequests to our fund from our millionaires we should by now be in a position to buy all Eretz Israel and to pay the Turk the full amount for it, to the last penny!"

"I know you will throw it up at me," he went on, "that we spent a lot of money and a lot of time on cultural work. My answer to that complaint is that till now we have spent much less on culture than we should have done. Our venerated rabbi was right when he told us in the synagogue today that one academy in all Eretz Israel is not enough. It would be more like it if we had three academies there, four, five!"

I was standing aside, somewhere at the back, watching these funny Jews. They want more academies in Eretz Israel! One isn't enough for them. They want ten, a hundred, a thousand academies! Give them millions of academies!

The smart-aleck finished and sat down, and another one stood up to complain of the unhappy state of the Jewish gardeners in Eretz Israel, who because of it had not been able to contribute more than half a million francs this year to the fund. But if conditions for the gardeners were not good, the condition of the artisans, the craftsmen in Israel was shocking. The artisans in Eretz Israel, he said, had always had their own library. Today they had no library! There had been a fire, and it was burned down. So the poor artisans had to go to other people's libraries! As for the Jewish workers on the railways in Eretz Israel, they were worst off of all. Till now they had run their own theater. Now their theater had broken up. Their best actors had gone abroad or had gotten married and gone into business. And the poor railway workers were left without a theater. (Their tears could have melted a stone! Imagine Jewish railway workers without a theater!)

This smart-aleck was followed by a young fellow from the Youth movement, who spoke with fire and passion. His attack was on a body he called the Carmel Society. It was, he said, the wealthiest of all the Jewish societies. It would be only right that the Carmel Society should provide wine free to all the Jewish hospitals in Eretz Israel. It wouldn't hurt anyone if the Carmel Society would make a few hundred thousand less in the year. It wouldn't harm them. Not to worry! They'll survive!

After that a young man read a long rigmarole in a paper about military service, about a Jewish army, with new plans how and when, and everybody listened to him, all eyes and ears. They asked questions, and he answered. And when he finished, everybody clapped, and called, Bravo, Hedad! It was deafening!

Next the host himself, the rabbi, stood up and read a letter from Rothschild. From his reading I gathered that Rothschild was asking them for a favor, flattering them, ingratiating himself with them. He wanted to join them, be a member, like all the others, equal, and promising them millions. I stood thinking to myself—if such a thing happened with us, a millionaire wanting to buy himself into our society, I know what would happen. We would go crawling to him on all fours. We would dance with joy. With us, when a rich man only says a nice word to us, without any money, we are delighted. "He spoke to us. He said. He took a pinch of snuff from the shammas, and he sneezed. Bless him!"

I thought they would all fall over themselves to welcome Rothschild into their society. No! There were some who wanted to know where Rothschild had been before? When they would have needed him. When they had asked him to join them. When Jewish tears and Jewish blood were being poured out. Then he had sat behind locked doors. Inaccessible. At that time he hadn't understood Yiddish. Now when God helped us, and we have our own funds, when God has found us worthy, and our nation is going to be again equal with other nations, now our bigwigs come along and want to buy themselves in with their millions, so that they can have their say. No! We don't sell honors for money. Honors must be earned, worked for! We don't need Rothschild! We don't need his millions!

I could no longer contain myself. I jumped up. "Rabosei," I screamed at the top of my voice, "don't take it bad that I who don't belong here, a stranger, a guest from the other side of the Sambatyon intrudes in your affairs. They say, where I come from, that a guest for a while sees for a mile. I beg you a hundred times to forgive me, but in my eyes you seem to be just plain mad!

"About that terrible tragedy of the railway workers in Eretz Israel left without a theater," I went on, "I'll leave that alone. But what that cheeky youngster just said about Rothschild—it takes some doing to be a Rothschild! Where I come from, we would have taken a young man like that, begging your pardon, and given him fifty or sixty strokes on his backside, to teach him to be respectful, how to speak about a man of wealth. If I had any acquaintance with Rothschild, I'd be the first to tell him what's been going on here. It would be only right to teach these impudent pups the way we do it! Don't you agree with me?"

Hearing words like these from me, they hid their faces in shame—so it seemed to me, since they made no attempt to refute what I said. They exchanged glances, smiled, and whispered something inaudible in one another's ear. Apparently they were afraid I would sit down at once and write to Rothschild to tell him all about it.

"We'll explain things to you, make it all clear to you, presently," the rabbi called over to me.

"There's nothing for you to make clear to me," I replied. "I have all my senses, thank God, still unimpaired."

The old man at the top rang his bell and announced that the meeting was ended. The whole crowd rose, and all together sang some song all in Hebrew, Hatikvah. Everybody sang—the old and the young, the men and the women.

"You were right with what you said," the carpenter remarked to me on our way back, trying at the same time to supress the laughter that was making him hold his sides. "I knew right away you were laughing at them!"

"That's right," I said. "Of course I was. You know more than a corpse knows, you understand as much as my boots do."

That made the carpenter go into fits of laughter. And the more I spoke about him as a fool, a dolt, the son of a clown, a buffoon, the more it made him laugh.

He nearly burst laughing. I spat at the mad carpenter and busied myself with my thoughts.

"Strange creatures these! That meeting with all those speeches and the talk of millions made my head swim. I had no idea any more what world I was in. Either, or—either they are mad, or I am! No! I concluded. It's they who are mad!

1900

Homesick

Not a thing in the world that doesn't get known in Kasrielevky. No news in the world that doesn't get known to the little folk.

True, it gets there a little late, and not firsthand. So what? It's no big tragedy. On the contrary, I think it's an advantage, a big advantage. Better so!

For, speaking among ourselves, what, for instance, do the Kasrielevky Jews lose if they hear today's news—what wonderful news! God help us! Such happy tidings, salvation and consolation—a month or two later, a year later even! No tragedy!

In short, the little folk got to know—a little late, indeed—that there is such a word as Zionism. Not everybody understood at first what it meant, this Zionism. Derived from Zion, which is in the prayer book, that Zionists are a kind of association whose desire is to pack all Jews off to Eretz Israel. It set the whole town roaring with laughter. People held their sides with laughing. All the wisecracks that were hurled at Dr. Herzl's head! And Dr. Nordau's head. And at all the other doctors! It would be worth collecting them all and publishing them as a separate booklet. I give you my word that they have a lot more salt and a lot more pepper than those sugar-sweet wise words that we get dished up every year in our Hebrew calendars.

There's one good thing about the Kasrielevky folk. As long as they're laughing, they laugh. But when they laugh their fill, they start to think about what they had been laughing at, and after a while they begin to understand. That's how it was with Zionism, too. First of all they laughed. Scoffed. Made jokes about it. Then they started listening to what was being said in the papers, and they repeated it, only the other way round, chewing it over and over. After all, shares are shares, and business is business. Money. And money talks. What can't you do with money these days? And that settled it. Money would do the trick, especially when you're dealing with the Turk, with the red fez; he was himself a real proper Kasrielevkite like all the Kasrielevky folk. That's when they took up Zionism in Kasrielevky. The Kasrielevky townspeople, thank God, are of such a kind that you can win them over to anything you wish. What looked to them yesterday crooked, and as hard to get as crossing the Red Sea, is today to them straight, as straight as can be. And buying Eretz Israel from the Turk looks as easy as eating a bagel or smoking a cigarette. For make no mistake—what can stand in our way? Nothing else, only money. And money is no difficulty with us. Our Rothschild—if only he wants to—can buy up the

whole of Eretz Israel, with Istanbul and all Turkey rolled into one. No need to
worry about money. Like all business deals there would have to be some
bargaining, some haggling. Right! A rouble more, a rouble less. The only
question left is—what if he doesn't want to sell? But if you think it over, aren't
we blood relations, near kin, Jews and Turks—Isaac and Ishmael! Think it over,
and we're blood relations. Really!

To cut it short—there was a meeting. And another meeting and a third. With
the help of God a Zionist society was formed, with an elected president and a
vice-president and a treasurer and a secretary and a corresponding secretary,
everything in proper order. And everyone pledged payment of a shekel. One
pledged a kopek a week. Another two kopeks. Young people delivered impas-
sioned speeches. The words Zion, Zionism, Zionists were heard increasingly.
And the names Dr. Herzl, Dr. Nordau, and all the other doctors were all the
time on people's lips. Membership kept growing, and money came in, a very
considerable sum. So they called a big meeting, and people sat down to consider what to do with the money. Whether to leave the capital where it was for
the time being, making it a separate fund for the Kasrielevky Zionists, or send it
to the central office, or perhaps wait a bit till there was a really big sum
accumulated, and Kasrilevke would become a shareholder in the Jewish Bank.

This meeting turned out to be one of the stormiest, most passionate meetings
ever held in Kasrielevky. Opinions were sharply divided. Many people wanted
a central office. "We are bound," they said, "to support the center. For if we
don't support the center, and you don't want to support the center, how will
the center exist?" There were others who took the opposite view. The center
could manage, they said, without Kasrilevke. "We're not expected to provide
for the whole world. Does anyone provide for Kasrilevke? Everybody should
look after number one! That's the ticket!"

Then Noah Reb Yossel's, the president, the rich man's son-in-law, stood up, a
young man of the Enlightenment, a Maskil, still beardless, and said a few warm
words, his tone pitched a little too high. "'Four thousand years'." That's how
Noah, the president, began, as if he was Napoleon addressing his troops when
he marched them into Egypt. "'Four thousand years.' With these same words I
should begin my speech to you today. With only a slight difference. For almost
two thousand years, brothers, we find ourselves not on the height of the Pyr-
amids, but deep, very deep down in the ground. For almost two thousand years
we have been looking out, not for our troops but for Messiah to come and free
us from Golus, to lead us to the land of our Fathers, to Eretz Israel. For almost
two thousand years we have fasted on the Seventeenth of Tammuz, abstained
from meat in the Nine Days, and when the Ninth of Ab comes round, we sit on
the ground in our stockinged feet, bewailing the destruction of the Temple. For
almost two thousand years we remember seventy-seven times a day Zion and
Jerusalem and ask ourselves, 'What have we done for Zion's sake and for the
sake of Jerusalem?'" It's a sin, as sure as I'm alive, that we have no stenog-
rapher in Kasrilevke who could have been at that meeting and taken down that

fine speech by Noah, the president, word for word, the way it's done in proper towns. So we must confine ourselves now to the few words we have given here from memory, and the conclusion, very briefly, of this remarkable address.

"Now," said Noah, the president, "now that we are privileged in our lifetime to see our frail old Israel waken from sleep, straighten his tormented limbs, look round to discover where in the world he is, and say, 'House of Jacob, come let us go!' We have no need, rabosei, to rely on the big men, on our notables. For if you leave it to them, you may well go on waiting. We don't need to wait for miracles. It is easier to be struck by lightning than to get a rouble or two for Zion out of a rich man's pocket. We must ourselves begin to build the edifice. If I am not for myself, who will be?"

"We may be proud," he went on, "that we have lived to see the day when Jews may think and speak of our own Jewish Bank. Of course we must see to it that Kasrielevky does not lag behind other towns, and that Kasrielevky Jews should also have a share in our own Jewish Bank.

"But I must tell you, rabosei, that according to the accounts which our treasurer will be presenting to you, we haven't enough money to buy even one share. We are short of nearly half the sum we need, about five or six roubles. That's why, brothers, we should now and here, right away get together and make up the deficit, each one of us as much as his means allow, and see to it that we have the full amount, ten roubles. Let our brothers, let the whole world see that there are in Kasrielevky too Zionists in whom the fire of Zion is aflame. Let Dr. Herzl see that his labor on our behalf is not in vain."

Clapping hands and shouting "Bravo" is not the way yet in Kasrielevky. Thank God it isn't. The noise and the clamor are loud enough as it is. If people clapped and shouted "Bravo," it would be deafening. In Kasrielevky if someone likes what you've just been saying, he comes over to you and slaps you on the back.

"What do you say of our president, eh?"

"Some lip, some tongue, some speaker!"

"And he's got learning! Did you hear the way he mixed up things, Gemara and Soferim!"

"You've got to have a head on your shoulders to remember all that by heart!"

"Don't be silly! That chap sits day and night over his books!"

To cut it short, the meeting decided to subscribe for one share. But it's easy to say, "subscribe for one share." How do you get this across, if Jews live stuck away somewhere in a hole called Kasrielevky, and the Jewish Bank is—know where? In London!

It started a whole correspondence. Letters here, letters there, letters everywhere! Shmaye, the secretary, who wrote our letters wrote his fingers to the bone before he got a clear answer where and how to send the money. But no sooner he knew where and how, then a new trouble hit him. The Kasrielevky postmaster! The Kasrielevky postmaster, a notoriously coarse fellow and very fastidious about his food, couldn't stand the smell of garlic. If a Jew entered the post office, he would hold his nose and say "Shalom Shlumke!" And when Shmaye handed him his packet, he slammed it back at him—"You haven't addressed it properly!" Or he told him to go and get some sealing wax. Or another time he would examine the packet from every side, read the address out loud, melt the sealing wax, and ask Shmaye, staring him straight in the face, "What sort of business have you got with London? Are you sending money out of the country?"

What Shmaye had in mind to answer the postmaster the way he did, I don't know. Maybe he wanted to impress the postmaster. He said:

"This money is going to our Jewish Bank, our own Jewish Bank."

The postmaster looked at Shmaye.

"Jewish Bank! Zhidovska Bank? How did Jews get a bank?"

That made Shmaye think. And in his mind said to himself: "If you are such an anti-Semite, I'll tell you what a Zhidovska Bank is."

And he told him a lot of boastful stories, exaggerated stories (all correspondents exaggerate). He told him that the Jewish Bank is the biggest bank in the world. It has two hundred thousand million pounds sterling. In pure gold. Hard to say how much that is in our money, because the pound is so much more than our money. A pound sterling would be almost a hundred roubles of ours.

At that the postmaster glared at Shmaye, and as he watched the sealing wax dripping down on the envelope, he said:

"You're lying. You dirty dog! A pound sterling is less than ten roubles!"

"That's an ordinary pound," Shmaye said, trying to get out of this new challenge. "A gold pound is worth much more!"

"Get out of here, you boob! Who do you think you're kidding? A Jew always tries bamboozling you! Anyone else in my place would give you back your packet and refuse to send it on! You know I have the power to put your packet under arrest, and you, and your whole community for trying to send our money to London. We work hard, we toil, and we plough, and you Jews come along when everything's finished and ready, and you guzzle and booze, and on top of it you send out parcels with our gold in them, devil knows where to—a Jewish Bank somewhere!"

Now Shmaye saw what a mess he had gotten himself into. He stood speechless for a while. What wouldn't he have given to retract his words! But too late now. (Many correspondents would like to take back their words, full of lies and deceptions. But that's nonsense! You can never take words back!) Our Kasrielevky correspondent was glad enough to pocket the receipt for his postal packet and get out of the post office, like a beaten good-for-nothing.

With the money sent off the Kasrielevky Zionists started looking out for their one single share to arrive. Day after day. A whole month passed, two months, and three and four, and still no goods for their money. So they turned on the secretary, the correspondent; perhaps he hadn't sent the money to the right place, hadn't written the address properly. Poor Shmaye got it hot and strong.

He hadn't stopped writing letters to the central office in London. And here in Kasrielevky people were going at him, sticking barbed words into his flesh, making all sorts of accusations against him. The honest, pious Orthodox Jews and the Hasidim, all those, that is, who didn't believe in Zionism, found it a good topical subject for discussion. "Didn't we know from the start that this is how it would turn out?" And they plagued and tormented the Zionists—"Didn't we tell you that they would trick you out of your money?"

Then God had mercy on our correspondent, and one morning he received a letter from London, to say that the one share for which he had applied was sent, was here. Not actually here, in Kasrielevky, but at the frontier. It only needed official stamping.

Then another month passed, two months, and three and four, and still no share! People started worrying the corresponding secretary again—"Where's the share? Still stamping it?" They didn't spare words, harsh stinging words and all sorts of innuendos. They all hit the mark. It hurt him more waiting for the stamping than previously for the share. It almost made him spit blood. So he rolled up his sleeves and started writing letters all over again, to all the corners of Israel.

"What's the idea?" he asked. "Taking such a time over stamping one share! If it needed stamping with ten thousand others, it should have been stamped long ago now!"

To the Zionist Society he said day after day—"Look! You've waited such a long time. Wait a little longer! It won't take long now, not as long as it's taken already!"

And that's how it was! In less than nine months a small packet arrived at the address of the rabbi, Reb Yosifl (our corresponding secretary didn't want any more trouble with the postmaster).

So they called a meeting of all the members, in Rabbi Reb Yosifl's house. And all Jews, certainly all Kasrielevky Jews being at all times everywhere in a hurry, everyone wanting always to be first, it was no wonder that there was a lot of pushing and shoving, everybody standing on top of everybody else, trying to snatch the bit of paper out of the other man's hand, so that he could examine the Jewish share certificate all to himself, "Our own Jewish Bank."

For a long, a very long time the Kasrielevky Zionists basked in the pride of their one share in "Our own Jewish Bank." First a deep, deep sigh, followed by each man coming up, one after the other, each with a different idea. It made things somehow more lively, jollier; it put people in a better mood. Like a wanderer in foreign parts feeling homesick, looking out for a word from home. Suddenly it has come. Bringing both joy and heartache. You feel like dancing, and at the same time like a good cry.

Afterwards, when everybody had had a good look, Reb Yosifl, the rabbi, who hated pushing his way to the top, even though he is the rabbi, said—"Now let me have a look!"

Rabbi Yosifl settled his glasses on his nose, looked and looked again, examined the paper slowly, from all sides, the "Jewish share in our own bank," saw the Jewish lettering, the Hebrew words. Then he put on his Sabbath cap, said the Shchecheyanu benediction, thanking God for having let us live to this day. Then he looked at the paper again and again, and his face grew sad. You could swear there were tears in his eyes.

"Why are you so sad, Rabbi?" he was asked. "This is a time for gladness. We should be dancing with joy! Why do you grieve?"

Reb Yosifl, the rabbi, did not answer immediately. He drew out of a pocket deep down at the back of his capote an odd looking scarf, pretended to blow his nose in it, but the truth of it is, I think, that he used it to wipe his eyes. Then he sighed, and in a broken voice he said:

"I am homesick!"

Doctors in Consultation

A Tragicomedy in Two Acts

Cast:

Dr. Herzl ⎫
Dr. Nordau ⎬ Professors
Dr. Mandelstamm ⎭

Achad Ha'am ⎫
Dubnow ⎬ Consultants
Ussishkin ⎭

Suvarin, a medical assistant
Rabbi Akivah, skilled in overcoming the evil eye
A Rabbi from Poltava
Krushevan, a masseur
Poor little Israel, ill, at death's door
Ica, Israel's distant but very rich relative
Press, a servant girl
Jews and Their Wives, Young Men and Girls, Israel's Family

Act One

Israel in bed, covered over with rags. Deathly pallor. Sunken cheeks. Both hands outstretched, as with a corpse. Only his sharp black eyes give any indication of continued life. All three doctors seated round the bed, lost in deep thought. A little farther off, the three consultants. Still farther away, the barber-surgeon, the masseur, and the good friend. Round the bed, the afflicted family. At the head of the bed, the rich relative.

Dr. Herzl: Respected colleagues! I have called you here to hold counsel regarding this very sick patient, so that we should all of us in counsel together consider his illness and find a remedy to save his life. My colleague, Dr. Nordau, will speak to you about the curriculum morti and will give you the sick man's life story. He will make things clear to you, show you how the matter stands with our patient. In short, I can only tell you the position in our medical language, "prognosis mal." His condition is grave, desperate!

131

Dr. Nordau: My colleague, Dr. Herzl, said, "Prognosis mal." His condition is desperate. It's an old trouble, long neglected and getting worse and worse. Look at the patient! Skin and bone! No part of him is whole. Not a single spot without disease. God alone knows how the soul still holds in this frail body.

Israel: (signs piteously)

The Family: (wringing their hands) Lord God, save us! Lord, help him!

Dr. Nordau: This is not my first case, thank God. I have treated all sorts of patients in my time, with all kinds of diseases. But never have I seen a patient in this state. I fear we are no longer treating a living person. He's like a dead man. Yet if we look at him properly, give him a thorough examination, we'll find it is still a living body, but it's terribly worn out, dilapidated, on its last legs. One must marvel at the ways of nature, how such a being still keeps alive. What force holds him still on earth, poor man? The only likelihood is that his forefathers plead and pray for him, and it is by their merit that he lives on the way he does.

The family are all beside themselves, with at the same time a feeling of pride that such a famous man as Dr. Nordau has something good to say about the sick man. The patient groans.

Dr. Mandelstamm: If you want to know about his life, ask me! I knew him longer than my colleagues. Poor man! He holds on to his life more because of the spirit, not his body, his wonderful spirit that came to him as his heritage. Mens sana in corpore sana. Meaning a sound mind in a sound body. You are surprised that he looks so ill. Lack of fresh air, my dear colleagues. Eating the wrong food, sitting all the time in the same place, cramped quarters, not moving about. Open the windows, somebody. Let him breathe! Feed him! Make him strong!

(Israel gives a painful, deep groan. The family, wringing their hands, keep crying, "Save us, Lord God!")

Dr. Herzl: I have seen all his prescriptions, all the medicines and treatments he had. Everything the various doctors ordered for him throughout his illness. What I have to tell you now, my friends and colleagues, is that it has all been a waste of time. I found prescriptions of Argentine grass and of Braziliano, with doses of assimilation. But all those remedies are now completely out of fashion. Yet my search was not without result. I found, with God's help, the real remedy. "Old-New Land," I called it. In pharmaceutics it is known as Zionisticus.

That caused a stir among the people present. One keeps hearing the words Zionism, Zion, Zion, Zionism. The family are beside themselves again, ecstatic.

Achad Ha'am: Zionism? Zion? No offense meant, gentlemen. Forgive me intervening between such great and famous authorities. But the truth stands above everything. I can see these people here are all swept off their feet— do you know what new thing that Dr. Herzl has brought here? I believe the same remedy was put forward eighteen years ago by Professor Pinsker, rest his soul. That time it had a different name—Palestine, Eretz Israel. Today it has another name, Zion. But the name is not important. Our much respected Professor Doctor has not discovered any new America. (A slight disturbance among the Consultants.) I only said that Professor Dr. Herzl has not achieved anything in my opinion, because Zionism is an old, very old treatment, almost as old as our patient himself. Zionism was known in medical practice for ever so many years under various names. It was given to the patient as a cure I don't know how many times. But it registered no results, because the disease was terribly neglected, and poor little Israel's body had been allowed to deteriorate to such an extent that nothing could really help. What Professor Dr. Herzl tells us, that Zionism and only Zionism is the sole remedy, is no great help to the patient. If Zionism is to have any effect, he must first have a strong injection of nationalism and a proper course of nursing, of care, and of culture.

The Consultants shrug. "Culture?" "You're surely not giving the patient any more culture! He's had plenty! More than enough!"

Dubnow: My colleague, Achad Ha'am, takes the view that Zionism won't do the patient any good now. He must first have a course of spiritual Zionism. For whatever is wrong with Israel's body, he says, it is much worse with his soul. So what we have to do is to heal his soul, to fortify his spirit, so that he can bear up under his severe suffering of the body. We have it all recorded in his case history, poor little sick Israel, going back ever so far.

Ussishkin: (sharp and brusque) I say, No! If the consultants here have decided to prescribe Zionism as the cure, let's have good, pure, clean Zionism, no spiritual this or that, just simple, straightforward Palestine air and Palestine soil!

Rabbi Akivah: (intervenes) There was some talk here of spirituality. In this field of spirituality I think we rabbis have more knowledge than the most eminent consultants. So I propose that we call together a conference of rabbis only, to consider this sole question of Israel's spirituality.

Laughter among the consultants. The family look pleased.

Suvarin: Having heard all the opinions of your doctors and professors, I think it would be useful to have an outside opinion. My colleague, Krushevan, and I go along with the view that all your controversies and quarrelings are pure waste of time. You just grope around in the dark, and you have not yet discovered what is wrong. I can't tell you what this illness is called in

Latin, but in our plain and simple language it is known as Jewish exploitation. It means that the sick man is not as sick as he pretends. He is not well, of course. There is pain in his arms and legs. His backbone is broken. His stomach is out of order. And one of his lungs is affected. He has jaundice. You can see that in his face. So why all the fuss? You can read all that from his face. But it doesn't require him to lie in bed and not be able to stand on his own feet. He must be told the truth in the language they used in ancient Egypt—"Israel, you're lazy! That's what you are! Bone lazy! Listen to me. I have a better cure than all your Zionisms! My cure is blood letting. I know it's an old remedy. Old fashioned. But it works!

Krushevan: Amen! What I say is massage. Nowadays we cure illnesses with massage. Massage your bones, and it makes a different man of you!

The Family: (wringing their hands, groaning) For your salvation we pray, O Lord!

Dr. Herzl: Don't let us lose more time, my colleagues. Here is my prescription. Send it to the chemists. A good dose of Zionism! It helps instantly. (He passes the prescription to Dr. Nordau.)

Dr. Nordau: (signing the prescription and passing it to Dr. Mandelstamm) One tablespoon every two hours.

Dr. Mandelstamm signs and passes the prescription to Achad Ha'am, who refuses to sign and hands the prescription to Dubnow.

Achad Ha'am: I would add one more word to the prescription—spiritual.

Dubnow: (refusing to sign) I'll sign, if you will only add one word—spiritual. (He passes the prescription to Ussishkin, who signs).

Ussishkin: I would have prescribed a larger dose. Two tablespoons. (He hands the prescription to Dr. Herzl, who calls over Press, the maid, gives her the prescription and tells her to rush it to the chemists' and have it made up.)

Press: And the money to pay for it? (goes from one to another asking for the money)

The Family: Money? (All heads turn to the rich relative, who moves aside. The poor relations search their pockets and put a few small coins on the table. Press snatches them up and runs off to the chemists'. The doctors all rush off, each to his home. The family disperse, the sick man is left alone.)

Act Two

A few days later. The same scene and the same persons. Nothing changed.

Dr. Herzl: (to the other doctors and consultants) Gentlemen! I have called you here again for consultation, to see if we can find another way of saving our poor little patient, whose condition now is worse than before. I regret I have no good news for you. The chemist refused to make up our prescription for a dose of Zionism. Not even half the dose we asked for. I went there myself several times and spoke to the dispenser. I explained to him that Zionism is one of the most harmless treatments. It can't hurt anyone. It can only do good. It was useless. After all, he is only a paid employee, the pharmacist. And all my pleas left him unmoved. Yet you mustn't think that all hope is lost. If not today, the chemists' will be open again tomorrow, and we will be able to buy as much Zionism as we want. The only worry is, what do we do with the sick man in the meantime? I thought about this for some days, and I think I have the answer, not, of course, for always, but for the time being, while it is urgent. This remedy that I have is a kind of drink, almost the same as Zionism. I got it from the famous English Professor Chamberlain, and the name for us and in the medical register is "Uganda Africanica."

All: Uganda? Uganda? East Africa? (This causes a near-riot, with everyone shouting and screaming at the same time. One says Uganda is a great idea. Another denounces it as hopeless and bad. Many protest. The family is in commotion.)

Dr. Nordau: (stands up) Respected colleagues, I am surprised that you don't want to prescribe Uganda. What is all the fuss about? Have you ever in your practice prescribed Uganda? You say you want a cure for poor sick little Israel through Zionism. Where shall we take it from if they won't sell to us? Do you propose that our poor sick little Israel should go to war against the dispenser? And what will the poor soul do meanwhile? Die in front of us?

Israel: (moans and groans)

The Family: (wringing their hands) Save him, Lord God!

Dr. Nordau: Brothers! Give a thought now to the condition in which poor sick Israel is living! Don't forget the prescription we have written out; Uganda, is only temporary, for the time being, for the moment, for now! Till God will give the dispenser enough sense and a good heart, and we'll get the real cure, Zionism. When a man is drowning, he will grasp hold at a finger tip, the edge of a sword. (takes the prescription from Herzl's hand and passes it on)

Achad Ha'am: Forgive me, gentlemen, if I offend you, with some of the things I say. I have some very plain, blunt words to say. I am not surprised by Professor Herzl, who seems quite ready to grab hold of a new kind of prescription in his own mind. Professor Herzl is well able, I should say, an accomplished master in writing out a new kind of prescription. Nor am I surprised that Professor Nordau seems always ready to sign new prescriptions drawn up by Professor Herzl. One who so lightly signed the earlier prescription, dry, sober Zionism will just as lightly sign the new prescription now, the new "Uganda" mixture that has as much relation with Zionism as I have with Egypt. Who can say if it is going to work, and who can say if it is bad? After the way this Professor Herzl had praised Zionism to the skies, you will understand what I mean. What confidence can the poor little man have in him? I don't claim to be a prophet, not even a half-fool, as the folk saying has it—Only I said it at that particular moment. If you praise Zionism with super superlatives, and you say that nothing can take its place, and then you come along with some other remedy, you are doing your patient the worst possible service. What faith can the patient have in this new medicine Uganda, when only a few days before the same Professor Herzl proclaimed that only Zionism can help?

Uproar. Everybody trying to be heard above the others. Some on the side of Achad Ha'am. A few against him.

The Family: What insolence for a Jew, an ordinary medical practitioner, not even a professor, to use such language about a world-famous specialist, Professor Herzl, and his discovery, Uganda!

Ussishkin: I don't like those fine-sounding words! Oratorical gifts. Platform addresses! I declare myself openly, I am against Dr. Herzl and his treatment, his Uganda! There is only one remedy, one treatment, one method—Zionism. This same Dr. Herzl once signed a statement for Zionism. And we won't hear of any other. What's the idea of changing the diagnosis every day?

Dr. Herzl: We will now ask our colleague, Ussishkin, to leave our consultation. For if he is against our consultation there is no point in having him with us. How can he help if he does not believe in our medicine? How can he help the poor sick man?

Ussishkin: I don't know who is against our consultation. The one who changes his prescriptions every three or four days, or the one who stands firmly by his belief. You know my record. I am for Eretz Israel.

Dr. Herzl: (beside himself, trying to fight down his anger) Our disputes won't make the sick man any better. Let's ask his family if they want us to give him a dose of Uganda mixture or not.

The Family: (all at once) Yes! Yes! No! No!

Dr. Herzl: One at a time, please! One at a time! Each of us separately.

The Family: (shouting and screaming, wringing their hands)

Dr. Nordau: (repeats several times over) One, two, three, four, five, six, seven, eight. Three hundred seventy-five, Yes. Two hundred ninety-six, No. So the yes-sayers are the majority. We'll send round to the chemists for some Uganda mixture. (Dr. Nordau hands the prescription to the maid to fetch the Uganda mixture.)

Rabbi Akivah: (arms raised prophetically) Poor Israel! Poor us! Woe to the pitcher that falls on the stone! And woe to the pitcher the stone has fallen on! Nice mess we've gotten ourselves into! That brought about the destruction of the Temple. The Churban! The profanation of the Holy Name! (turning to the masseur) The Third Churban! First was the Temple. Then came Zionism. Now it's Uganda. Chillul Hashem! Profanation of the Name! (turning to the masseur and the medical assistant) We must call an assembly! Immediately! At once!

Suvarin: Blood letting! That's what we need now! Letting blood!

Krushevan: Massage! Always massage! Yes, all the time massage!

Israel: (moans aloud)

The Family: (wringing their hands, weeping and wailing) God, help him! For Thy salvation we wait!

Achad Ha'am: A strange family, Israel's! Only a moment ago they were shouting, "Yes, Uganda, Yes! Uganda! Uganda!" Now they weep and wail; they faint! They cry to God who alone can save!

The Family: Easy for you to talk! Look at poor sick Israel! He's ill! Will the Uganda medicine help? Will it do him any good?

A clamor of voices: Zionism! Zion!

Dr. Herzl: (speaking to the family, gently, reassuringly) Calm yourselves! Be quiet! I know myself that Zionism is the best method. The best cure. But what can we do if the dispenser won't hand over the medicine! I swear to you that I shall go there myself and speak to the dispenser. And I'll keep urging him, demanding from him, till I get the medicine from him. I promise you that! I will not forget! If I forget thee Jerusalem, let my right arm wither!

The Family: (Grow no calmer. Some whisper, "Bravo!" Many shout protests. Some outside sing Hatikvah!)

Dr. Nordau: (gruffly) I am surprised at my colleague Herzl arguing and pleading with you, when it is as clear as day that we can't leave the sick man like this. We must work out a prescription, at least for now, for this moment, to hold his soul and body together. So we have now this prescription Uganda. That's what we had this consultation of doctors for.

A bullet shot is heard suddenly, fired at Dr. Nordau by one of the family. Dr. Nordau is not hit. But Rabbi Akibah is, in the right cheek. Members of the family try to explain it was no bullet, but a cork being pulled out of a bottle of soda water. Some go over to Dr. Nordau and press his hand. The masseur and medical assistant whisper to each other and laugh at the panic caused by the shot.

Rabbi Akivah: (points out to the medical assistant where the bullet landed in his cheek) Look at it! What did I do to deserve it?

Suvarin: (shakes his head and murmurs to the masseur) The dog deserves the stick!

The door opens, and Press, the maid servant, flies in, empty-handed.

Dr. Herzl: Well?

Press: (words pouring out in a torrent) There isn't any! He gave me none! The
    chemists won't give us any Uganda medicine! Why? I don't know! They say
    Professor Chamberlain hasn't said anything about issuing Uganda
    medicine. So I've got none!

All are struck dumb by Press's news.

Israel: (loud moan)

The Family: (wringing their hands) May God help him! Ani Vaha Hoshiana!
    Save Thou us!

Curtain.
1903

Dr. Theodor Herzl

1

Thursday, 24th June 1904, twenty-four days in the Jewish month of Tammuz, a rare, wonderful, vast, tumultuous funeral. It was in Vienna, and following the funeral, millions of Jews, almost the whole Jewish People. Silently, step by step, with bowed heads, with reverence, accompanying one of the greatest, one of the best and most loved, one of the dearest of our People. And when a thirteen-year-old lad stood up for Kaddish—Yisgadal ve-Yiskadash—several million Jews, almost the whole Jewish People, wept bitterly. When they returned from the cemetery millions of Jews, almost the entire Jewish people, sat "shiva." Then there broke out a weeping and a wailing and wringing of hands and a beating of breasts.

Why? Why? Why didn't we know what we had and what we have lost? Why? Why? Why were we not told that he was so ill, so near death?

Risen from shiva, the Shloshim (the thirty days of mourning) soon gone, and the orphans, several million Jews, almost the whole Jewish People, have not stopped wailing and weeping. Every time they remember what they had and what they have lost, they do not cease to mourn and to beat their breasts. Why? Why? Why did we not know what we had and what we have lost? Why? Why? Why were we not told that he was near to death?

Many days will pass, and the poor bereft orphans will not forget, will not cease to moan and lament, why was it kept from them, why were they not told that he was near to death? They seem to feel themselves guilty of not having been adequate to help him, one of the greatest, one of the best, the dearest of our People. Why did they not rise to the height he had expected of them, why had they failed him? For they know that he had sacrificed himself, all of him, heart and soul, on their behalf. And the more they know that, the more their regret, so much greater is the pain, their resentment against themselves and against others, against each other, for not having sufficiently prized him, not looked after him enough, but on the contrary, criticized him, disparaged him, looked for faults in him, buttonholed him in the old Jewish way, asking him the same old Jewish question, "Who made you a ruler over us? Who sent for you?"

For indeed, how come a man suddenly gives up all his affairs, wife and children, and devotes himself entirely to the good of the People? Nonsense! Nobody does things like that nowadays! There are no fools about like that. The clever Jewish people won't believe that there are fools willing to sacrifice themselves, heart and soul, with no other intent, with no personal gain for themselves in their mind. And if there is someone like that found, you criticize him, sneer at him, find faults in him, till you drive him to his grave. Then, when he is in his grave, then and only then, you look round and cry, "What have we done! Why didn't we know what we had and why were we not told that he was dying!"

It was a tremendous, a vast concourse, this funeral of Dr. Herzl. It was an endless mourning. But even greater was the remorse because he did not get from us what he expected from us. Here lies the real tragedy. The Jewish People were not destined to produce a true hero and to know him as such. If they do have a hero sometimes, they can't hold him, they can't keep him, they don't know what he is, and they don't want to know. They become aware of him only later, when he is on the way out. And he leaves behind a glorious legend.

Indeed a legend. Our ancient history, which is packed full of legends, has now added another legend, Herzl. And here I would like to quote something that appeared in the Hebrew journal, "Hador," when he died (no. 21, 1904), some very remarkable words that might well be inscribed over Herzl's grave, in letters of gold. This is what the editor of "Hador" wrote in his lovely Hebrew:

"As we were putting this issue to bed, we received the stunning news that we have lost this great and wonderful man, Dr. Theodor Herzl. The message came suddenly, without any warning. No one had foreseen it. Like a legend he flashed before our eyes. Mothers will tell their children this amazing legend. One generation will pass it on to the next. As he appeared to us suddenly so he has disappeared suddenly, like a legend. There was a good fairy at his birth, an angel, who showered all the gifts on him that are usually divided among thousands. She bestowed them all on this one man. A fine presence, magnetic eyes, sweet lips, a tender heart, a powerful intellect, the kind heart of a child, straight thinking, a strong character, the rare ability to dream, to see visions, and a tremendous passion to do great things, things which are beyond a man's reach. And the angel gave him cheerfulness and a tear, the power to dominate and rule, with a strong will and with a charm that could win him the favor of the greatest in this world—all the physical and mental gifts a man can have. And she gave him also a rare death, sudden, unexpected, a death that could only add charm to a legend, the charm of a true hero. What he could not achieve in life, the fairy said to herself, he will achieve with his death."

Yes, what Herzl could not achieve in life he will achieve with his death. Sad though it may be, we can't escape the truth. Now after his death Herzl has many more Hasidim, many more followers than he had in life. Many anti-Zionists have become Zionists, and many Zionists now after Herzl's death have become more Zionist than they had been before while he was alive. We are no longer surprised when we read in the Pentateuch that the people murmured against Moses while Moses lived. Not only murmured. They wanted to stone him. Yet when Moses died, they wept for him thirty days. We are no longer surprised now that the same Jews who not long ago had challenged Herzl, had demanded to know "who made you a ruler over us?" now compare him with Moses and comfort themselves with the thought that in the same way as Moses was not considered worthy to see Eretz Israel, and he handed the Israelites over to Joshua, so Herzl was not deemed worthy to see the charter in Eretz Israel and handed us over. To whom? To Joshua? Well then, let God work a miracle, and let a Joshua arise among us now, the true Joshua whom we need. He would soon be asked the same old Jewish question—"Who are you? How do we know you are the Joshua?" And he will be watched, spied upon, criticized, driven into his grave. And then there will be weeping and moaning, wailing and lamenting, tearing of the hair and beating of the breast.

"Woe! We did not know what we had and what we have lost!"

And so that we should know it, I shall tell our friends in plain, ordinary language who this Dr. Theodor Herzl was, what he was for us, for our People, for our history.

2

In all the eighteen hundred years that poor little Israel has been banished, in exile, wandering around with his beggar's pouch from land to land, unable to find a place anywhere, his eyes never stopped turning back to that land where he had spent his best years, to sigh and long, like a child torn from his mother at an early age and abandoned, left to wander, to stray in strange places, his road cut off for evermore. Sometimes, seldom, he remembers that he had a mother. But only dimly, hardly at all, as if in sleep. When he reminds himself, it hurts, and sometimes when there is no one near to see, he drops a tear. Time after time he makes up his mind to break his way out and go to his aged mother, but always he remains where he is—"Please, God, next year!" He repeats it quietly to himself, knowing that he is only fooling himself. Yet he does not forget to repeat those same sweet words, "Next year! In God's good time, next year!"

For hundreds of years we have been repeating the same sweet words, "Next year in Jerusalem!" "And to Jerusalem, your city, return in mercy." "Let our eyes behold your return in mercy to Zion." And many more such sweet and loving words, that we repeat automatically, by heart. We say these words without hearing what we say. Our minds are full of other things. Only sometimes, rarely, a sigh breaks out, "Jerusalem! Zion!" And the heart faints, and we long to be there, back in the old home, with our ancient mother. Rarely, only rarely, one of us rises up and in a loud voice cries: "Why do we sigh silently? How long must we wander around, homeless, astray on the face of the earth? Stand up! Let us return to our ancient mother!" He speaks and we hear! We hear him, and we watch his face. "How beautifully he speaks! What a lovely song he sings! A sweet dream has come true!"

In the closing years of the nineteenth century the words Jerusalem, Zion, Palestine, Eretz Israel came to be heard more and more often. There were some who were not content only with words, who rose from their places and went there, went back to the old, sweet land, where old Jews used to come to die. And these took up work there, hard work, which made them ill—in the Holy Land. They did what they had come to do. There were among us also a few rich men, who poured out money, lots of money, established agricultural colonies for poor workers, turned traders into land workers, artisans into keepers of vineyards. Frail little old Israel began to revive, stirred—but that was all. No more.

Till suddenly, just a few years back, a doctor from Vienna appeared to us, with a little book in his hand, which made a terrific noise in the whole Jewish world. Several million Jews, almost the entire Jewish People, spoke about this little book, spoke about this remarkable doctor. Some laughed. Some made jokes about him, dismissed him as a dreamer, a madman.

Dr. Theodor Herzl, this doctor from Vienna and his little book, *Der Judenstaat, (The Jewish State)*, proposed to the Jewish People a Jewish State. Not colonies, but our own Jewish land. In Eretz Israel.

It started a hullabaloo. A Jewish land? Our own Jewish land! Where? With the Turk? With whom? With Jews? Funny sort of a doctor!

But this funny sort of a doctor wasn't content only with little books. He soon started talking about calling a big meeting somewhere or other to discuss his plan. To try to find a way of helping poor little Israel to return home. And this Dr. Herzl had a habit of not only thinking and speaking, but also doing. So he called together a congress of representatives of the Jewish People as a whole, of all the millions of Jews who are scattered and dispersed all over the world. It was in Basel, at the First Zionist Congress, that he proclaimed his plan, openly and clearly, before the whole world:

"Brothers, back to our old home, for the unfortunate, the distressed of our People, to our own land, our own state, in what was formerly our own land, Eretz Israel!"

And the whole assembly rose to him, enthusiastic, fascinated by the Herzl plan. Not so much the plan as its open, public proclamation. Dr. Herzl grew, became a giant, a hero to several million Jews, almost the entire Jewish People. No longer the funny sort of a doctor from Vienna, but "our Herzl," or just simply "Herzl."

Meetings were held to discuss Herzl's plan. In every country the Zionist shekel was sold, libraries were opened. Everything was done as Herzl instructed, to organize, to prepare the Second Zionist Congress. And when the time came for the Second Congress it caused such a stir that the entire world, Jews and Christians, spoke of the Jewish Congress and of the Jewish hero, Dr. Herzl. The power of this Jewish hero was such that those who had once seen him, had ever heard him speak, clung to him, could not take their eyes from him, were magnetized by him, by the way he stood, the way he walked, the way he spoke. It was a festive day when he appeared to his followers. Going to Basel was a joyous pilgrimage. "I am going to see Herzl," people said. And those who could not make the journey envied those who could. "I envy you—you will be seeing Herzl!"

Everybody knew the Herzl portrait. It hung in Jewish homes. Like the picture of Moses Montefiore, but loved and prized even more. Hardly a Jew in the world who did not know that picture of Herzl, with his beautiful black beard and his magnetic eyes.

Naturally it also made him many enemies. Those who couldn't understand him, and those who grudged him his fame. They called him "False Messiah!" They denounced him! As we always did! And the worst of all were the pietists, the God-fearing Jews, the rabbis, long life to them, who look out for Messiah, want him to come riding on a white horse. In short, Herzl became a true hero. Everywhere and always you would hear among us the words "Herzl!" "Dr. Herzl!"

3

Where did this Dr. Herzl come from, and what gave him such power? I am reproducing here the short biography he wrote himself and published originally in English in the "Jewish Chronicle" on 14 January, 1898:

> I was born in the year 1860 in Budapest, close to that synagogue in which the rabbi recently criticized me with the utmost severity because I wanted—really and truly—to obtain for the Jews more dignity and freedom than they at present enjoy. But in twenty years there will be a "To Let" sign on the door of the house where I first saw the light of day, a sign saying that the resident has moved—to Eretz Israel.
>
> I cannot deny that I went to school. First I went to a Jewish preparatory school, where I was treated with a certain respect because my father was a well-to-do merchant. My first memories of this school center round the thrashings which I got because I did not know all the details of the Exodus of the Jews from Egypt. Today there are many schoolmasters who would like to thrash me because I remember it too well. At the age of ten I went to the realschule, where, in contrast to the gymnasium, which specializes in the classics, the main emphasis is laid on modern studies. At that time de Lesseps was the hero of the day, and I completed a plan for the cutting through of that other Isthmus—the Panama. But I soon lost my first love for logarithms and trigonometry, for at that time there reigned in the realschule an outspoken anti-Semitic tendency. One of our teachers used to define the word heathen with the following classification: "Among them are idolators, Mohammedans, and Jews." After this extraordinary explanation I had enough of the realschule and wanted instead to go to a classic institution. My good father never kept me to a hard-and-fast program of studies, and so I became a student at a gymnasium. Nevertheless, I did not give my Panama Plan up altogether. Many years later, as the Paris correspondent of the Vienna "Neue Freie Presse," I had a great deal to report to my paper con-

cerning the unsavory incidents which accompanied this scandalous episode in modern French history.[7]

The Jews were in the majority at the Evangelical Gymnasium, and for that reason I found too little to complain of in the way of Jew-baiting. When I was in the seventh class, I wrote my first newspaper article—anonymously, of course, or else I should have been kept in. While I was still a student in the higher classes of the gymnasium, my only sister, a girl of eighteen, died. My mother fell into such depression that in 1878 we moved to Vienna.

During the week of mourning Rabbi Kohn visited us and asked me what my plans for the future were. I told him that I wanted to become a writer, whereupon the rabbi shook his head with the same disapproval as he did years later over my Zionism. A writer's career is really no sort of profession, the dissatisfied rabbi concluded.

In Vienna I studied law, took part in all the crazy student tricks, and wore the colored cap of a student Verbindung until one day the society decided to cease admitting Jews as members. Such Jews as were already members received generous permission to remain. I said farewell to my noble young colleagues and sat down seriously to my work. In 1884 I graduated as Doctor of Law and took a post as unpaid official under the guidance of a judge. I found employment in the courts in Vienna and Salzburg. The work in Salzburg seemed to be more attractive: the scenery around that city is known for its beauty. My law office was in an old tower in the castle, right under the clock, and three times daily the bells rang pleasantly in my ears.

Naturally I wrote more plays than briefs. In Salzburg I spent some of the happiest hours of my life. And I would gladly have remained in the beautiful city; but as a Jew I would never have received an appointment as judge. And for that reason I said farewell simultaneously to Salzburg and to legal learning.

I was again destined to distress profoundly the rabbi of Budapest; for instead of looking around for a real profession or a real job I began to travel and to write for the theater and for the newspapers. Many of my plays were accepted and played in various theaters, some with more and some with less applause. Until this day I fail to understand why some of my plays were received with applause while others were hissed. But the difference in the reception accorded to my pieces taught me one thing—to pay no attention whether the public applauded or hissed. Conscience must be satisfied; nothing else matters. Today I have no use for any of my dramas—even those which are still produced successfully at the Imperial Burgtheater.

In 1889 I married. I now have three children, a boy and two girls. In my opinion my children are neither bad-looking nor stupid. But, of course, I may be mistaken.

During my travels in Spain in 1891 the Vienna newspaper "Die Neue Freie Presse" offered me the position of its foreign correspondent in Paris. I accepted, even though up to that time I had despised and avoided politics. In Paris I had an opportunity to learn what it is that the world understands by the word politics, and I expressed my own opinion in a little book, "Das Palais Bourbon." In 1895 I had had enough of Paris and returned to Vienna.

---

7. A concession for building a canal in Panama was granted in 1878 to a French company under Ferdinand de Lesseps. Work was begun in 1881, but disease among the workers, construction troubles, and inadequate financing drove the company into bankruptcy in 1889. There were charges of corruption and a great scandal.

During the last two months of my stay in Paris I wrote the book, *The Jewish State.* I cannot remember ever having written anything in such a mood of exaltation. Heine tells us that he heard the clapping of eagles' wings above his head when he wrote certain stanzas. I too seemed to hear the flutter of wings above my head while I wrote *The Jewish State.* I worked at it daily until I was completely exhausted. My one recreation was in the evenings when I could go to hear Wagner's music, particularly Tannhauser, an opera which I go to hear as often as it is produced. And only on those evenings when there was no opera did I have my doubts as to the truth of my ideas.

My first idea was to let this little essay on the solution of the Jewish question circulate privately among my friends. It was only later that I thought of publishing it; it was not my intention to begin a personal agitation on the Jewish question. The majority of my readers will be astounded to learn of this reluctance on my part. The whole matter seemed to me to be one in which action had to be taken, but in which discussion was impossible. An open agitation was reserved as a last recourse, only when my private advice was ignored or repudiated.

When I had completed the book, I asked my oldest and best friend to read the manuscript. In the midst of the reading he suddenly burst into tears. I found this natural enough, since he was a Jew; I too had wept at times during the writing of it. But I was staggered when he gave me an entirely different reason for his tears. He thought that I had gone off my head, and since he was my friend, he was touched to tears by my misfortune. He ran off without saying another word. After a sleepless night he returned and pressed me hard to leave the entire business alone, for everyone would take me for a lunatic. He was so excited that I promised him anything in order to soothe him. Then he besought me to ask Max Nordau whether this plan of mine could possibly have entered the mind of any man still capable of making calculations. "I shall not ask anybody," I said. "If this is the impression my ideas make on an educated and faithful friend, I shall give them up."

It was thus that I went through my first crisis; the only comparison I can find for it is the plunging of a red-hot body into a basin of cold water. It is true, however, that if the body is iron, it becomes steel.

My friend, of whom I have written above, had to cast up my expenses for telegraphic messages. When he handed me the account, which was made-up of a great number of items, I saw at a single glance that he had miscalculated. I drew his attention to the error, and he added up the total a second time; but it was only at the third or fourth attempt that his figures agreed with mine. This little incident returned to me my self-confidence. If it was a matter of calculation, I seemed to be capable of greater accuracy than he. My reason, then, had not left me entirely.

On that day began my restlessness concerning the Jewish state. During the two years and more that I have passed since then, I have lived through many sorrowful days, and I fear that other days even more sorrowful are still in reserve for me. In 1895 I began to keep a diary, and by now four thick volumes are already filled. If I were to publish these volumes, the world would be astounded at what efforts I had to put into this work, to know who were the enemies of my plans, and who were the men that stood by me.

But one thing I regard as certain and placed beyond the reach of all doubt: the movement will endure. I do not know when I shall die, but Zionism will never die. Since those days in Basel the Jewish People has a national representation once again; as a result the Jewish state will once more rise in its own country. I am at present engaged in the task of creating the bank, and I expect it to be at least as great a success as the congress was.

4

That is Herzl telling us about himself and about his idea, for which he worked and for which he died. We will now see what the world says, our own people and strangers, Zionists and anti-Zionists, Jews and Christians. While Herzl was alive, many who saw him said they had never seen a man like him. Even those opposed to him confessed that it was enough for Herzl to look at you, with his magnetic eyes, to say a few words, to appear on the platform, for the whole assembly to feel it was under his spell. He dominated them all.

A young doctor from Kiev has told us that he went to Basel as an opponent, against Herzl, to speak against him. Arrived in Basel he waited for his first sight of Herzl.

"As soon as I saw him," he has recorded, "as soon as I heard him speak, say the first few words, I gave up. I surrendered to him. I felt a tremendous force drawing me to him irresistibly, like a magnet. I had become completely his— wherever he would send me, I would go. What he told me to do, I would do!"

Everyone knows with how much respect Herzl was received by kings and princes, by the pope in Rome, by ministers in government. The king of Italy sent a telegram when Herzl died, full of his sorrow and regret. Dr. Max Nordau expressed the common feeling when he wrote in the Petersburg "Novosti"—"I am asked on all sides to write obituaries, appreciations of Herzl. How can I write now about my friend, who was ten years younger than I, with whom I had hoped to work together for a long time to come? What can I say? Unhappy People! Out of ten million chances with ten million white lots, we had the calamitous misfortune to draw a black lot—for Herzl, whom it is impossible to replace. Impossible! He united in himself everything—complete firm faith, independence, immense will, and the energy of a hero, ready to sacrifice everything, right to the very end. No sacrifice was too much. He had the mind of Moses and the tongue of Aaron. Where shall we find such another? One lacks enough faith, another the will. One hasn't enough in him, the other hasn't the physical presence or the oratory."

Speaking of the condition of the Jews in the different countries, Nordau returned again and again to Herzl: "There is no Herzl," he kept repeating. "There is no Herzl. The Jewish People has one more holy grave. And graves don't grow flowers."

5

Among all the messages, letters, and telegrams that came flying in from all the corners of the earth, there was one from the Russian woman writer Tesia, expressing the grief that was felt "Not only by Jews, but also by Christians, and by Jews who are anti-Zionists, by writers who had never concerned themselves with Zionism, by dukes and princes and government ministers. No wonder, for a great man has gone to his grave. All those who knew him loved him. In the street, among the people he passed as he walked there, in the theater, where they played his plays, in the office of the newspaper where he was the literary editor, everywhere in Vienna and wheresoever he went, this marvelously handsome man, with his majestic appearance, his magnetic eyes, his noble beard. He stood out among them all, among all who stood near him. There was a gentleness in his eyes. He had such beautiful, gentle eyes!"

"I saw Herzl," she continued, "for the first time at a big meeting of Zionists in Vienna, held in honor of Max Nordau, who had arrived from Paris. Though Nordau was the guest, and the meeting was called for him, all eyes were turned on Herzl. Nordau spoke well. Everybody was delighted. But it was enough for Herzl to stand up on the platform for all eyes to turn away from Nordau to Herzl. All eyes were on him, all hearts beat in unison with his heart. And on the faces of all those poor harassed people who bear the unmerited hatred of the whole world, appeared a happy smile—this is Herzl, their pride, their glory, their hope of better, happier days.

"I knew an old man in Vienna. He had a grey beard, he was a wise man, and he was a fine speaker. This old man had grown up from childhood under the spell of Herzl. When talk turned on Herzl, he forgot his wife and his children and the whole world. If anyone said a bad word about Herzl, he was ready to scratch his eyes out, to kill him. You could see that this old man would have sacrificed himself, would have given his life for Herzl. This old man, one of the ordinary people, a man of the folk, was in the crowd. I though Herzl had impressed him with his wisdom, with his learning. That was what I thought before I had known Herzl myself. There was an engineer in the crowd, an able man, a man of brains. He too was under the spell of Herzl. It is true too of another man I knew, a pianist, a great name in music. He too was under the spell of Herzl. And the same with another friend in Switzerland. 'Mark my words,' he said to me, 'this man Herzl has not yet been appreciated as he deserves. He was a genius. Not only the Jews but all mankind should be proud of him.'"

Tesia continued: "A few years back I got to know Herzl myself. A Russian paper in Moscow asked me to get for it the feeling of a number of people abroad about Gogol. One of the first I looked up was Theodor Herzl. I am not exaggerating by one iota when I say that no one else of all those I approached got into the heart and soul of Gogol as Herzl did. That was when I met Herzl in person. In Ischl. We both had acquaintances there. He was interested above all in what was going on in Russia. Everything. Russia was closer to Herzl than most other countries. So many of his own people lived there. He was receiving letters all the time from Russia.

"Herzl did not stay long in Ischl. He had come there to see his mother. I was struck by the sadness in his face. He looked as though he had a deep hurt in his heart. A worm was gnawing at his vitals.

"Theodor Herzl had a golden pen," she concluded. "It so happened that I was looking for a German writer to translate a Russian work into German. I turned to one of the best German writers at the time, and he said 'There is a man in Vienna whose German is outstanding—Theodor Herzl!' "

6

Herzl gave his golden pen to the Jewish People. He gave it with his heart and with his life. Not only his own life, but the life also of his wife and his children. Those who knew him closely, men like Sokolow, Reuben Brainin, Dr. Mandelstamm, tell wonderful stories of Herzl; he was all on fire, they say, all burnt up, and snuffed out like a candle. For the sake of the Jewish People, for the sake of Zion, he forgot everything that should have been dear to him. Only a man like Herzl could work as he worked, for his goal, which was the restoration of the Jewish People, which had long ceased to be a nation, as a nation again. He wanted the ancient Jewish People to have its own country, its own Jewish land.

The Yiddish paper, "Der Freind," gave a detailed account of Herzl's life and activity, step by step, as diplomat and as the founder, the architect of Jewish policy. Till Herzl came, we had no Jewish politician.

"Dr. Herzl," says "Der Freind," "created diplomatic Zionism. He put forward the idea that the Jewish Question, which brings so much misery and disaster to the Jewish People, is also a great difficulty for the nations among whom the Jews live. Their sufferings drive the Jews from one country to another. Hundreds and thousands of Jews make their way from east to west. And the countries to which the Jews go have to consider this question of Jewish immigration. That being so, the European nations must be interested also in finding an answer to the question which will settle it once and for all. Most of all, more than all the European states, Zionism should interest Turkey. A poor, weak country, Turkey is now on the verge of collapse. Yet Turkey is a country with a great deal of natural wealth, rich agricultural land. But it hasn't the people to work the land. Turkey can't lift itself up by its own efforts. It has no developed industry. Its level of education is low. Its financial state is deplorable. It can be saved only by the influx of a new population, bringing in fresh forces and fresh capital.

"Where will Turkey find these new fresh forces? Only in Jewish colonization, which would bring a revival of Turkey.

"But if we Jews are the one people on earth who can in this way benefit the Turkish state, we Jews must have in return certain Jewish national rights.

"Jewish settlement in Palestine would be of immense benefit not only for Turkey but for the whole world. It is important for Europe to create a corner of life and culture in this land of Palestine which lies by the Mediterranean, and where the roads are open to all western Asia. All these considerations were part of Dr. Herzl's plans, with which he came to the different states of Europe and to the Turkish government. The aim of all Dr. Herzl's reasonings and calculations and of his diplomatic activities was to obtain a charter for a large-scale Jewish colonization in Palestine. The idea of the charter was to give the Jews the right not only to settle freely in the land and colonize it, but also to give the Jews the opportunity to develop their own autonomous administration in their own internal affairs.

"Naturally the granting of special publicly-secured concessions to the Jewish People in Palestine would depend entirely and exclusively on the Turkish government. Of all the European powers, Germany has in recent years gained most say in Turkey. The German kaiser became the sultan's friend, and his word counts in Constantinople. That is why Dr. Herzl made his first important diplomatic approach to the Kaiser. The Kaiser received Dr. Herzl, with a deputation from the Zionist Actions Committee, in Jerusalem. Present also was the German Chancellor, Von Buelow, which gave the meeting a political character. The Kaiser gave the Zionist deputation a very friendly reception and promised to help and support.

"Dr. Herzl left with the impression that the time was now ripe for obtaining the charter. He made his way to London and Paris full of hope, in the belief that he would be able to raise there the millions that were needed. His hopes were dashed. The Jewish millionaires were deaf to his pleas, and their wallets stayed closed. . . Herzl could not forget it till the day he died. He often recalled with bitterness how the favorable moment immediately after the meeting with the kaiser had been allowed to slip by. But it never cooled his ardor. He did not give up hope. What he had failed to get from the rich Jews he hoped to get from the Jewish masses, in whom the true fire burned.

"Herzl went on without a break with his diplomatic work. He met all the great figures in Europe, and all were most friendly to him. He came a second time now to Constantinople. The first time he had come before the First Zionist Congress, as a journalist. Now he was the Zionist leader. He explained the Zionist movement to the sultan and spoke of Zionism as good and important for both their parties, the Jews and Turkey.

"From that time on Herzl kept negotiating with Turkey. He was twice invited to Constantinople. But the negotiations brought no result. The sultan wanted to permit Jewish colonization only in several different parts of Turkey, and without a charter. Since this was not in line with the program of the congress Herzl had to reject the offer, and the negotiations had to be broken off.

"Then Herzl started looking for other ways. In 1902 he was invited to present his views on Jewish immigration before the British Royal Commission. This brought him in touch with British politicians and with members of the British government, and he tried to interest them in Zionism. He proposed a charter for colonizing Al Arish, lying between Egypt and Palestine. Britain, (which was then the suzerain power in Egypt) was friendly to the idea, and a Zionist commission went to Al Arish. It reported back, however, that the area, through which Moses led the Jews out of Egypt, was not suitable for colonization. That was when Britain offered Dr. Herzl Uganda. Dr. Herzl submitted this offer to the Zionist Congress, which after much stormy discussion rejected it. That did not stop Dr. Herzl from further search for settlement possibilities in Eretz Israel. Only a few months back Dr. Herzl was received in Rome, by the king of Italy, and by the pope. It was his last political journey . . ."

7

Dr. Herzl's diplomatic work condemned him to be continually on the move, traveling from land to land. He seemed to carry with him the curse of the Jewish People doomed by God to wander over the face of the earth. He accepted happily the Golus imposed on him and on all his fellow Jews. A well-known Zionist, Hillel Zlatopolski, speaking in Kiev at one of the many Herzl memorial meetings, said: "Weep not for him who has died; weep for the Dr. Herzl who was always traveling on your behalf, always on his way from one land to another, from one ruler to another, to plead for his People Israel. No one could have known at any time where Herzl was. Now he was in London, now in Constantinople, now in Rome or in Petersburg or in Eretz Israel. Always moving about, on the go. Never for himself." And Zlatopolski concluded, with tears in his eyes and the eyes of all the Jews there, "Who knows whether his constant traveling has yet ended. Perhaps he has now made another journey to the heavenly Beth Din, to plead for better fortune for his People Israel."

There is a letter from Boris Goldberg in Vilna: "You can see how far the masses of our People were bound up and tied together with the great leader of our Zionist movement, and how Herzl was dear and precious to the Jews in Eretz Israel. I was in Palestine recently, and I could not help wondering why Herzl's name is so loved and sanctified even in our historic land. We have had great Jews who did much more—at least, in the practical sense—than Herzl, men who have left an everlasting mark in Palestine. There is Baron de Rothschild, who has spent millions in Palestine and is still giving more millions now. He gives his heart to Eretz Israel. There was Moses Montefiore, who gave all he could to revive and improve the life of the Jewish people living in Eretz Israel. Yet Herzl's name stands higher among the Jews of Palestine than either of these two great Chovevei Zion. One can hardly imagine the emotion with which they told me in Rehovot, with every detail and particular, about Herzl's short stay there during his Palestine visit. The colonists built a great Triumphal Arch in Herzl's honor, and all the way from the Arch to the house where Herzl stayed there were flowers laid under his feet, the whole road lined with the colonists and their wives and children. Not a single one was missing. Everybody had come. Even the babes in their cradles. They all wanted to see with their own eyes the leader of the Jewish People. As for Herzl, when he saw all this, he wept, wept with joy when he saw this small section of Jews living a free Jewish life on their native soil.

"And the colonists of Rishon le Zion too, they also cannot forget Herzl's stay. Turning the pages of the Visitors Book, I was struck by a couple of lines written there by a colonist named Braze, who had the honor of having Dr. Herzl plant a tree in his vineyard. That colonist holds that tree holy. He shows it with pride to every visitor. And the tree has grown strong and beautiful. My wife broke off a few twigs, which now adorn the portrait of Herzl.

"If you travel with a Jew from Rishon le Zion to Jaffa, he will point out to you the place by Mikve Israel where Dr. Herzl presented himself to the German kaiser. All Jewish Palestine is proud of Dr. Herzl, the Jewish leader, all he said and did.

"Herzl is great not only in Jerusalem, but also in Safad, in Tiberias, in Jaffa. In Jaffa where the bank is, the bank which is of such importance in Palestine. The bank that he, Dr. Herzl, created."

Herzl's love of Eretz Israel was demonstrated to all of us at the Sixth Congress in Basel, when during the debate on the Uganda offer he raised his right arm and swore, "If I forget thee, Jerusalem, let my hand wither!" And in his will he wrote, "I wish to be buried beside my father, till the Jewish People carry my bones to Eretz Israel."

Eretz Israel, the Jewish land—these were the words most dear to him. They were God's greatest gift, with which he lived and with which he died. It was not only the Jewish land that he loved. He loved the whole Jewish People. He loved even the Jewish language, which he hardly knew. He often told those near to him how much he regretted not knowing Hebrew. He tried to put it right by having his children, at least, especially his son, Hans, whom he regarded as his heir, learn Hebrew. How happy he was when Hans (Simeon) at the age of thirteen showed a knowledge of Hebrew. Herzl was looking forward to the boy's Bar Mitzva, which he did not live to see.

Nahum Sokolow, speaking at Herzl's graveside in the name of the Hebrew writers, said: "Loshen Kodesh (the holy tongue, Hebrew), the ancient Jewish language, the language of Jeremiah's Lamentations and Yahuda Halevi's Zionides, the language that was long since buried by her own children, and has risen in recent years from the grave, Hebrew weeps now at Herzl's tomb. The best of her sons, he did not know her, but with all his heart and soul and all his actions he made her live, and she began to stir, to move, to sing new songs, with a strong vigorous voice. And when he pointed his hand towards Eretz Israel, he spoke Hebrew words, and everything was alive again, everything was glad and happy and in bloom.

"Some time passed," Sokolov went on, "and his son says Kaddish, and the whole Jewish People weeps. But we Hebrew writers will not weep. We drop our pens in mourning, as soldiers drop their spears. But we lift them up again, as soldiers do, who know that they must return to the battlefield. Herzl's life was to us a golden era, a time of revival. Our sorrow is great. The very stones weep. Let the stones weep. But not the Hebrew language. Hebrew must not weep any more. Weeping is no way to honor Herzl. He loved the Jerusalem of King Solomon, the sun, the clean pure air, the Jewish freedom. The day will come when we will take Herzl's bones to Eretz Israel. His spirit is already now in our Hebrew literature."

Jews are fond of comparisons. There are those who compare Herzl with Moses Montefiore. That is not right. Dr. Gaster in London put it this way— "Montefiore was more the philanthropist. Herzl created a great movement among the Jewish People. Montefiore gave Palestine a great deal of help. But Herzl tried to create for the Jews of Roumania a home in Palestine. He found the right word for it, Zionism. And with the power of this word, Zionism, he performed miracles, as Moses did. And like Moses Herzl died on the mountain from which one could only see the beloved land. Herzl is not dead," Dr. Gaster concluded, "No one can persuade us that he is dead. His body has vanished from our sight. But Herzl, the leader of Zionism, lives forever with his People."

It is hard to find another man in Jewish history and in Jewish literature whose death caused such a stir as the death of Herzl. There is hadly a town all over the world where Jews live which was not sitting in mourning for Herzl. Reports came in of memorial services, memorial meetings, obituaries, appreciations from all the five continents. A collection of all the material about Herzl published in those first weeks of mourning would have made a big, bulky book. It was endless. From London, from Vilna, from Jerusalem, from Paris, Munich, Riga, Homel, New York, Montreal, Irkutsk, from far and wide, mourning, tears, grief, weeping. The whole Jewish People sat in mourning for Herzl. It was no exaggeration when the Hebrew poet, Yehalel, said, "Such a man as Herzl has not been known among Jews for almost two thousand years."

Such was Dr. Herzl, as a Jew, as a writer, as a diplomat, as a Zionist. It is fascinating to read what men like Sokolow and Brainin had to say about Herzl as a man, as a human being, about his way of life, his relations with colleagues and with people generally. He emerges from it all as a man, as a gentleman. He had a noble character, a kind heart, and a generous hand. He was not conceited and proud. He was considerate of others. He gave more than his wealth, his fortune, much more than our men of money give, who had to have it torn from them, or tricked out of them, with promises of the next world, or the fear of Gehenna. Herzl could not see others suffer. He had to do what he could to help. There was no pretence about him. He genuinely wanted to be of service, to help. There was always a welcome on his face, an invitation to come nearer, to approach. He was a good, friendly, warm-hearted man, a warm-hearted Jew.

And this good, warm heart of his, with his golden pen, and his dreams, he gave it all to the Jewish People. "Take it, hold it. I and all that is mine are yours, yours to use!"

It broke too soon, this good, warm Jewish heart. Too soon the magnetism in his eyes faded and died. It was a bitter experience to stand by this dear, young grave. The pain is too great.

That is why we mourn. The whole Jewish People, almost five million Jews mourn, because we have lost a hero, whose greatness we did not realize. We did not know what we had, and God knows if we will ever again have such a one. It was not granted to us to have a hero and know that we had him. For if we do have a hero sometimes, we don't know him, and we learn about him only much later, when he is already on the point of leaving us, and he becomes only a memory, a wonderful legend.

A legend indeed. Our great ancient history that is full of legends has now another legend, whose name is Herzl. Our great ancient history which is full of magnificent pages has added another page, a magnificent chapter which will be known by the name Herzl.

Ugandaade

A Congress Picture in One Act

Cast:

Madam Palestine, a widow, not so rich as of high lineage
Zionism her son, very gentlemanly behavior
Miss Uganda, rich orphan girl, comely black beauty
Territorialism, a land-searching shadchan
Max Nordau, personal medical attendant to Madam Palestine
Israel Zangwill, cousin to Miss Uganda
Zion-Zionists, Madam Palestine's family
Porter
Scene, Basel. Time, 1905

A large hall in the Hotel Casino in Basel. Madam Palestine seated in front. Zion-Zionists moving around her. Zionism, her son, at the table, absorbed in a book. Knock at the door. Madam Palestine calls, "Come in!" Zion-Zionism (loudly), "Come in!" Enter Territorialism.

Territorialism: (very politely) I am the widely-known land-searching shadchan. My name is Territorialism.
Madam Palestine: (inclining her ear) Eh? Territorialism?
Territorialism: (turning in her direction) Territorialism!
Madam Palestine: Funny name. Take a seat. Do sit down.
Territorialism: Thank you! I can stand. (sits down, looks round at the family, who eye him in no friendly manner)
Zion-Zionists: We have heard of this shadchan.
Madam Palestine: Well? And what good news have you brought us, Mr. Territorialism?
Territorialism: What can a Jew, a shadchan, tell you? Only I've heard that you are in Basel, and as is often the rule, not so much for the spa as to find a match for your son. So it came to my mind that I might perhaps have a likely match for you. I have indeed! Just the right thing! A jewel of a girl! (kisses his fingertips appreciatively, looking round) Why! There's your young man himself!

Zion-Zionists: Did you hear that?

Madam Palestine: (to Zionism) How this shadchan can arrange things! He's got all the pieces to fit in! Come over here, my son! Meet Mr. Territoria—Toria—I can't get the word right! Toria, Territoria . . .

Territorialism: Thank you! What more can I tell you? One lives. One works. And what are you doing? Still sitting over those books of yours? Studying?

Zionism: What else?

Madam Palestine: (to the Zion-Zionists) Tell them to bring refreshments. (Immediately the table is laden with Israel fruit, carobs and figs, dates and olives) Help yourself, Mr. Territorialism! Lovely fruit! What sort of match have you in mind for my son? What kind of bride have you picked for him?

Territorialism: Brides I have aplenty. But I wouldn't even suggest to you any of the local girls. I'm a land-searching shadchan. And I have a bride for your son, do you know, one and only one in the whole wide world. Not from these parts! All the way from Africa.

Madam Palestine: As far away as that! All that long way!

Zion-Zionists: (excited) All that way, from Africa! All that way! What do you say to that idea of his! No! We say, No! No! All together now, No! (noise in the hall)

Territorialism: Distance doesn't mean a thing nowadays. If I were blessed for every marriage arranged much farther away! So long as the quid pro quo is sound!

Madam Palestine: (thinking hard) You may be right! Who is the girl? Where does she come from?

Territorialism: She is an orphan. But not a poor orphan, God forbid! She lives with an aunt of hers. They call her the "English Aunt." Fabulously rich. And her ancestry is something out of this world.

Madam Palestine: I've got enough ancestry! What's she got in dowry?

Territorialism: Wish I had a tenth of her dowry. She owns land. Large tracts of land. Fields and forests—ever so much! Empty spaces. Not yet occupied.

Madam Palestine: Empty spaces? I've got plenty of that myself. What's her name?

Territorialism: Uganda. That's her name.

Madam Palestine: I don't seem to know that name. Uganda?

Zion-Zionists: (starting a hullabaloo) No! "No" to Uganda! We want no Uganda!

Territorialism: Why are you shouting, "no"? Do you know the girl?

Zion-Zionists: We don't know the girl. But we heard a lot about her.

Madam Palestine: Tell me, what does your Uganda look like? How old is she?

Territorialism: I can't tell you exactly how old she is. But I have a near relative of hers, a first cousin. The name is Zangwill. Your son knows him well. If you want me to, I'll call him in.

Zion-Zionists: (shouting) No! We don't want him here!

Madam Palestine: Why not? Call him in!

Territorialism: (opens the door and calls) Reb Israel Zangwill! We want you! Please come in.

Zangwill: (enters, introduces himself) Israel Zangwill! An old friend of your son's.

Madam Palestine: Do sit down. Please take a seat. (pointing to a chair) Help yourself to some fruit. Those figs are delicious.

Zangwill: No, thank you! I don't care for the fruit.

Zion-Zionists: Did you hear that? He doesn't care for the fruit! The impudence of him!

Madam Palestine: Tell me about the girl! The match that you propose for my son. She's a cousin of yours?

Zangwill: Second or third cousin. But a real relative.

Zion-Zionists: Like my left foot!

Madam Palestine: How old is she?

Zangwill: As young as fresh milk.

Madam Palestine: Good looks?

Zangwill: A very clever girl!

Madam Palestine: I asked you if she is good-looking?

Zangwill: She's clever.

Madam Palestine: Good-looking?

Zangwill: Spirited!

Madam Palestine: Her face?

Zangwill: Wonderful housewife.

Zion-Zionists: What do you make of that man? Ask him this, and he answers that! Keep shouting, "No!" All together, "No!"

Madam Palestine: What can she do?

Zangwill: She can do everything to please!

Madam Palestine: What does she need?

Zangwill: A husband.

Zion-Zionists: This relative of his must be terribly clever, or he's a fool.

Madam Palestine: Call her in here. Let's have a look at her.

Zangwill: (to the Zion-Zionists) Go and fetch her, one of you. She's in the next room, waiting.

Zion-Zionists: (grumbling) The cheek of him! Go and fetch her! You go! (Several Zion-Zionists go to fetch Miss Uganda. They soon return, with Miss Uganda following. Her face is covered with a thick veil.)

Miss Uganda: (looks round, confused) Why have you brought me here?

Zangwill: (presenting her) Miss Uganda!

Madam Palestine: Come here, my child! Let me look at you. (Miss Uganda goes up to Madam Palestine but does not remove her veil)

Zangwill: I think this would interest your son more than you.

Territorialism: (holding Zionism by the hand leads the young man forward, presents them to each other) Mr. Zionism. Miss Uganda.

The young people stand silent for a while. Then gradually they start talking, becoming quite animated, flushed, as though sickening of chickenpox.

Territorialism: (to Zangwill) Something seems to be hatching out.

Zangwill: Not so fast! The family won't have it.

Madam Palestine: (to Territorialism) Look! You're the shadchan here. Could you get her to lift her veil? Let's have a look at her face.

Territorialism: Who cares about looks these days? So long as they share the same outlook, have the same temperaments.

Madam Palestine: That's where you're wrong! Zionism is my only child. So I want his bride to have all the good qualities.

Territorialism: All things in one are given to none!

Zion-Zionists: A very apt saying! And it rhymes too! But it's no patch on a good-looking girl.

Zangwill: That's what I always say.

Madam Palestine: (to Zangwill) So as you and I say the same thing, please persuade her to remove her veil. Let's see her face. You know I wouldn't buy an ethrog in the dark.

Zangwill: Ethrog is something they use for trading in Eretz Israel. And we are good at everything but not in trade! We think our cousin is just right for your son. They make a fine couple. A match made in heaven! We told you before that the girl is black but comely. As we say in the Song of Songs, "I am black but comely."

Zion-Zionists: What was that you said? Clean-shaven, and he spouts Biblical texts! No! I tell you again and again, No!

Zangwill: Why must you always run ahead? Before we started to discuss the matter. Let's leave it to the young people to decide.

Territorialism: In our shadchan talk we say, if it's from peas, it'll increase. If it's blight, it will vanish in the night!

Zion-Zionists: Why do we stand around and listen to him repeating folk sayings and folk rhymes? These people think they can sell us a pig in a poke! (Several go up to Miss Uganda and tear the veil from her face.) Look! Just you look! What do you make of this beauty? A real Gypsy! That's what she is! (Loud laughter. Madam Palestine falls in a faint.)

Territorialism: (comes running up) God save us!

Zangwill: What's happened!

Zion-Zionists: (shouting and clamoring) Doctor! Bring the doctor! At once!

Dr. Nordau: (enters) What's been happening here? The old lady has had a bad fright. She can't stand such things at her age. (bending down to examine her)

Madam Palestine: (feebly) Oh Doctor! (looking towards Uganda)

Dr. Nordau: I see! Miss Uganda!

Zion-Zionists: We won't allow it! No marriage with a Gypsy! No! No!

Dr. Nordau: (to the shadchan and to Zangwill) Please go, gentlemen! Please leave us alone. The poor woman is old and ill. You could kill her, the way you're going on. (Zionism eyes Miss Uganda sadly. Miss Uganda turns a long passionate gaze on Zionism.)

Territorialism: (wringing his hands) I knew it would end like this! Always the same trouble with these aristocratic families! Our grandees! Our upper crust! Nobody's good enough for them. They want dukes and princes.

Zion-Zionists: (shouting) Tell him to get out! He started the whole trouble! We don't want Uganda! We don't want Territorialism!

Zangwill: (trying to calm the crowd) No shouting, please! We'll be leaving soon. We have an old custom that before we go, we sit down and say a few words. I ask you only for a few minutes to listen to me quietly. Whoever you are, you must not behave to a guest as you are behaving to us. I don't know what you call it here, but in our language we call it discourtesy. We call it bad manners, swinish behavior. True, my friend, Territorialism, proposed this match to you. You sent for the girl, wanting to see her. You've brought her in here yourselves. I came with her. True, your young man is a fine young man. But we all know what he is short of. He hasn't, forgive me, a pair of shoes he can go out in. He hasn't a decent shirt to his back. Beggars, we say, mustn't be choosers. A stuck-up beggar is one of the three despised by God himself. True, Zionism is precious to you. But believe me, heart and soul, he is no less precious to me. In the short time I have known him, I have come to love him like my own. I fear that if you go on being so choosy, he will be left, poor chap, on the shelf, an old bachelor. True, the bride is black. But don't forget what fortune awaits your young man when he reaches that new land. He will be throned and crowned there. Exalted. He will, as we say, have the small dish in heaven brought down for him. He will then come to you well-fed and well-satisfied, rested, elegant, newborn, a new man! Don't forget where he is going, into what hands. No haggling little market woman. This is Aunt England, her very self!

Zion-Zionists: (passionately) So what! We've got our own rich aunt. The name is Ica (Baron de Hirsch's Jewish Colonization Association). But we've had a taste of these rich aunts. Shout, "Down with the rich aunts!" Let God himself help us, each with his own! Back home, bridegroom! Back to the ancient mother! Long live the ancient mother! Hedad!

Zangwill: (passionately) Take care you don't have to regret what you are doing. That people won't be pointing their finger at you! Won't be repeating the words of the Psalm—"The stone that the builders rejected." You have to no purpose debased the cornerstone! To no purpose you have wasted your good fortune. We part now! We leave you! But not, I hope, forever. I hope we shall meet again. Au revoir!

Zion-Zionists: (many-voiced) Let those yearn who want you to return!

Territorialism: (banging his stick on the table. Wants to speak, but is shouted down.

Porter: (enters waving his arms about and shouting; chairs and hats flying through the air) Stop this noise! Or I'll clear the place. (No one pays any attention to him.)

Madam Palestine: (in tears) This is dreadful! Shameful! If that other doctor— Dr. Herzl—lived now, he would have never allowed such things! (Madam Palestine faints. Dr. Nordau fusses around her. Brings her round.)

Somebody sings Hatikvah:

> We raise our hands
> To the East, and swear
> By Zion, by her flag we swear,
> By her soil that is sacred and dear.

Curtain

1905

Impressions From a Zionist Congress

The Zionist Organization of America had appointed Sholom Aleichem as a delegate to the Eighth Zionist Congress held at The Hague in 1907. His "Impressions from the Congress" appeared in the New York "Tageblatt."

Arrival at The Hague

If you have never been at a Zionist Congress, it is best to arrive at night and not look for any reception committee and the like waiting for you. These are dreams that exist only on paper, in the news-sheets.

I don't, for instance, know what would have happened if a Jew like me, without the word "Zion" written on his nose, and without the Magen David round his neck, came along with some other travelers in the same compartment, without shouting and fighting; who doesn't care about Zangwill having turned from Zionism and become a Territorialist, and Ussihkin becoming a Chovev Zion, and Ish-Hurwitz thundering away—Make up your minds, one way or the other, here or there.

What would happen, I said, if a Jew like me arrived at The Hague. I'd surely do the same as my father did—take a cab and find a hotel, have a meal, look at the surroundings, and so on and so on.

But the Lord had blessed me with a delegate's seat at the congress. When the congress is over, I'll tell you the name of the Zionist society I represent. At this moment I don't know it myself. As a delegate, traveling with other delegates to the congress I must, of course, keep to the spirit, the hospitality of the Zionist Organization, receiving us with honor, with music and singing, with noise and bustle, excitement and pomp. What could I do? Humble as I am I must give way to the preparations made for our glittering reception.

So we traveled to The Hague, to the Eighth Zionist Congress, in high spirits. We and the ladies traveling with us. And so we arrived, with God's help, at The Hague.

There was no music, no singing. But there was a lot of noise and bustle from the arrivals and from the porters and the cabbies. Lots of people, and not a single Magen David. Not one Zionist! Not one Jew!

I stood there with my baggage, sunk in sad thoughts, on the threshold of this small but boisterous town, The Hague. The town where Baruch Spinoza once wandered around, working out the greatest, the most liberal ideas in the world, for which he was repaid with the most cruel blows in the world. Suddenly I heard a good, sweet, familiar word—Shalom! A Hebrew word. But not only a word—a whole poem recalling a land named Canaan, that once belonged to us, and where Arabs live now, and it sits there and waits for us, like a widow for her children.

The word Shalom wakened me as from a sleep. I saw another Jew in front of me, like me also carrying his baggage, like mine, and lost in thought like me, and we got talking together, in the same language. "Hague? Delegate? Yes, delegate."

We understood each other, speaking our national tongue. We asked and we answered each other in Hebrew, asked and answered the same question. Then we picked up our baggage and went wandering through the town of the Eighth Zionist Congress.

The ladies in our party were much worse off than we were, poor things! They hadn't brought their husbands with them. So they had to find their way themselves to the Congress Bureau. Like all of us. And there a new life started.

The Congress Bureau

What would you call the Congress Bureau? A market place! Passover Eve or the Eve of Yom Kippur need not be so noisy, so uproarious as this Congress Bureau was. Girls with blue sashes and handsome young men with Magen Davids, and all so friendly, all smiling nicely at us, and all asking us, "What can we do for you?"

Everything has a special window to serve you. Everything in Yiddish and German. Post. Accommodation. Information, etcetera. The only trouble is that all these girls with blue sashes and all these nice young men with Magen Davids keep getting in each other's way. Make your head turn. Of course, I wanted help to find a place to stay. One of the young men with a Magen David came over to me. Said he knew me and promised to find somewhere for me to stay, as the information card in the bureau promised.

Our walk was most interesting. For instance, I discovered that in Holland, though it is a much smaller place than Russia, you can easily find somewhere to stay, more so than in Berditchev or Vilna. If you want to drop deep down into a dark hole, you just walk down there or four steps, and you're there. In The Hague you have to grope your way down a winding staircase on all fours, almost at the risk of your life. You wouldn't believe that you were in Holland.

The end of it was that I abandoned all hope of finding accommodation through the bureau. I was saved by the same means we use at home, in our glorious Russian land where you can find help at any time, if only you have enough money or a check on your bank or a money order.

The Pre-Conferences

White flags with blue Magen Davids. Loud cries, Shalom! Shalom! Jewish eyes, Jewish faces, Jewish runnings-around, Jews catching hold of you. And where? Somewhere in Holland, where the light of the sun competes the whole time with the cleanliness of the streets, in this country ruled by a woman, Queen Wilhelmina, God's angel, whom I fell in love with even before I got to know her.

I went into one of those houses with a white flag and a blue Magen David. There was a notice on the door, "Hebrew." There were some young men and some young girls busy arguing, debating. All in Hebrew! The chairman, Levinsky, recognized me, and banging down his gavel, called across to me.

The speaker was Brainin, who went on undisturbed with his speech. It poured out of him like from a barrel, our holy tongue. One felt like patting him on the cheek and saying: "You're a cheeky rascal, Brainin! You speak Hebrew as easily as German!"

There was a young man sitting near me, a nice, neatly-dressed young man, perspiring all over his face, who kept getting up every few minutes and calling out in Hebrew, "I don't agree!"

The chairman kept banging down his gavel and refused to let him speak. That shut him up, this young man. But not for long. He sat there on pins and needles. It made me want to find out who this young man was.

That moment the chairman announced a break, and everybody rushed to the door, all talking together, and all in Hebrew. And a young man came over to me and took me to the perspiring young man about whom I was so curious. He gave me a broad smile and said to me, of course, in Hebrew, "You're Sholom Aleichem. I'm Bialik."

"Bialik?"

"Sholom Aleichem?"

And we fell on each other's neck and kissed, a long lingering kiss, like a newly betrothed couple, who really love each other.

The Great Moment Has Arrived. The Congress Is Open

If you think that the greatest of all moments at the congress is the opening, you are mistaken. The greatest of all moments at the congress is the *not* opening of the congress. Meaning the half hour from nine till half past nine when all the doors are closed, and three thousand people in festive dress and festive mood stand with beating hearts, staring at the clock.

If we said Kol Nidrei not on Yom Kippur Eve, but on the morning of Kippur, it could not be more festive an occasion, more hushed and solemn than this opening of the congress. Gentlemen in black frock coats, Jews with long capotes, beautiful, elegant ladies. Faces you know, and faces you don't know, people from all the corners of the earth. They are all here, all in high spirits, all wanting to get inside, as for Kol Nidrei. Truly a great moment, a holy moment!

So the congress is now open! The presidium are in their places. The public have taken their seats. Like in the House of Commons, like in Parliament. Everybody hanging on the lips of the speakers, the orators. The legacy Herzl left us.

Wolffsohn's opening speech transported me to the reality of a Parliament, official, dry, as these things should be. Among the faces I recognize one with a high forehead, a little too severe. Ussishkin, who truly regards himself as a future Iron Bismarck of the Jewish state, in Eretz Israel, of course. Only in Eretz Israel. I am very much impressed by the appearance of the young-old Anglo-Jewish philanthropist Moser from Bradford. I am impressed too by two rabbis seated at the top, Rabbi Dr. Gaster and Rabbi Reines. And by Nahum Sokolow, by Tchlenov who comes from Moscow, and Engineer Temkin, with his Russian beard.

But whose face can vie with the shining bright face of Nordau? All eyes are turned to him! All hearts beat in time with his. Nordau is here! He will soon appear on the platform, rise in his seat. He will raise his hand! He is about to speak!

It would be wrong of me to fail to single out two veterans, two old men, great men—the painter Josef Israels and the Dutch Senator, De Pinto, who welcomed the congress in the name of the Jewish communities of Holland. And after him—Nordau!

Who is this Nordau? A Prophet in a frock coat. A doctor in Paris between the nineteenth and twentieth century. And what language does he speak? High German! Real literary High German! Sweet, poetic, only for the intelligentsia, the aristocracy of thought! And what words does he use? Carefully prepared and memorized, a simple ABC language, a magnificent sound. Words of gold created by a genius, like blades of green grass warmed by the rays of the sun. Fantastic sounds coming from a heart that feels, from a noble soul in Golus!

Dear Friends! I am not going to profane this brilliant speech of Nordau's. You will be able to read it later on, the whole speech, complete, with nothing left out. There are only two things I want to say about this great speech of Nordau's. The first is that it was not spoken in our ancient Hebrew language, and the other, that 90 percent of the delegates and guests don't understand Hebrew.

There's a delegate from America sitting next to me, a well-known Russian personality, not, God forbid, an ailing, sick man, a man with strong nerves, and I saw this man wiping his eyes as he listened to Nordau's speech, when he told us that there are only two ways for Jews—Zionism or national bankruptcy.

In the Corridors of the Jewish Parliament

Like every Parliament the Jewish Congress has its corridors, its side rooms, the buffet, post, telegrams, etcetera. All with the same wording,—"For Your

Assistance." Assisting you how? With what? Breakfast, dinner, very nice of them! Take your seat, if you please, at one of these small tables. If you have a chair, that is, of course. For if you haven't a chair, you must get one, grab hold of one from somebody else. If he won't let you, take it by force. If he slaps you over the hand, slap him back. And take your seat at the table. Not like some young newlywed, afraid to say a word for yourself, because if you don't, you may sit here till the congress closes, and all your shouting and whistling and stamping your feet won't help you!

Yet if you do know somebody who is a real somebody, and he puts in a good word for you, you'll soon get a waiter to serve you, a Jewish waiter who will run up to you suddenly, flushed and perspiring, to explain something to you in some queer language, very similar to our Jargon, Yiddish. Till after a terribly long wait he suddenly shows up with a quarter duck—a poor, solitary duck, I'm sorry to say, without knife or fork, and no bread. If you take my advice, you'll not wait on ceremony but will start at once on that duck, for if you don't somebody else will have lifted your duck to his plate and is ticking in for all he's worth, and you can go whistle for it.

If you want wine—Carmel wine of course, you should order it, and it will not take half an hour, and another waiter will come over to you, clean-shaven, and with a skullcap on, and he'll bring you a bottle of wine, sealed with a Magen David. The first thing he draws your attention to is the notice on the wall behind you, in Hebrew—"Payment in Advance." And he won't let the bottle out of his hand, in case your holding it makes it forbidden.

The buffet is in a state of chaos, God forgive us! I was sitting with Nahum Sokolow, having tea with him. Sokolow asked the waiter for a spoon. Since the waiters understand only their own Jargon, he thought we wanted milk to add to the tea. So he pointed to the notice on the wall which said that milk was not allowed with meat. It was not kosher. And he brought no spoon. Not for me either. So we stirred our tea with one of those tiny congress flags.

The whole place was in such a muddle that a wedding in Mazepevka would have looked like a quiet, well-behaved, orderly gathering in comparison.

Yet after all that, it was pleasant to eat there. You felt you were having a meal in your own Jewish Parliament, the place where Jewish history was being shaped, where our Jewish state was coming into existence. In a word, you were eating at home, in your own home, where the waiters and everybody else speak your language. True, your home is yours only for a while, no more than one week. So it is dearer and more precious!

The Congress Ladies

The Jewish Parliament would have been the poorer without these fine truly-Jewish women, the reliable ladies of the Bnoth Zion, on whom the Goyim would cast their envious eyes if they could. God created them (the women, not the Goyim) to adorn, to sweeten our lives. Dressed simply, but with taste, no jewelry, they looked like lovely flowers in the Jewish garden, giving a special charm to the whole assembly. Only a pity that not one of them can or wishes to stand up on the platform and speak. What a power of attraction it would be to our national movement if we now had one of our Miriams, our Deborahs, our Judiths, as we had them of old! I say this very seriously. Our Zionists might well give a thought to this idea for our future congresses. How beautiful, how attractive our national tongue Hebrew would sound on the lips of these ladies! I couldn't hear enough of it! I found it remarkable that some spoke Hebrew with a Sephardic accent, so that we felt they were Italian or Spanish or French. I felt that if all our sisters and our daughters could speak Hebrew as these women did, it would bring Redemption to our People. Then Max Nordau would not need to be so pessimistic about our national liquidation and bankruptcy, and Ish-Hurwitz would not need to tell us that there are only two ways for the Jewish People—Zionism or assimilation. There would be only one way—Jews an independent nation.

Congress Caricatures

Any big collection of pictures must contain some caricatures. Any gathering of earnest, dedicated idealists must include some who, for no fault of their own, make people laugh at them. Queer people. An odd lot. I'll give you two examples.

We, the American Landsmannshaft, were holding a meeting. Dr. Magnes was delivering an important speech on a very important question when the door was suddenly pulled wide open, and a handsome young man tore into the place like a whirlwind. A young banker, a German, well-dressed, well-fed, with red cheeks, and in high spirits. He turned on his heel and proposed that our American Landsmannshaft should participate financially in a project he was putting forward, because if we didn't, it would be the end of Zionism. The tone in which he delivered his speech was the kind of tone in which a man would come to a group of people out on a picnic and tell them to go on an excursion in the forest or to take a boat out on the river. When he had finished his proposition, the young, smooth-shaved banker laid two fingers to his forehead, smiled sweetly at us, like a man well-satisfied with life, who had come to a ball to have a jolly time, and all he had got to worry about was a toothache.

Out in the corridors there is a man going up and down, with burning eyes and an enormous briefcase, who stops you short and grips your hand, and won't let go till you have heard him out and he has read to you his whole project which he has been carrying about with him for the last eight years, the right way to help the Jewish People, and nobody listens.

Outside, at the front door, there are two young men, both of them together not quite forty years old, running down the whole congress, condemning it with the most damning words. They say they have long given up the Jewish People—time now to say goodbye to it. Unless God works a miracle, and Ussishkin and his policy collapse.

You look hard at these two young men, and an involuntary smile hovers on your lips. And you say to yourself—"Poor, silly children!"

There's another young man with a nice face who goes round with a pack of postcards, stopping everyone who passes, pulling at their coattails, and he says to everyone—"Sign please!"

And though you haven't a moment to spare, you stop and sign.

What will he do with all those cards? He caught me in the buffet, having a bite.

"Sholom Aleichem?"

"Aleichem Sholom!"

"Sign please!"

And the young man with the nice face pushed one card after the other in front of me. Till I had to take the fork in my left hand and let the young man hold my right hand, and do with it whatever he wanted. Signed cards from the congress became almost as much a fashion as sending Rosh Hashona cards. Or having your photograph taken at the congress.

On the third day of the congress there was a photographer waiting for customers, outside in the courtyard, with his stand and an umbrella, and delegates lining up in groups, waiting their turn. Landsmannshaften separately, journalists separately, each to his own group. Naturally, lots of people wanted to be photographed with Nordau. And, of course, the various groups were very concerned to keep their group safe from intrusion. No amount of money, for instance, could buy the right for a member of one Landsmannshaft to appear on a photograph of a different Landsmannshaft than his own.

There was one young man who wanted to smuggle himself into a picture of our American Landsmannshaft. He was told three separate times to be good enough to smuggle himself out again. No sooner he was out than he was in again! What was it that drew him to us? The American flag? Or President Wolffsohn and Max Nordau on the same card? You could see it had become a matter of life or death for this young man! I felt that we should all, for pity's sake, make room for him on our card. But the Americans are, forgive me, a tough breed, and they wouldn't have it. One of our delegates, Dr. J. L. Magnes himself, made it his special mission to get this unfortunate young man ejected from our group. I am giving you here a word for word stenographic record of what transpired.

Dr. Magnes: "Please! I beg of you!"

Young man: "What difference does it make to you?"

Dr. Magnes: "Our group doesn't want you!"

Young man: "Doesn't cost you anything, does it?"

Dr. Magnes: "It's not a question of money. It's a question of you on the photograph."

Young man: "My what?"

Dr. Magnes: "Your picture. Your face!"

Young man: "My face?"

Dr. Magnes: "Your face. We don't like your face!"

The young man took to tidying his hair and his beard to make himself more presentable. But I'm afraid I haven't seen the picture yet. Somehow the young man did, after all, smuggle himself into our picture, among us American citizens.

1907

Sholom Aleichem's concluding article from The Hague carried with it the following editorial note:

The most interesting series of articles from the congress was interrupted at this point. Sholom Aleichem received a telegram in The Hague to come at once to Switzerland, to his mother-in-law's sickbed. He went off at once to Switzerland, where she closed her eyes for the last time.

The bereaved writer put away his pen for the days of mourning, and he is unable to say whether he can continue these congress pictures.

The First Jewish Republic

One Who Has Returned from the First Jewish State Tells of All He Has Seen and Heard There

i
Thirteen at Sea

The first few difficult days of our great journey by water, thank God, we got over long ago. Each of us gave the sea its due, not, God forbid, left anything owing, one more, one less, one sooner, one later. One of us whom we knew, not knowing him, only as a brother shipmate, who had professed himself a man not afraid of anything, and whom we had therefore named, "The Atheist," was the only one whom the sea had not disturbed. He ate enough for all of us and strode about the ship like a demon, whistling a tune, till one day he disappeared for two whole days and nights. When I saw him on the third day, he looked a little pale. He was, true enough, walking about the ship and whistling as before, but it wasn't the same walk, nor the same whistling. He found it better to sit half reclining, with his feet up, watching the ship rocking from north to south, and from east to west, and the waves chasing each other, looking like white sheep, arriving without number and without end, you don't know from where, and vanishing without your knowing where to. If you sit like that for a good while, you get sick of looking, and you lift up your eyes to heaven, and you meet the sun, looking lonely on the water, without earth, without trees, without houses or roads or railways or people running to and fro. You close your eyes and start counting how many of you have been on the ship, and how many days you still have to stay on the ship. Till you drop off to sleep, and you dream of red flowers nodding their heads.

We were on this ship a whole colony of acquaintances, half-acquainted, unacquainted, some complete strangers. Among them undoubted Jews, and Jews who are doubtful Jews—Jew or German. One of them said to be a banker and a multimillionaire. Traveling first class, but he often came over to us in second class, just to talk. His unassuming ways, no pride, behaving like any ordinary human being, won us all over, made us his devoted slaves, hypnotized us. On top of that he was a cheerful fellow, an amusing talker, and he loved a good story. When you looked at his bald head, his slightly raised shoulders, his fleshy nose and fleshy lips, and his dark pince-nez, his simple black tie on his plain white shirt, without any gold or diamond tiepin, his simple flat watch which he keeps taking out and holding up to his short-sighted eyes, you thought to yourself—"This a millionaire? Impossible!" But when you heard him talk, and you heard him laugh, and you saw how his eyes close when he talks and his white teeth sparkle, you realized that he must be one of those people on whom conditions smile, and people flatter them, and luck pursues them, and care avoids them. The only thing they lack is honor given to them, homage. Or rather they have honor and homage enough. But they want more.

One of those who really did not suffer on the boat and just laughed at the sea and the stormy waves was an unacquainted acquaintance, a passenger traveling between decks, a strapping young man, butcher or cobbler or carpenter, some sort of workman, with a pair of hands on which the whole man stands. When he spoke, he chopped off the ends, as with an axe, and then banged them down with his hand as with a hammer. He kept coming up to us, on the second class deck, hanging around our Jewish colony all the time. He was delighted when one of us spoke a word to him. And if we asked him a question, he was in seventh heaven.

There was also a lady in our little colony on the ship, a young lady, nearly thirty. Tall as an Englishwoman, talkative as a Frenchwoman, and beautiful as a daughter of Israel. Dressed up she was almost taller than a man. And she bore herself like a man. She loved being in male company. She herself confessed that she couldn't stand women and womanish nerves. Who she was and where she was going nobody knew, just as we didn't know who the other people were, who without question were Jews or Germans. I mean they were Jews rather than Germans. And if you want me to, I can assure you that I am myself convinced that they were Jews. Bet you any amount you like. I can recognize a Jew, if you know what I mean, by his eyes. Jewish eyes ask questions, want to know. They may quite possibly be asking you—"So you have found out! You have spotted us!"

But that is not the point of our story. All I want to say is that as it is on land, so it is at sea. Each one is drawn towards his own. Poles, Turks, Blacks, Chinese. Each forms a separate group. We didn't arrange it beforehand. Nobody came to us with such a proposal, that we should get together, in a separate group. I don't know how it happened. Our handful of Jews quite quietly, without words, formed into a separate colony, sat down separately at the rear of the boat, and started to talk. At first about just anything, trivia, and then, I don't remember how, the talk drifted into what pinches each of us; we spoke about Jews, about our past, about the Jewish condition in different countries, and about the future of the Jewish People. At first only those spoke who were openly Jews. Then those too who were doubtful, whether they were Jews or Germans, also joined in our talk. And since we spoke German, fools might still go on thinking that these half-Jews were Germans. But as we talked on, their secret came out.

All the members of our group were Jews, from different countries, with different professions and different ideas and opinions. We were thirteen in number, thirteen Jews from thirteen different worlds. It meant that each of us was a world of our own. And our talk progressed, I can tell you, at first very soberly, cold, but gradually becoming warmer and warmer, till it finally became quite heated, so hot that the other passengers on deck grew interested and stopped, apparently to look down at the sea, but in reality to overhear our discussion. In plain Yiddish you would call it a row, an altercation, a squabble. Like a market place. Every single one of us was trying to convince all the others that his opinion was the only right one. And to prove that your opinion was right you had to shout louder than anyone else. So we all shouted at the top of our voices. It's an old story that he who shouts loudest is more likely to convince. So we all shouted, made a hullabaloo, thrashed our arms about, and in our excitement we didn't notice that the sea had begun to rage. A lot of small but thick black clouds suddenly appeared out of nowhere. So it seemed. And they spread in length and breadth, crept all over heaven and swallowed the sun. The sea sang a sad tune, and the waves clapped in time. The ship began to roll, went up and down, there and back, as though it was going to turn turtle. Bells were ringing. The music had stopped. People and crew were running. Before we could look round, we heard a terrific bang, as from a thousand thunders. Then it seemed as if the void under us had split and turned right over. The next moment and all of us, all the passengers on the boat, were lying in various postures, one on top of the other. Then suddenly a cold, wet stream swept over us and carried us away, huddled together on a big broken-off plank, wet through, flung into some limbo, God knows where! All this happened with such swiftness that we had no time to give ourselves an account of what was happening to us. We behaved like so many sheep caught in a panic. We didn't know where to run. We were in the water, hanging on to each other, clutching at any broken spar floating by. We lost all sense of time, day and night. Of everything round us. We only knew that we were lifted up and banged down, up and down. The blood froze in our veins. We stopped hearing and seeing and feeling. We were no longer ourselves.

Of course, I tell you all this in the name of my fellow observers. As for myself I can tell you (you will hardly think I'm boasting) I stood firm in one spot, and I had the opportunity to observe how each of my fellow passengers, struggling with the waves, refused to give up.

Well, there's nothing I can say about our millionaire. Do you know of any millionaire who wants to die? Unless one whose millions and the honors that go with them and all the good things of this world have grown stale and wearisome, and he feels like having a try at the next world, to see what that tastes like. You should have seen our skeptic, the Atheist, who on the boat denied God and demolished the entire world, with all its pleasures, which, in fact, are not worth a pinch of snuff. Now he was flinging his arms about, moaning and groaning, calling to God to help him. The woman who on the boat had borne herself like a man had now lost all self-control and kept fainting every few minutes, and was each time revived by the water splashing in her face. A woman remains a woman.

Our workman, with powerful hands, kept turning his head towards me all the time, to make me understand that I must hold on with both hands, where he was clinging with only one hand. Because with his other hand he was holding up the woman, who otherwise would have slipped into the sea and found an early grave there.

I can't say how long all this took. None of us had a mind to look at his watch. I remember only that for a long time it was very dark. A darkness that could be felt. And time dragged ever so long, a whole day perhaps, maybe a day and a night, possibly two days and two nights. I can't tell you, because there are such readers who, when you tell them an unusual story, will exchange glances with their neighbor and smile. I know what that smile means: "What's he going on about? Jaw, jaw, jaw! We take his word as much as we trust this board!" I can well picture how these smart-alecks would grin if I told them all the wonders I have seen, as we floated on the plank after our shipwreck. The fish and the waterfowl and the sea monsters, all those strange beings half fish, half human. They would surely say, as they say in America, I'm bluffing, meaning I exaggerate, am telling them fairy tales. Rather than listen to them better to keep quiet and go on to tell what happened afterwards.

Thank God, the afterwards was good. Very good! Better than we could have expected. There was a sudden big bang, and we were all cast out on a sand and pebble shore. We suddenly felt a caressing warmth on our wet frozen bodies, and a bright light penetrating our half-closed eyes. A strange heat poured into our veins. Our limbs began to straighten one by one.

We opened our eyes slowly, and began to see and hear and understand what was happening to us. It was hard to get a word out of us. We could hardly speak.

"Where are we?" said one.

"Where are we?" said another.

We didn't know where we were. But we could see. We felt that we were on dry land. And one after the other we sat up. And presently we stood up, on our feet. We shook off the wet on our bodies, and looked around us, on all sides, up to the sky and down to the ground, and we saw: above, a beautiful clear blue sky, and a bright warm sun; below, a green earth, with grass and trees, forests and birds flying, birds singing over our heads, and flowers of all colors adorning this Garden of Eden. We felt a strange pang, a pain in the breast, and our legs shook under us; perhaps from hunger. And again we asked each other, repeating the same refrain: "Where are we? Where are we?"

Our senses gradually came back to us, and we began to realize that the sea had cast us out in a land foreign to us, an island whose name we did not know. We looked at each other, and I counted. Imagine it! We were thirteen, just thirteen. The same thirteen! The same millionaire, the same Atheist, the same woman passenger, the same workman from between decks. All the same. Our whole Jewish colony from the ship. Not one outsider. And involuntarily a sigh burst from the breast, and the eye dropped a tear. We all lifted our hands to heaven (except one, the Atheist, who had just then turned away from the rest of us). And we thanked and praised God silently, without words, each deep down in the heart. We said: "Thou art great, O God, and great are Thy marvels."

ii
Thirteen on Dry Land

Each one of you, of course, was once a child, and each one of you surely read that lovely story, "Robinson Crusoe," how the sea had cast him out on an island, and he spent some years there all alone, except at first with a parrot, whom he taught to speak a few words, and then with the savage Man Friday. How he lived on nuts and sewed clothes for himself from leaves, and many more such fine tales that you have read in "Robinson Crusoe," a book that is immortal, famous throughout the world.

It was like that with us, the thirteen luckless passengers who had survived the shipwreck and were cast out somewhere we don't know where. The difference between us and Robinson Crusoe was only this—he was one, and we were thirteen. Thirteen brothers (actually twelve brothers and one sister), all of one people, only from different countries, different classes and different opinions. Thirteen Robinson Crusoes on one island! Of course, we were much better off than poor Robinson Crusoe all alone, on his own. Yet what was the good of it that we were thirteen, when we had no idea where in the world we were—in a large country, on an island, in a desert, in a wilderness? Though judging by the grass, the trees, and the birds, we concluded that we were not in a desert. There may be people here. The only question was, what people? What if they were, God forbid, wild men of the Taratuta tribe, cannibals? It reminded me of the book I had been reading on the ship. A Yiddish book, as it happens, written in Yiddish and published in America. Seventh printing! So it says in the book. It has a very long title.

"Captain Coribaba, or: They Travel for Diamonds and Fall Into the Hands of Cannibals on the Island Kukuruso, Where You Find the Wild Men of the Taratuta Tribe."

The book caused such a sensation all over the world (it says so explicitly in the Foreword), that there wasn't enough paper in the factories and not enough type in the printing presses, and more had to be brought from Europe, on special ships. Pity I never finished that novel. Because the storm on the sea had caught me in the middle, just where I was reading about how the ship had wandered over the ocean, and the food stores had given out. They had decided to cast lots, to see which of the sailors should be first put into the pot, for soup. They went one by one, till there were no more sailors left, only Captain Coribaba. He swam over to an island with the name Kukuruso, where the savages of the Taratuta Tribe live. Would be nice if we ended up with the savages of the Taratuta Tribe, and they took it into their heads to make a roast out of us, or human cutlets, cooked in women's milk. If so, it would have been better a thousand times to have drowned in the depths of the sea or been swallowed by a great fish.

This thought nagged all thirteen of us. Nobody wanted to be a roast for the savages of the Taratuta tribe. Each of us would much rather have devoured one of those same Taratuta savages—we were so hungry! And we were worn out by that lovely excursion on the broken plank. One question stuck in our throats: "What are we going to eat!" And we looked at one another with hungry eyes that seemed to say, "Let's cast lots to see whom to eat first!"

"But what's the use of standing around here? We must get something to eat," cried one of our thirteen, the millionaire, I think, who couldn't put up with going hungry. "Must eat!" said another, angrily.

"Easy to say 'Must eat!'. Where are we to get it? Can't you see we are in a wilderness!"

"How do you know that?" asked a third, glaring at the second. "Almighty God who saved us from the wild sea will not forsake us now!" This from the only religious Orthodox Jew among us. It only got him a dirty look from the man we called, "The Atheist." It started us off on a long debate about where to get food. Till one of us (I won't say it was me, in case you say I'm boasting) got an idea. That all thirteen of us should set out in different directions, thirteen different roads, looking, searching. One in the field, another in the forest, a third on the hills. We might find something to eat.

This plan was almost adopted, when suddenly one of us raised an objection. "Suppose we get lost? Here, at least, we are all together, all the thirteen of us. Thirteen is not one!"

That was a very important point. We all agreed that thirteen is not the same as one. But the question remained—where should we go, all thirteen of us? Right or left? Field or forest? It led to another discussion over several points, and our opinions divided, here on dry land, as at sea before. As many people, so many opinions. Thirteen people, thirteen opinions. One said, "if we go in the forest, we're sure to find fruit." It made one of the others sneer—"First time I've heard of fruit growing in a forest." A third thought it was quite likely that fruit grew in a forest. Not perhaps the kind of fruit we knew. Not apples and pears. But fruit, eatable. He was sure of that.

"What makes you so sure? What pledge do you give?"

"Anything you like."

"Against wild beasts?"

"And aren't human savages worse than wild beasts?"

"Much worse!"

So we had a long and bitter argument whether to go into the forest to look for fruit, and God knows how long it would have gone but for the passenger between decks, the workman. "Friends!" he said. "If you don't mind, I'll tell you something. I'm only a simple working man. I don't know any roundabout talk. Why should we quarrel over something we don't know. It may happen that there is a lot of fruit in the forest. Maybe there isn't any. If you will allow me, I'll go into the forest, and I'll tell you. I'll bring some back with me if there is."

This sounded so honest and straightforward that nobody said a word against it. We all sat down against the sun, warming ourselves and drying ourselves, each full of his own thoughts. No one spoke. Not because we did not dare to intrude on the sacred silence, nor because there was nothing to say, but for a very natural reason. We were starving. And when a man wants to eat, he can't talk. If everybody felt as I did, I am afraid that we dared not even look at each other because we could have swallowed each other up alive, no better than the savages of the Taratuta tribe. A hungry man is a wild beast. I saw that when our messenger in the forest came back laden with fruit. The whole colony flung itself at him. God knows what they would have done to him if he had returned empty-handed. The biggest gentleman among us, the millionaire, would have been the first to jump at his throat. But luckily our messenger came back from the forest loaded with fresh sweet bananas and with piles of nuts. We flung ourselves on him, tearing everything out of his hands. Those nuts and bananas tasted wonderful. A thousand tastes. Each one of us found a different taste. Our people couldn't praise it enough. They didn't stop lauding it. They were full of talk now. The more they stilled their hunger, the more it loosened their tongues. Their faces lighted up. Their lips smiled. We became altogether different people. One of us said bananas were the best fruit in the world. Another asserted he could live on bananas all his life. Bananas were the most filling of all fruit. A third tried to show that, according to Darwin, primitive man had lived only on fruit. A fourth denied this, on the authority of the same Darwin. He was supported by a fifth, who argued that it couldn't have been soft fruit, because then we would not have developed such strong teeth. And our one religious Orthodox Jew stood up and said the blessing, "Lord God, King of the Universe, who createst the fruit of the tree."

"Why," he said, "do you argue and bicker? Have you forgotten what is written in the Torah? What God said to Adam, 'Of every tree of the garden thou mayest freely eat; but of the two trees thou shalt not eat.'"

Of course, that brought out our Atheist in opposition. And the two went into a wrangle. Good-humoredly, as it happens. We know that after food people are generally more tolerant. Especially after such a long and hard fast as ours on the sea. The bananas and the nuts had satisfied us. They were balm to our bones. Joy in our hearts, and a light in our eyes. We now wanted to rest, to lie stretched out on the green, soft grass, staring up to the blue sky. And that was what all the thirteen of us did; we lay there stretched out on the grass, staring up to the sky. Our eyes began to close, and we slept. For some time it seems, for when we woke, the sun was already far down in the sky. Our first call was, "Water! Where can we get a drink of water?"

As was our way, we began to argue and dispute about the question: There should be lots of water here. Where there are hills, there must be water. Others contended that this didn't prove anything. You could have hills and no water. Each of us gave his own opinion. Thirteen people. Thirteen opinions. The thirteenth to speak was the plain workman, who always liked being the last. He had apologized first, in his way, for putting his word in when there were better qualified people present, much more competent. But if they would allow him, if his interference wouldn't offend, he would give his opinion. Very likely there was a lot of water. Or there might be no water. If we allowed him, he would jump over to that hill and see if there was water there. And he would tell us. Of course, we accepted his offer. Almost unanimously. He didn't take long. He was soon back with a beaming face, bringing good news. Not far off, behind that hill, there was a running stream. Water, good clear water, a taste like the Garden of Eden. Pity he had no bucket to bring some back. He was afraid we would all have to make an effort and go ourselves to the stream. All thirteen of us.

Naturally, we made the effort. All thirteen. We found a running stream, with crystal clear water, snaking along down the hill and round into the forest. We fell on our knees and dipped our faces in the water, as our forefathers had done in olden times, and quenched our thirst. Again it was balm stealing through our bones, a joy in the heart and light in our eyes. We sat down, all the thirteen, on the grass beside the stream, and stared up to the flaming sun descending over the forest. The warm day was departing, yielding its place to the cool of the evening, hanging over our heads, and putting a new fear into us—where will we sleep this night?

Naturally our opinions were divided—thirteen people, thirteen opinions. One said, sleep in the forest. Another objected. There may be wild beasts in the forest. A third advised we should go up the hill. We might find something there. A fourth said: "We'll find nothing there except stones." The fifth suggested putting stones together to make a shelter. "It will keep us dry if it rains."

And talking like this we kept going on, walking farther till we came to a big cave that nature had dug out of the rock, or maybe human hands, a long, long time ago, and gone away and left it.

This too started off a number of differing opinions. Thirteen people, thirteen opinions. But on one point there were no differing opinions. We all agreed that this was where we would spend the night. What choice had we? And if you want to know, it was not so bad as you might imagine. True, there were no pillows and no blankets and no covers. But each of us took his place among the stones and covered himself with freshly plucked grass. For the woman in our group we found a spot far removed from all the rest. We built stones all round it; bedded it with grass and leaves.

All this work, collecting and building the stone rampart and bringing the grass and the leaves, all this work was done by our workman. Not because we told him to, not because we ordered him about. He did it all of his own free

will. He liked doing it, was glad to do it. He asked us to forgive him, but that
was his nature. He was a workman, a born workman, and he was used to work.
He couldn't sit idle. I can't say that we made any particular protest. We didn't
tell him not to. And we didn't sit idle ourselves either. We were busy with a
very important question—where in the world were we? There is nothing worse
for a man than not to know where he is. Odd! We had in our group lots of
scholarly people, thinkers, philosophers, but not a single one who remembered
his geography and could name the islands. One did have a hazy memory, and
he started pouring out names at us—Sicily, Sardinia, Sumatra, Java, Borneo,
Cuba, Jamaica, Madagascar, Newfoundland. Islands galore.

"Not so fast," one of us tried to halt the flow. "Look where your geography
has landed you!"

"If we don't know the name, let's invent one," said one of us. "A name that
will suit our island. A special name, a name with distinction."

The proposal was acceptable to all, and each of us started to look for a special
name. Thirteen people—thirteen names. The millionaire pined for the name
"Paris," the city in which he had spent most of his life. Our Orthodox Jew, who
had just finished reciting the afternoon prayers, was of the opinion that the
island should be called "Help of the Lord." The Atheist mocked him and said
that as far as he was concerned they could call it "Devil Island." . . . The
woman, of course, wanted it to be called "Eve," after Mother Eve, but since
she was the only woman there, no one wanted to support her. One argued that
the island should be named "Zion," whereupon another asked why "Zion,"
rather than Argentina, Brazil, Uganda, or some other country?

"If you would listen to me, you would call the island 'Karl Marx,'" one of us
called out, probably the socialist.

"Why suddenly 'Karl Marx'? another throws in. "Why not Moses our
Teacher, Mohammed, Spinoza, Byron, Heine, Pushkin, or Spenser?"

From these arguments we found that there were exactly thirteen different
principles among us, as follows:

One Zionist, one territorialist, one capitalist, one atheist, one socialist, one
nationalist, one assimilationist, one materialist, one worker, one woman, and
one writer (the author of this account). Thirteen people—thirteen principles.

An idea suddenly popped into my mind (great ideas always pop up suddenly). I rose and asked for the floor.

"Lady and gentlemen, permit me to tell you what I think about the name to
be given to our island. Since each one of us is standing firm on his own
suggestion and refuses to defer to anyone else, and perhaps rightly—since each
one thinks to himself: Why should I give in to him? Why shouldn't he give in to
me?—I therefore suggest since the thirteen of us have thirteen different ideas
and thirteen different principles, why shouldn't we call the island "Thirteen"?

Here I must make a brief comment, and note the fact that no orator in the
world, neither in Europe nor in America—not even Bebel, Jaures, or Bryan—
ever received the thunderous applause I earned from my colleagues on that

great night on that wonderful island. I do not say this, God forbid, to boast. I simply want to prove to the reader that the greatness of an oration and what it accomplishes depends on its brevity—the shorter it is the better, and for that reason I now conclude my second tale.

iii
Thirteen Robinson Crusoes on an Island

When I was a child, reading with my teacher the world-famous, delightful story of Robinson Crusoe, I would stop the reading from time to time and pose challenging questions: What would have happened if Crusoe had not found nuts to eat? Or what if he had not succeeded in striking fire from the rock? If the parrot had not made its flight to him? If he had not met the savage he called "Friday"? These were some weighty questions I presented. My teacher got fed up with me and began to tear his hair (he seems to have been a somewhat nervous type).

"How is it possible," he raved, "for a child not to understand that if those things had not happened the book would never have been published?"

After this brief introduction, I think my readers will pay attention to the events I am describing for them and will refrain from asking questions. I also hope that no one will even suspect, God forbid, that there is any exaggeration at all in what I write. You cannot compare me to Robinson Crusoe, since he was alone and so could make up whatever he felt like, whereas I was not alone. There were thirteen of us, thank God, thirteen different points of view and characters, all of one people, all subject to one fate, all having travelled in one ship that was wrecked, and all cast up together on one island about which we knew nothing and therefore named "Thirteen Island."

I can assure you that we never spent a night like that first night on "Thirteen Island." After we had stuffed ourselves with sweet bananas and ripe nuts, and washed them down with the tasty waters flowing in the crystal clear brook bubbling down the hillside to the nearby forest, we stretched out in the cave, each of us in his own corner. Bedded down on fresh grass pallets, we were overcome by the sweet sleep that comes after prolonged suffering, after a bout with death, after long hunger and thirst and a variety of misadventures. Such sleep is not disturbed by nightmares. Such sleep is quiet and lasts until greeted by morning and the smile of the rising sun. You open your eyes slowly, stretch your aching but rested limbs, and yesterday's events and adventures pass before you mind's eye like pictures in a gallery. You ask yourself:

"Where am I?"

Each of the Robinson Crusoes got up slowly, slowly dressed himself in his still-damp clothing, and made his way out of the cave into the bright world of the Almighty. We marched to the bubbling brook to wash our hands and faces in the pure crystal clear water, and marveled at the beauties of nature as we walked, observing the dense forest and the towering mountains. The rising sun made you think of a beautiful princess in an enchanting story. We all stood facing the forest, to give our one and only woman the privacy fitting a "madam" of her station, to wash and dress herself. Only then did we wish each other a "good morning" and ask each other how we had slept. And then, suddenly, the same question burst forth from each of us:

"Now what do we do?"

The primary, fundamental questions of food and drink had already been answered. Thank God: there was an abundance of sweet bananas on the trees, ripe nuts, and flowing water in the crystal brook bubbling down the hill. We realized that we would not succumb to hunger or thirst on this island. Still, people are creatures of habit, and it is hard to break them of their habits. For example: a cup of tea in the morning, or coffee with a little milk, followed by a cigarette—things which at first glance seem to be unimportant, trivial, are really very good. Man cannot do without them. But it is a well-known rule that it is just what we do not have that we yearn for the most!

I don't remember who it was who first cried out: "tea with milk." In any case, once it was said, it served as a topic for a lengthy debate that lasted half an hour. One said tea with milk, another said coffee with milk; one cried that it could be without milk, as long as it was tea, and another asserted that milk without tea was better than tea without milk. And a third agreed with him, arguing that for tea you need sugar as well, but milk could be drunk without sugar.

All this time, of course, we were not standing in one place. We were strolling, leisurely, on the green, fragrant grass of the hillside, breathing the intoxicating scent of the yellow-dotted red flowers under our feet, marveling at the heavenly scenery of the blessed island on which the sea had cast us up. As we strolled and debated—with gestures—we sudddenly saw some shapes off in the distance, moving and glistening in the sun. We stood and wondered what they were: people? Little children? Dwarfs? Midgets? And just then I recalled the book I had been reading on board ship, but did not get to finish. It was published in America, under a very long name:

"Captain Coribaba, or: They Travel for Diamonds and Fall Into the Hands of Cannibals on the Island of Kukuruso, Where You Find the Wild Men of the Taratuta Tribe."

To the best of my memory, the wild men of the Taratutu tribe were not so small. Furthermore, they were black, and not at all white. Each one of us, of course, voiced his opinion of these white creatures. Thirteen people—thirteen opinions. But since we were walking toward them, and they were walking toward us, we quickly saw them to be a herd of goats, goats with the usual beards and horns and agile, clattering feet and silly faces. It was obvious that these were not wild goats because they not only did not run away from us but, on the contrary, came right up to us as if to old friends, lifting their foolish chins and wagging their beards as though asking us for something. Stupid goats! They could give us a lot more than we could give them.

"What do you think, are they milk-goats?"

"Where are your eyes?"

"If we only had some kind of receptacle . . ."

"If you don't mind," our worker turned to us, "if you permit me, I will milk a few of the goats. Why are you so surprised? I had a goat at home, and I used to milk her myself."

"What will you milk them into?"

"I'll milk them for each of you into your hats."

At first the suggestion provoked a lot of laughter, as though it had been suggested that we put one foot in heaven, but then the laughter died down. The yearning for a little warm milk was stronger than all other feelings, and each of us handed his hat to the workman—or, as we called him, the Proletarian. First came the millionaire, who presented his hat with a flourish, like a king—or at least a minister—presenting his goblet at the spring somewhere in Carlsbad or Marienbad for it to be filled with hot mineral water which has no taste but, what can he do, he must obey the doctor's orders to drink a cupful every morning on an empty stomach. . . . We all followed, each of us hat in hand, including our lady with her hat, each of us with a pleasant word, and each of us pounced on the bit of milk and refreshed himself as though it was some kind of magic draught.

There was a minor incident when it was the turn of the religious man, the one we called the Orthodox. First, he was doubtful whether he could drink milk that way. Then, when he accepted the majority opinion, with a great deal of hesitation, that one must not exclude himself from the community and must behave in keeping with the verse "to follow the many," he wrestled with the question of how could he drink with his head bare? However, a scholar can always find a solution: he covered his head with the hem of his capote and handed his hat to the Proletarian, like the man who says, "what can I do, it is the decree of the Almighty . . . ." The non-believer, of course, or as we called him, the Atheist, poked fun at the Orthodox, accused him of hypocrisy and religious pretension, but the Orthodox paid no attention to him, made the proper blessing over milk, and drank it down to the last drop and was, as the Americans say, "all right!"

Later, after everyone had slaked his thirst with milk, the proletarian sat himself down on the ground under one of the goats and simply drank from its teats. The sight shook us, and we turned away and sat down on the fragrant grass and launched into a lively discussion about the island on which we found ourselves. One tried to prove that in view of the fact that the goats were not afraid of us, one must conclude that there are people on the island. A second came to the opposite conclusion: precisely because the goats were not afraid of us and let us milk them it was evident that they had never seen people at all—and proof for this conclusion was the silly look on their faces when they looked at us.

In any case, we were all pleased, all satisfied, and all many times better off than poor lonely Robinson Crusoe was. We had food—sweet bananas and ripe nuts. We had drink—streaming water and fresh goat milk. And we did not have to work ourselves, as poor Robinson Crusoe did—we had our own worker, our Proletarian, who tired himself out in our behalf, did not let any one raise a finger, and even asked us not to complain about him. In the morning he would milk the goats (after a while they grew so accustomed to us that they did not wait for us to come to them but would come to us and wait to be milked), then he would go and pick bananas and nuts and bring back enough for the entire day. In the evening he would pick fresh grass and make our beds on the boulders in the cave. Then he showed us a practical trick: he pounded one stone on another, over and over again, and hacked out a kind of bowl into which he milked the goats, and then another, which he filled with water. In brief, he became our right hand. Everybody gave him jobs to do, and he glowed with pleasure when someone asked him to do something because—as he said—he was accustomed to work. . . .

Yes, it is all a matter of what one is accustomed to. For example, we thirteen Robinson Crusoes on the Island grew accustomed to the fact that when we got up in the morning and emerged from the cave we would find milk, bananas, and nuts all ready for us. It was all prepared for us by the worker (the Proletarian), and if something was missing we would tell him and he would immediately provide it. Otherwise, he would be reprimanded and chastised as a lesson for the future. He would accept the reprimand humbly, in silence.

Note that despite his simplicity, he understood that not one of us was like him: we were not created to do hard work, our work was refined work, brainwork, head-work. Every day we walked about the island exploring it, looking for people, investigating where we were, trying to get to know the sea before us and the surrounding lands, in hopes that we might find some populated place and thus be saved, or be picked up by a passing ship, or be saved by one of those miracles that do happen in our world.

And so days passed, and weeks and months—and there was no salvation! We met no one. We lost all hope, and we decided to settle there permanently, to create a community, establish a culture, pass laws, establish a division of labor with each one assigned a task, adopt a constitution and fix procedures for a division of the wealth so that each one would know what was his. In a word: to set up a government, a state, a kingdom, a constitution, or perhaps a republic. And so we set to work with great enthusiasm and laid the corner-stone for our republic, the first Jewish republic on earth. But it is much easier to talk about doing something than to do it. I therefore ask my reader to gird himself with patience until the next tale.

iv
Thirteen Colonies

Wise folk who study the nature of beast and fowl discovered long ago that the most ungrateful creature in the world is man. Take us for example, the thirteen

Robinson Crusoes on Thirteen Island. What were we short of? For whose sake did the bright sun shine? On whom did the clear sky look down? For whom was the green grass made? Or the trees blossom? The stream flow? The birds sing? The sea roar? For whom had God sent the goats to be milked? And the caves— why had God provided them? Wasn't it so that we should protect ourselves from the heat by day and from the cold by night? And yet we were dissatisfied, terribly dissatisfied! Let me picture a morning with our Thirteen.

Rose early. Left the cave. Washed. Our workman (the Proletarian) came over, looking very pleased with himself, to say that breakfast was ready. The table was a huge stone that our Proletarian had dug up somewhere. Round underneath and flat on top, as though someone had used a plane on it. Our Proletarian must have worked very hard to place this stone where he wanted it. Then he had gone hunting for some smaller stones for us to sit on. He hadn't long to look for them. Our island was full of stones. He collected thirteen stones and worked on them till he had fashioned thirteen chairs for us, which he placed all round the table. He wouldn't let any of us help him. Never! Work, he said, was his job. "I'm used to it. I can do it!"

"Everybody should work. Every man is obliged to work." That's what the Socialist in our party said. He made quite a speech about it, developing a whole theory of social life. Every man, he insisted, is bound to work for his own needs. Our Proletarian listened, and then with a self-effacing smile, he said: "If you won't mind my saying so, it seems to me that work and work are not always the same. There is work, and there are workers. One works with his hands, another with his head, brain-work."

What can you do with a man who has made up his mind about these things? When did our Proletarian do all this work? We didn't know. He was a quick worker. By the time we got up in the morning, he'd got everything ready. Water in the basins that he had made out of stone, goats' milk he had milked for us ready to drink, bananas and nuts and blackberries that he had found in the forest.

It was a sight to see us, thirteen Robinson Crusoes on our island, walking single file towards our table—first Madam, the only woman on our island, with the Capitalist next, the man who considers himself the most elegant gentleman in our colony. Following him the Atheist, the Orthodox Jew, the Zionist, the Territorialist, the Socialist, the Nationalist, the Assimilationist, the Idealist, the Materialist, and after them all, I, the Writer, and behind me, last of all, the Proletarian. We settled ourselves, all thirteen of us, round our big table, on our primitive chairs, and we ate and drank and talked, discussed all sorts of things, religious, social, political. Each of us spoke his mind freely and frankly. And everyone's opinion was the complete opposite of the other man's. Thirteen people, thirteen opinions. Of course, each of us would have liked all of us to adopt his opinion, for each of us was convinced that his was the right opinion. It often lead to a clash and sometimes to an unpleasant scene. We said nasty things to each other, spiteful remarks. We were sometimes very rude. We were fed up, were on each other's nerves, sick and tired each of all the rest. We went out of our way to avoid each other. We got ideas about breaking away from the others, setting up separate groups, spreading out to cover the whole island, so that each of us would have his own separate corner. Thirteen people, thirteen corners.

Everybody liked the idea of breaking up and spreading out. We spoke about it at first as an idea, which veiled words. For instance—wouldn't it be nice if we could arrange things in this way? Presently we found ourselves speaking about it openly, without disguise—a separate "homeland" for each of us. Thirteen people, thirteen homelands.

"If you don't mind," said our Proletarian, in his usual apologetic way, "if you don't mind, I have a suggestion. This hill here is big enough, with caves enough for us all. They can accommodate not only thirteen people, but thirteen whole families. If you will allow me, I will place a separate stone at each cave to show which is whose."

This was followed by a short discussion, lasting no more than a few hours. For each of us had to explain his attitude. Finally the suggestion made by the Proletarian was adopted, and everybody was satisfied, even the Proletarian himself. It turned out that he too had got sick of us. Which was not at all surprising, for each of us had his own whims and fancies. One wanted a lot of sun. Another wanted shade. One insisted that his share of goat's milk must be fresh and warm, just milked. Another demanded that his should be cool. One wanted his bananas skinned. Another wanted the skin on. The same with our sleeping arrangements. One liked a lot of soft grass under him. And over him. The other wanted it hard and high under his head. Madam had the woman's privilege of capriciousness. Which is not a bad thing. As long as it isn't over-done. What Madam particularly wanted was a bunch of freshly picked flowers on her table every morning. If it wasn't there one day, she sulked, wouldn't say a word to anyone. And when she sulked, the very ground under us sulked as well and so did the forest and the birds in the forest. And so every one of us sulked too, turned his face away, and detested his companions even more than before.

So it is easy to understand the sort of life we had, and how glad we were to settle in, each of us in his own cave, in his own territory. Thirteen people, thirteen territories. The largest territory went, naturally to the Capitalist. He, our millionaire, was brought up, so he said, to sit comfortably, with plenty of room. It wasn't his fault, he explained, but he had been used to it from child-hood, everything big and bright. Large, comfortable rooms. The smallest terri-tory fell to the Proletarian. For when did he sit around in his cave? From early morning to late at night he was outside, working. "When one sleeps only a few hours at night, there's little difference where one sleeps," he said. "I slept no better at home."

Too much work didn't come to him either, except the cleaning. So far he had only one cave to clean. Now he had thirteen caves. To sweep, to put sand down by day. And by night to bed down with grass, for each according to his liking, to his taste. A bit of luck for him, at least, that he didn't have to lay a different table for each of us. It might easily have been thirteen separate tables. After a lot of bitter and heated arguments we decided that the big table should stay as one table, a general dining room on God's earth, under God's heaven. The best place where all thirteen of us could see each other every day at a fixed time in the morning and in the evening.

Strange! When we all sat together, all thirteen, in one territory, we hated each other. Then when we separated, and each had his own separate territory, we began to long for each other, to hanker for each other, impatient for the morning when we all got together, all the thirteen, round one table. And when we were together, we argued, lost our tempers, found fault, swore and cursed, reproached each other, leading to open quarreling and wanting to get away from the whole stupid crowd. Till we came to the conclusion that the only way left to us was to divide up our island into so many separate colonies. Thirteen people, thirteen colonies.

The first to propose separate colonies, and thus introduce private property, was the Capitalist. He had practical experience of this, he told us, quoting examples to show how much better it would be for us all on our island if each of us knew that he was the owner of his little corner, his own bit of land, his own bit of forest, his own animals (the goats).

In a word, the Capitalist concluded, property is the perpetum mobile. Without property no progress is possible.

"You're right!" the religious Jew exclaimed, a typical Litvak, with a scruffy thick beard and a paunch. "Our Talmudic sages," he went on, "said that every man is bound to look after his well-being in this world. Every Jew should build a house, plant a garden, establish a home. We see this in our father Noah."

And our Orthodox Jew went on quoting text after text, and parable after parable, till our Atheist roused himself, brushed aside all the texts and the parables, and said he agreed with the Capitalist, but from the standpoint of convenience. "Man," said he, "was created from the earth. So he must organize himself on this earth."

"A clear text that!" cried the Orthodox Jew. "From the earth you were taken."

That started an argument between the Idealist and the Materialist. The Idealist said he agreed with the Capitalist on idealist grounds. The Materialist said he too agreed with the Capitalist, but from the materialist standpoint. Next to claim the right to speak were the Zionist and the Territorialist. Two young intellectual hotheads.

"Give me a chance to speak," said the Zionist. "If I am not mistaken, we are now talking about land, about community settlement, about colonization. I don't understand how Jews can speak of any land other than Palestine! How can one talk about community settlement and about Yishuv, and not about Yishuv

Eretz Israel? How can Jews go to colonize an alien land when the land of our forefathers lies idle for nearly two thousand years, like a widow, waiting for us, her children, orphaned in the long, dark Golus, scattered and dispersed in all the four corners of the earth!"

"Just as the text says," the Orthodox Jew interrupted, "Rachel weeping for her children!"

"That's lyricism," said the Territorialist. "Sentimentalism. All that about weeping, the poor orphaned child, singing dithyrambics to the Holy Land of our ancestors. That won't achieve anything. Eretz Israel is only a name on paper, found in ancient books. The land itself belongs to others. You'll be singing songs to yourselves, and poor little Israel will still be dragging around in exile among foreign nations who don't want to know of him. Go and hear what is going on in the great big world outside. In Russia, Roumania, Morocco, and other countries. No, little Israel can't wait any longer! He asks for a land! Give him a land! A bit of the earth! A small corner of the earth, small but his own! Where he will not be beaten and knocked about. Where he will not be hunted and persecuted, harassed and oppressed. That will be our Eretz Israel!"

"As the Gemara says, "the Orthodox Jew explained, 'Eretz Israel, the Land of Israel, will spread and expand over all countries!'"

"That is our mission!" cried the Assimilationist, a real Pole of the Mosaic faith. "We Israelites must be in all places, everywhere. We must rub shoulders with other nations, get together, mix and mingle with them, so that we will lead them to the fount of true progress."

"Mix and mingle?" the Nationalist, a Russian Jew, repeated questioningly, looking round at all the others as if to say, "You don't agree with that! Shouldn't you cry out against such a thing? Mix and mingle! Assimilate? Get lost! Was it for this that we suffered through the centuries, driven from land to land, burned at the stake by the Inquisition, to mix and mingle at the end, cease to exist, assimilated? Let our national flag drop from our hands, discard our national dress! Delete the word, Jew! At our age commit suicide! Why don't you say it openly? You want us to do what the Christian missionaries want—get baptized, and you'll be rid of all your troubles! Jews turn Christians and end it all!"

"God forbid!" the Orthodox Jew called out. At that the Socialist stood up, a Russian-Jewish student, wearing a black shirt and speaking a language that was more than half Russian. They were not now, he said, "concerned with religion, nor with nationalism. What we are witnessing here is a social process, a question of colonizing an island, or more correctly forming a state, according to the ancient rules and customs, based on the principle of property." That's how the student started very heatedly to set out his theory about property, emphasizing that though he was a Socialist, not an Anarchist, he could demonstrate to us, with the support of the greatest authorities, that property is robbery. The word property must be expunged from the dictionary. "Hurrah for Socialism!"

"That's right!" the Orthodox Jew chimed in. "It's written categorically, 'Your gold and silver are mine!' So God said."

Then when all the others had spoken to the full, I rose and said it seemed to me that the question of colonizing our island had been sufficiently ventilated. In such cases it was customary, among people who knew these things, to take a vote. Would all in favor of colonization raise their hand?

But here we had unexpectedly hit against a hard rock. We had, for the first time in our island history, encountered the woman question; and it started a new series of heated discussions. There were some of us who held that only we twelve men on the island were entitled to vote. Others spoke up strongly for women's rights. Especially the Atheist. He was, he said, a free American citizen, and he stood firm as steel for women's emancipation!

"Mister Chairman, lady and gentlemen," the American Atheist started his speech, in the big American way. "In no country in the world are women so emancipated, enjoying all equal rights, just like men, as with us in the United States of America. There are parts of our country where women share freely in all business concerns, in all stages of human endeavor. Our first law is Ladies First. I want to tell you a fact, something that happened to us in America. No bluffing! It's straightforward fact, taken from the history of the United States. It was in 1851. Anyone who doesn't want to hear about it is free to leave. Shall I tell the story, or not?"

"Go on! Tell us!"

"Very well. It was in the year 1851, in the month of July, in our real hot period, over a hundred thousand women fighting for women's rights assembled in Washington, to give their opinion about hundreds and thousands of ideas for new coats for women, which would not be much different in appearance from men's coats. All the garments were rejected, with a single exception. It was not invented by a "lady," but by a "gentleman," and he was not even a tailor, only a simple butcher. He presented a jacket, not particularly unusual, with a pair of baggy trousers, forgive me for mentioning the unmentionables. And the trousers, excuse me for mentioning them, attracted the attention of one of the women there, Mrs. Amelia Bloomer, and the baggy trousers, please forgive me, were named after her, bloomers. There was an outcry against the bloomers. Every woman who dared to wear them was in danger of being lynched. With the result that the president of the United States of America had to issue a manifesto ordering all emancipated women not to wear bloomers."

Immediate comment came from the Capitalist, who had, unbidden, assumed the role of chairman at all our meetings. "I think," he said, "that a gentleman like you would be more delicate with what you say in the presence of a lady."

The American Atheist went red in the face right up to his ears. The interruption had visibly upset him. But he went on with his speech.

"All right! All right! Lady and gentlemen! I could tell you thousands of such facts in the history of the United States of America, to show you how high the standing is that we give to our women. But since Mr. Chairman interrupted me, and since I don't want to hold up the vote, I'll leave all that for another time and end my speech with the hope that we will not have to bow our heads in shame. Lady and gentlemen, it would indeed be shameful if we in this free territory would not recognize our ladies as our equals, with equal rights, the same as us. What would the press say? What would Europe say? What would the world say? They would point the finger of scorn at us! Don't let yourselves be influenced by those hypocrites who hold fast to the Bible and won't see what the Bible says about Eve, the first woman, that she is 'bone of our bone and flesh of our flesh.'"

That was the end of the Atheist's speech, for which he received long and loud applause, and then we proceeded to the vote. By ballot. About colonizing. Should we divide our Thirteen Island into thirteen separate colonies or settlements? The result was just what we wanted: The great majority voted for. Twelve hands were raised in favor. Only one did not raise his hand. So we had twelve yes-sayers and only one who said no. Only that did not end the work of organizing our society. There was still much to do on our Thirteen Island.

The one and only no-sayer was the Zionist.

v
Thirteen United States

Anyone with a knowledge of cultural history and the evolution of human society will not be surprised that we thirteen Robinson Crusoes on our Thirteen Island wanted to divide up our possessions. That's what our forefathers did. First, when they were nomads. Finding pasture for their cattle, wandering free with their sheep and oxen through forests and fields. Later, when they began to settle on the land, when they took up agriculture—that was when the quarreling started, with armed raids, with bloodshed, with wars. Everyone wanted to grab more and more. The one who was stronger won. We thirteen Robinson Crusoes, too, were at first nomads, feeding our goats on the hill, living on bananas and nuts that grew on trees. And we were content. It was later, when this way of life palled on us, that we began to think of settling down, organizing a community, colonizing our territory, dividing up the earth, the forest, the trees, the livestock (the goats) and all else that we had. The difference was that our forefathers in times of old did it with force, with bloodshed and war. We managed, thank God, without fighting, without wars, without bloodshed. We had no enmity, no resentment, no casting lots to divide the land among the tribes. Like Moses. There was nothing for us to quarrel about. We had plenty. We were not short of anything. Each of us had chosen his bit of the hill, his trees, his bananas, his nuts, his goats.

That was how each of us became a settler, possessing everything we needed.

Thirteen settlers. Thirteen living like princes. We were all satisfied with what we had. Previously we had lived one on top of the other. And nothing had pleased us. Now that we had split up, everything became precious to us. Each of us had grown to love his bit of land, his colony, his territory, his piece of forest, his trees, his goats, his cave. Each of us liked the idea of eating his own bananas, cracking his own nuts, drinking his own goat's milk. Do you know what I'll tell you? There is something very sweet in having possessions. Let our Socialist fume as much as he likes! I had time enough to keep an eye on him, as well as on the others, all the thirteen Robinson Crusoes on our Thirteen Island, to study each one's character, the good points and the bad. I had noticed something strange about our Socialist, the one who kept telling us, backed with the most famous authorities, that property is robbery. This same Socialist, if he caught someone straying by mistake into his clump of trees and helping himself to his bananas, he would forget all his Communist ideas, and give the intruder a proper telling off.

Indeed, dear friends, say what you will, theory and practice are poles apart.

I am myself a good example. In theory I am a great believer in vegetarianism. I am against eating meat. And surely, what can be more repulsive than taking a chicken, for instance, a living creature, innocent of anything, killing it, cutting it up, putting it in the pot, boiling it, and eating it? How am I in this regard any better than a savage?

All of us, all the thirteen Robinson Crusoes on Thirteen Island, were so convinced of our vegetarianism that we swore an oath in case we were ever, with God's help, rescued from the island, we would never eat meat or fish. Never! Yes, indeed, but how we longed for a steak and roast potatoes! I must confess that we were getting fed up with bananas and nuts and goat's milk. We would have gladly given it all up for a freshly baked loaf of bread with garlic rubbed into it, with a bit of herring and an onion. And a plate of chicken soup. There is nothing better than to be a vegetarian, and eat meat once a day!

But that's all dreams. We thirteen Robinson Crusoes were torn away from the wide world by that terrible storm on the sea, and now we must be content with what we have, satisfied with our bananas and nuts and goat's milk for years, for as long as we are destined to go on living here. So that time shouldn't drag too much here, not to let ourselves feel how lonely we are, we concentrated on every little detail of our lives, each in his own hole, or his territory, as we called it, or his colony or possession. Every day we met in a fixed place, where we could sit and talk, a suitable spot, on the hill, under a big tree, sitting on the ground, with flowers before our eyes, and the angry sea teasing us with the thought that over there, on the other side, each of us has a home, parents and children, brothers and sisters, friends and acquaintances, who want us back with them, look who for us, with tears in their eyes. Or maybe they have forgotten us! Every day we met under that tree, talked for a while, or just sat and looked at that angry sea, roaring constantly, the waves speaking to us, and we telling one another for the hundredth time the story of our lives, of our pasts. Each of us repeated a long list, the names of his family. We repeated that list so often, so many times, over and over again, that we all know it by heart.

So we had come, all of us, to this spot, under our tree, all thirteen of us, to consider our situation and to work out a way of ordering our life day by day, politically, socially, and economically. To arrange things so that each of us thirteen would organize himself to be ready, a landed aristocrat, a landowner, independent in himself, and yet all one family, one political power if we should be attacked by savages or wild beasts.

Of course, the idea provoked, as always, a heated discussion. Each of us had his own ideas and plans. Thirteen people, thirteen plans.

The first to produce a plan was the millionaire, the Capitalist, as we called him. Odd! The spirit of capitalism has in our century fastened its iron grip so firmly round the whole world that even we on our Thirteen Island lived under its influence. Always and everywhere, every time there was something to discuss which affects all of us, who was the first to have his say? The Capitalist! He seemed to have been brought up like that, from childhood, to be everywhere first. He took it for granted. Of course, it annoyed some of our people. For instance, the Socialist once made a formal protest. He put to him the old question, "Who made you a ruler over us? Always you take it upon yourself to act as chairman!"

But our Capitalist is a slow, calm, easygoing individual. So he listened to the Socialist with a smile on his lips, then he got up and very politely said, "Here you are! You be chairman!"

That gesture made such a good impression on us that we all (except the Socialist) begged him (the Capitalist) to stay there, in the chair. And to oblige us he stayed.

The plan which the Capitalist submitted to us was very simple—a kind of bourgeois constitution, as the Socialist said, dismissing it. According to the plan all thirteen of us, all the thirteen colonists, would form a state of thirteen provinces, governed by an elected president. The president, as the representative of the people, was to govern all the colonists, to look after their interests, hear their complaints, and judge them according to his reason and his conscience.

The Socialist found this more than he could stomach. He jumped up and started shouting, "Absolutism! Autocracy!"

"What's up!" said the Orthodox Jew. "If you're going to have a state, you must have a ruler. No kingdom without a king! As the text says, 'Behold, the King walketh before thee!'"

"So that you can have someone for whom to say the prayer for royalty at the Sabbath synagogue service!"

"Indeed, yes," the Orthodox Jew retorted. "Our sages said, 'Pray for the welfare of the Ruler, but for the fear thereof men would swallow each other alive!'"

It's worth pointing out that this last intervention by the Orthodox Jew was greeted with laughter from all sides, including even our friend the worker, the Proletarian. There wasn't anyone in our group, apart from the Orthodox Jew, who wanted a monarchy. Very possible that even the Orthodox Jew himself didn't particularly want an autocratic king.

At this point the Atheist from America rose and submitted another plan—that we, all thirteen colonists, would form thirteen separate states. Each colonist would be autonomous, master in his own place. But all thirteen states, meaning all thirteen colonists, would unite, "as thirteen states, as in the United States of America," and we would elect a president, one of us thirteen. A different president every four years. He would be called, "The President of the United States of the First Jewish Republic of the Thirteen Island of Israel."

"That would be fine!" cried the Idealist. "I have dreamed of a Jewish republic for ever so long!"

"Not practical!" the Materialist objected. "It would take up all our time and all our notepaper to write all that long name. Consider it! 'The President of the United States of the First Jewish Republic of Thirteen Island of Israel.' What a rigmarole!"

"Allow me, please!" the only woman among us cut in. "Why must we copy America? As far as I know America is not a modern country. Not up to date. All the fashions come from Paris. So why not the Republic of France? Or the Republic of Switzerland? I was in Switzerland last year. With my late husband. We went everywhere—Zurich, Montreux, Interlaken. We saw Mont Blanc. There is no country like Switzerland in my opinion. Though Nice is a lovely town. And Monte Carlo is beautiful. But if you want to live cheaply and well, go to Switzerland. The best milk. Costs next to nothing!"

"Excuse me, Madam," the Capitalist intervened, "we're not looking for a country for us to live in, but for a state to establish here, on this island of ours.'

The woman went red in the face. She felt that she had made a fool of herself. Let her tongue run away with her. And doing so she had shown us that though she was a modern woman and held herself like a man, she was still a woman.

"Excuse me, gentlemen," she said. "When I speak of Switzerland, I remember my dear dead husband. And I meant to tell you that I would prefer a Federal Republic like Switzerland."

"I don't like your United States of America," the Nationalist said, "nor the Federal Republic of Switzerland. Do you know why? Because it is neither nationalist nor Jewish. We should find a name that will give us a taste of nationalism, that will be Jewish!"

"If it's Jewish you want," said the Zionist, "I propose that we name ourselves after Theodor Herzl."

"Why Herzl?" countered the Territorialist. "Why not Zangwill?"

"Because! Having Herzl as the name, we would call it 'The Herzl Republic'."

"How would Herzl Republic sound?"

"And how would Zangwill Republic sound?"

"Herzl is dead. Zangwill is alive!"

"So what did you want? That Zangwill should be dead as well? May he live to be a hundred and twenty!"

"If you don't mind," the Proletarian interrupted in his quiet modest way. He had just finished preparing a meal of bananas and nuts for the whole group. "If you don't mind, I'll give you my opinion. I'm only an ordinary working man. But it seems to me that we don't need anybody's name. It'll be enough to call it, 'The Jewish Republic,' or 'The First Jewish Republic,' or 'The First Jewish Republic of the Thirteen United States'."

This proposal was so acceptable to us all that we started shouting, "Bravo! Bravo!" The Socialist, delighted that all our talk was about a republic, not a monarchy, jumped up on a big boulder and called out, half in Russian, half in Yiddish:

"Long live the republic, brothers! Love live the proletariat! Cry aloud, shout, brothers! Hurrah!"

And we all joined him, shouting, "Hurrah!"

The next step was that all thirteen of us, representatives of the Thirteen United States, seated ourselves round the table and fell to on the bananas and the nuts and the fresh goat's milk that our Proletarian had prepared for us, and started a long discussion about the future awaiting our First Jewish Republic of the Thirteen United States, and the laws and statutes that we would have to draft, and whom we would have to make our president. All eyes turned involuntarily to our millionaire, our Capitalist; and he felt that all eyes were being turned to him. He straightened up and was about to say something. But the Socialist, the cheeky youngster among us, always in opposition against capitalism and capitalists, stopped him.

"I don't understand," he said, "what you have in mind. We should do what all progressive states do—have elections. Whoever is elected with a majority of votes will be the president."

"So we'll elect a president?"

"Yes, we'll elect a president!"

vi
Thirteen Presidents

Anyone who has traveled the world as I have, will agree with me that humanity is still very far from perfect. The biggest parliaments in the freest countries can't boast that they are anywhere near the political ideal. Look and see how republican France seethes and fumes when they have an election for president. Or take free golden America, the great democratic republic. Good Lord! What a to-do there is in election year! Party conflicts, Tammany bosses, and lots more such nice things that a stranger would never have credited and will never understand. Political warfare waged with such bitterness that people forget that they are human. Brother against brother, father against son! Help us, good God!

So what is new, then, in our Thirteen United States of the Jewish Republic going on a rampage when it came to electing a president? First of all we had to nominate our candidates. Each of us, the thirteen Robinson Crusoes—thirteen colonists, thirteen representatives of the Thirteen United States, naming each one's candidate for president. Of course, we had all the different parties among us, and each party had its own followers, those for and those against. Our Capitalist, for instance, had his own Capitalist party. His colleagues were the Orthodox Jew and the only woman on the island, also the Nationalist, the Idealist, and the Materialist. So he had five supporters in all, campaigning for him all the time. They almost won over the Polish Jew, the Assimilationist. And if they could have captured two or three more supporters the Capitalist would have been elected president. As a last hope they counted on our workman, the Proletarian. In order to gain his support the Capitalist party issued a proclamation pledging their president, the Capitalist, to pursue three aims—to protect property, defend religion, and secure the rights of the workers. This proclamation, which they displayed in all the thirteen colonies of the Thirteen United States, set off a furious attack from the opposition, which meant the Russian-Jewish student, with his black shirt, the Socialist. He stopped at each point in the proclamation, one by one. And in his half-Russian, half-Yiddish he said:

"I want to draw your attention to the insolence of this capitalism, this Capitalist! He wants to defend religion! And to protect the rights and interests of the workers! It sticks in your gullet!"

Then the Socialist went off to look for the Proletarian. He found him busy at work. He was milking the goats for the thirteen colonists. The Socialist started talking to him about the capitalist order of society, which exists everywhere in the world now, and which is oppressive of the working class, the proletariat. He told him that he was involved in this—he was the only one on the island who single-handed did all the work for the whole thirteen colonies. Nobody spoke of it. Nobody came to help him. The Proletarian's answer, in his usual blunt way was, "That is what God created workers for. To work!"

"For themselves! Not for others!" the Socialist cried out and followed on with a long lecture of the division of labor and the abolition of capital. He spoke to him so long and so persuasively till he got the Proletarian's promise that he would under no circumstance vote for the Capitalist.

"And for whom am I to vote?" he asked.

"For yourself!"

The Proletarian lifted his eyebrows. "What do you mean, for myself?"

"Very simple. I will agree to have you as president. I'll be the first to cast my vote for you. The working man! The Proletarian! Long live the common folk! The workers!"

And with those words the Socialist clasped the toilworn hand of the Proletarian and went off to continue his election propaganda in the other colonies of the Thirteen United States.

It is easy to imagine what impression the Socialist's last words left with the Proletarian. He put down the bucket into which he had been milking and laughed, held his sides laughing. He laughed so much that the goats looked at him as though he was mad. Then when he had finished laughing, he sat down on a stone, put his head in his hands, and lost himself in thought. What he was thinking I don't know. Perhaps he dreamed with his simple mind that he, the Proletarian, an ordinary working man, was indeed really president of all the Thirteen United States of the First Jewish Republic. But who would then do the work? Pick bananas? Gather nuts? Cut the grass? Milk the goats? Keep the colonies clean?

The second strongest party was the American, the Atheist's party. The American issued another proclamation, with huge lettering, like in America. It started with a load of screaming slogans. "Lady and Gentlemen! The First Jewish Republic is in Peril! Save the Honor of the Thirteen United States of the First Jewish Republic of Israel!"

He had on his side the Socialist, the Territorialist, the Idealist, the Materialist. The Assimilationist too had promised him his support, on condition that if he nominated a candidate of the Polish Parliamentary party, the American would support him. The Polish party—the Assimilationist, the Pole of Mosaic Faith, had his own party, the Kolo, consisting of himself, the Idealist, the Materialist, and madam, our only woman on the island. He had won her vote by paying her compliments, telling her that she looked like a real Warsaw lady, and everybody knew that a Warsaw lady was something outstanding. As sure as twice two!

The Polish party's proclamation started with, "High and Well-Born Electors," and ended with the Polish National Anthem, "Poland is not yet Lost!"

This Polish proclamation provoked fierce antagonism from three powerful parties, who joined together for this purpose—the Nationalist, the Zionist, the Territorialist. And these three brought in a fourth—the Orthodox Jew (naturally), and the Idealist, the Proletarian, and they tried hard to win over the one and only woman on the island, to secure seven votes, the majority. It's worth mentioning that each of the partners, in addition to their opposition to the Polish party, ran a campaign at the same time for themselves, each one separately as an individual. It didn't hinder the Zionist in any way, for instance, from coming out against the Territorialist, fighting him, daggers drawn. While the Territorialist, in turn, did all he could to lure everyone away from the Zionist party. I must confess that the war between these two was so bitter that it brought no credit to either of them. They did their utmost.

The Zionist put up a poster with a Shield of David on it and the wording:

"If I forget thee, Jerusalem,

> May my right hand
> Wither!"

The Zionist proclamation listed the names of all the great personalities who had worked for Zionism from the Patriarch Abraham to Ussishkin. It did not forget to mention the Jewish National Fund and our own bank and our Carmel wine, which had made itself world-famous. Nothing was left out. And it ended with Imber's Zionist anthem, Hatikvah.

The Territorialist came out at once with another proclamation carrying the slogan, "The World is Our Home." "Old Dreamer!" it said. "Thousand Year-Old Dreamer! When will You waken from Your Slumber, from Your Golden Dreams, into which the Eternal Dreamers, the Zionists of all Times, have lulled You, rocked You together with Your Children into the Ancient Ghetto!" (a hint at Zangwill's "Children of the Ghetto"). And it all ended with the words, "Seek and You Will Find!"

The elements on whom the Zionist could count were the Nationalist, the Orthodox Jew (naturally), the Idealist, and the Proletarian. There was hope, too, of the one woman on the island, who sided with Zionism only because the Zionist Congresses met in Switzerland (the First in Basel). It brought back memories of her late husband, with whom she had traveled all through Europe. He had died in London. Therefore she cursed this black, smoky, foggy town, with its filthy streets and its automobiles. Though her husband had not died because of London's squalid streets, nor because of its automobiles. Nor because of its fogs. He had died because he was a sick man. And that made her wander off into a story about her late husband and the nature of his illness. Why he had fallen ill, and much more, on and on.

I hope my readers will forgive me, but I must make a very necessary digression at this point. The woman who held herself like a man, had nevertheless, deep inside her, a flood of talk that never seemed to stop—like all women. But that only by the way. What really matters, what is important is the election campaign as it was reflected in our Thirteen United States of the First Jewish Republic.

The Territorialist had very poor prospects of success. He had on his side only the Atheist, the Assimilationist, and the Materialist. The Territorialist kept hanging round the woman, but he got very little out of it. She was more inclined to Zionism, for the reason I have given below. So the Territorialist saw things looking very grim for him. And he went for the Orthodox Jew, argued with him, persuaded him that the Territorialists keep the Sabbath no less than the Zionists, and if there was any hope of a Jewish autonomy, the Territorialists would achieve it before the Zionists, because they had the sympathy of the richest people and the most outstanding Christian opinion. The Zionist saw the Territorialist too much in a huddle with the Orthodox Jew, and as he passed them together, he dropped a remark, "What about mixed marriages?"

Nobody will be surprised if I now reveal a secret, that the Orthodox Jew, too, was hankering after the presidency. Why shouldn't he? Why not? He was not a nobody either. And he had his own party, too. You won't guess who his party were! The Nationalist was somewhat on his side. But his strongest support came from the woman. You didn't expect that, did you? You wouldn't have guessed? He had won her vote by calculating for her the exact day to correspond with the anniversary of her husband's death in the Hebrew calendar, his Yahrzeit. And on top of that he had won over the Proletarian. By talking to him about God and the next world and hell and Paradise. He had almost completed his catch when the cheeky fellow, the Socialist, got wind of it and joined up with the Atheist, and they launched a combined operation against the black forces of clericalism. "Down with the Black Reactionaries!" they shouted, and all the progressive elements shouted with them.

At this point I must say a few words about myself. You wonder why if everybody did, I didn't put myself up as well as a presidential candidate. First of all, as a writer I wanted to keep away from the political hurly-burly. Secondly, I admit that I saw clearly that I stood less chance of election than any of the other candidates. I am not easily taken in, to go thinking more of myself than I am. I know my colleagues detest me (nobody likes a writer, especially a humorous writer, who laughs at you and makes others laugh at you). True enough, they all made a fuss of me, paid me compliments, even those who haven't read me. I know it's all false. They flatter me because they are afraid of me. They are afraid of me writing them up in my stories. They like me writing about other people. Not themselves! So in short, I withdrew my candidature.

The end of it was that when it came to electing a president for the Thirteen United States of the First Jewish Republic, the voting list contained the names of all but one of the thirteen representatives of all the Thirteen United States. Then one of us stood up (note that I am not saying I was the one. I reckon the reader will himself realize who it was) and addressed the gathering, as follows:

Lady and Gentlemen, it is almost two thousand years since we lost our own country, since we ceased to exist as a state. Have we in that time ceased to be a People? No! By what force have we maintained ourselves until now? I don't know! By what force will we continue further? I don't know! Where till now was our territory? Where till now was our Fatherland? Where till now was our home? I'll tell you! Our territory was ourselves. Our Fatherland is our history. Our home is the great social ideal that the earlier prophets gave birth to and the later prophets preached, and their fulfillment will come in God's good time when Messiah arrives. The fact that each of us thirteen wants to be president of our United States indicates that none of us thirteen wants to give in, to submit, to yield to another. There's a Yiddish saying, "You're no moneybags, and I'm no pauper." Brothers! There are thirteen of us here. We were thirteen on the boat. Thirteen were brought here by the sea. Thirteen were cast out on this shore, on this Thirteen Island, to found thirteen colonies, Thirteen United States. I ask myself, why shouldn't each of us be president in his own state? Thirteen emigrants, thirteen Robinson Crusoes, thirteen colonists, thirteen representatives of thirteen United States. Long live the thirteen presidents of the Thirteen United States of the First Jewish Republic! Hurrah!"

"Hurrah!" everybody responded. With one exception, the Socialist student, who shouted, "Hurrah for equality!"

That was how the assembly ended. And we left our Political Club till tomorrow. We now had no more before us than to draft a constitution or laws and statutes for our United States. This should raise hope in our readers that very soon, in God's good time, we will be finished with our descriptions of the First Jewish Republic.

vii
Thirteen Constitutions

"A politician is a drunkard." So said Napoleon Bonaparte. Or Prince Bismarck. Or some other great man. "Go into politics. Give up your business." That was said by a plain, ordinary businessman, who got politics-drunk, drank with all the drunkards and became a drunkard himself, plain and simple. I endorse the statement fully, give you both my hands on it, whether Napoleon said it, or Bismarck did, or the ordinary businessman.

Let us consider our situation once again—thirteen people, thirteen travelers, thirteen different persons with thirteen different occupations, set out on their travels, thirteen different persons on their travels, in different directions on the same one boat. There is a sudden storm which breaks the ship in bits. The sea snatches them up and casts them out, all thirteen of them, on this our island, where they find everything is good—first, caves where to shelter from the sun by day and from the cold by night; secondly, trees growing bananas and trees growing nuts; thirdly, a crystal clear flowing stream; fourthly, a whole herd of goats, who let themselves be milked. Looks as if these thirteen Robinson Crusoes have nothing to grumble about. What's wrong, if there is food and drink, and not much work to do. The air here is better than in the best spa. There's the sea to bathe in. There's a forest to walk in. There are hills to climb. Flowers to delight the eye and to spread their aroma. The blue sky over us. And the sun warming us by day, and the moon lighting our way by night. No worry about earning a living. No one to envy. No taxes to pay. No money needed. No one to fear. No army, no police, no wars. No rush and hurry, no turmoil, not a sound from the outside world, no running, no riding, no flying. What do we lack, what are we short of?

Others placed as we are would, like the real Robinson Crusoe, have sent out an expedition to explore our new territory, length and breadth, to see where in the world we are, and what we have to do. No! What we decide is to colonize the land, to divide it up into thirteen separate colonies, to settle in thirteen United States, to elect thirteen presidents, and to work out a suitable constitution for the Thirteen United States of the First Jewish Republic. In short, what we did was to decide to go into politics! What else? That's how God made the world! Or rather, the people in the world. That they should never be content with what they have. They should always strive for more, further, higher, and better. Learned men call this progress and say the world couldn't exist without it. I don't want to vie with anyone. I certainly don't want to polemicize with learned men. They say it's progress. They, no doubt, know better. I only give the facts.

So it was left at that—we thirteen elected presidents of the Thirteen United States of the First Jewish Republic would all of us together meet at a certain time at a certain place, in our Political Club, that is, under a tree, on the hill on our Thirteen Island, and there we would work out our constitution, the basic laws of the First Constitution of the Thirteen United States of the First Jewish Republic. And naturally, when each of us arrived at the appointed time, in our Political Club, we brought with us each our own platform, our own constitution.

The first speaker at our meeting was the Capitalist. He came ready prepared with a project of strange, absurd "Freedoms," which I reproduce here exactly as they were presented to us at our meeting in the Political Club. Here they are:

1. All citizens of the Thirteen United States of the First Jewish Republic are recognized as free citizens.
2. The free citizens of the Thirteen United States are divided into three free classes: first class, second class, and third class.
3. Citizens of the first class are free to eat and drink and sleep.
4. Citizens of the second class are free at any time to entertain the citizens of the first class with conversation, telling short stories, jokes, or whatever they can. In a word, the citizens of the second class are free to see that the citizens of the first class will always find conditions agreeable.
5. The citizens of the third class are free to work for the citizens of the first class and second class.
6. The citizens of the third class may freely state their views whenever they are asked to do so.
7. If they are short of anything, or they need advice, they are free to turn to the citizens of the first or the second class.
8. Should they be dissatisfied with anything, they are free to think what they wish, and so forth.

Of course, the opposition howled down this bourgeois plan. Opposition means here the student with his black shirt, or the Socialist, as we called him. He also went for the "hypocritical" plan submitted by the Orthodox Jew, who had made his first point "the Holy Sabbath." He rejected all the other plans: all equally bad. Each had faults. This was too nationalist. That too materialist. The two constitutions submitted by the Zionist and the Territorialist were both equally bad. And he presented his own Socialist project, drawn up out of all the best bits in the best constitutions of Europe and America.

Alas, his project was also rejected. Not because it was so bad, but because each of the Thirteen United States wanted its own constitution to be the one adopted. Till it came to me, the writer.

The reader has more than once had the opportunity to convince himself that I am not a man given to boasting. But when one is writing a true story, not some sort of invention, one must not misrepresent the facts. I must tell you at once that my project was adopted with enthusiasm, with applause. Not because it was so original. For quite another reason. I had stumbled, if you please, on a secret in the popular voice. If you want to be popular in the world, you must keep in with the popular voice. Not to flatter anyone, but neither to attack anyone, not to hurt anyone's self-esteem. Believe me, my good friends, I speak from experience, from what I saw and heard during the whole time I spent in the Thirteen United States of the First Jewish Republic. After long and protracted thought I came to the conclusion that the more you want to push an idea of yours, the more you must adopt the other man's idea. And if you take it into your heart to fight for the idea, you should know that you'll only get your bones broken for your pains, and you will make enemies of the whole world.

So what, all in all, what was my project? Simply that all the projects of all the presidents of all the Thirteen United States are good, fine, right, and that we are obliged to accept them all. But since it is impossible to adopt thirteen constitutions, I propose herewith that we take one point out of each project and make of it a mixture, a sort of fruit salad, a tutti-frutti of constitutions. This very original project was so acceptable to all, that not only was I showered with applause, but everyone had to come up separately to shake my hand and thank me for what I had done for the Thirteen United States of the First Jewish Republic. One even, I think it was the Idealist, fell on my neck and kissed me, and if I saw rightly, there were tears in his eyes. Madam too, the only woman on our island, came over to me, smiling, and asked if I think long about my ideas, or do they spring from my head spontaneously, instantaneously. I said that when an idea occurs to me, I consider it first from all aspects, and only after I have done that, it bursts out of me, impromptu. Madam was highly satisfied, it seems, with my answer. She gave me a charming smile, showing at the same time her dazzling white teeth, made by the best dentist in Paris.

There was one thing that remained to be done now—to put the mixture, the tutti-frutti of all the thirteen constitutions on paper, to have it made public in a manifesto, or announcement. Who was to write the manifesto, or the announcement? Naturally I, for wasn't I the only writer in the Thirteen United States of the First Republic?

They allowed me time—three whole days in which to do it. We mustn't load too much on one man, they said. Before we dispersed, we ate bananas and nuts and washed them down with goat's milk that had all been prepared by our Proletarian. And meanwhile, as we munched and drank, we listened to more speeches. This time the first speaker was again the Capitalist. He was followed by the American, the Atheist, as we called him. In his speech he drew a parallel between us, with our search for a constitution, and the colonists of the United States of America. He concluded with these words—"Lady and Gentlemen, I give you the toast of the United States of the First Jewish Republic of the Thirteen Island of Israel."

After him came speeches from several other presidents, representatives of the Thirteen United States, each, of course, setting out his particular point of view, the Zionist from the Zionist position, the Territorialist from his position, each finding what he was looking for. The Assimilationist, for instance, the Pole of the Mosaic Faith, informed his noble-born, highly-esteemed colleagues that he was very happy now because the Constitution of our Thirteen United States reminded him of the ancient Polish Sejm and the noble legislation it promulgated. This did not hinder the Nationalist from drinking at the fount of the Jewish national idea, which illuminates our constitution. The last speaker was the Proletarian. Then when everybody rose, and we were all about to go home, each under his own vine tree and under his own fig tree, it suddenly occurred to me to ask the gathering in what language the manifesto or announcement of our constitution should be written.

It was like a stone dropped into water, making ripples that grow and expand endlessly, ripple after ripple. The question I dropped so innocently raised endless ripples—a storm, conflict, uproar and shouting that reached to high heaven.

Tomorrow I'll tell you what happened with the language question.

viii
Thirteen Languages

The Bible tells a story about people who tried to build a tower with its top in heaven, and were punished by God, who confounded their languages so that they did not understand one another's speech. That is what happened with us, the thirteen Robinson Crusoes on our Thirteen Island. Seems to me that thirteen people belonging to one nation, even if they come from different countries, might have one language in common, their own language. I imagine thirteen children of one father who left their father's house, settled in different countries, and at some later date returned home. How would they understand each other if not in their mother tongue, the original language of their old home? They would surely not resort to such madness as trying to speak to one another in thirteen different languages, each one separately. Is it possible that each one should have to understand all thirteen languages?

Such were the sad thoughts that came to my mind at that time, when we were all busy with the question—in what language to write the Constitution of the Thirteen United States of the First Jewish Republic?

The first speaker, as always, was our Capitalist, a Jew of the so-called German Yahudim. He said he was surprised that we had made an issue of the language question. "Who didn't know," he asked us, "that our language was and will be the pure, beautiful, ancient, rich German language? How could we speak at all if not in German?" That brought his sworn antagonist, the Socialist, the Russian-Jewish student with his black shirt, jumping to his feet, to intervene with his queer mixture of Yiddish and Russian words. He was, of course, all for Russian. He was sure that the majority of those present would agree to use Russian. Sure as twice two.

"Excuse me!" cried the Assimilationist. He was the Pole of the Mosaic Faith. "I protest," he declared, "against using the language of the Muscovites. I ask my colleague presidents to take my advice and to use the language of Mickiewicz who wrote *Pan Tadeusz.*"

"Merci beaucoup," intervened Madam, the solitary woman on our island. "Who will understand your Mickiewicz language? Our language must be French. The language of diplomacy. Everywhere you go in high society, the language everybody uses is French."

The American Atheist started off again with "Lady and Gentlemen! I want to ask you to excuse me," he went on, "for taking up your time again and bringing in statistics. We have a saying in America, 'Time is money.' Lady and Gentlemen, what is the most widely used language in the world? English, of course! English is spoken by six hundred million people in the United States of America!"

"Where do you get your six hundred million from? As far as I remember my geography, the figure is no more than—"

That interruption came from one of us. I think it was me. The American took it calmly. In no way abashed, without any sign of discomfiture, even with a self-assured smile, he turned to me:

"Excuse me, Mister! The best thing you can do with your geography book is to throw it into the sea. It knows as much as you know! Where was it published? Europe or America?"

All the time God has been dealing with impudent, cheeky youngsters, he hasn't had one like this to deal with. I turned my head away with shame, for all eyes were turned on me, and every face had an amused grin on it. There was nothing I could do but bite my lip and shut up.

And all this time the American gentleman was going on unperturbed with his statistical speech, trotting out his millions. According to him there should be a billion two hundred million people living on this earth, of whom English-speaking Americans count six hundred million. On top of this there were four hundred million English speakers in England, with eight hundred million in India, three hundred million in Australia, and two hundred million in various countries in Europe and elsewhere, making a total of nearly as many English speakers as there are people as a whole throughout the world. Then, having come to the end of his statistical calculation, he turned to us all, and speaking with great pathos, said:

"Name any other language in the wide world that has a Shakespeare, as we have, or a Milton, a Byron! Lady and Gentlemen, it would be only right that we, the thirteen presidents of the United States of the First Republic of Israel should recognize English as our national and our political language."

"National language!" the Nationalist jumped up, speaking with passion and waving his arms about. "It's a shame and a disgrace! How can Jews propose in our own territory that we should use a foreign language when we have such a beautiful, ancient, holy language as Hebrew! Isn't it absurd that Jews should get worked up about foreign writers like Mickiewicz and Milton and Byron and forget our own great poets! What about Isaiah? And Jeremiah! Ezekiel! And Habakuk! Tell me, what sounds better? Me speaking broken Russian? Or saying in English, 'The First State of the First Republic of Israel'? Or saying it in the holy tongue, in Hebrew?"

"I ask you—how long will we still be slaves, with regard only for what others have, not our own? We came here thirteen, cast up by the sea on this shore, thirteen children of one People, of one faith! We have just founded Thirteen United States. Only the good Lord knows how long we are destined to stay here. Why shouldn't we unite all thirteen under one flag? Why shouldn't we all thirteen have one language, our own holy tongue, Hebrew!" We thirteen should all of us have one God, one faith, one Torah, one language, one history, one land!"

"Hedad!" the Zionist called out, and the Idealist and the Orthodox Jew joined in, and all three started singing the Zionist national anthem. And then Madam joined in.

Odd! No one disliked the Hatikvah so intensely as the Territorialist. He simply squirmed. He got up, sat down again, then he rose once more and called out—"My dear colleagues, it is true that the language question is as important as the question of a territory, but it is all the same to us which territory we will have. So the language question, too, is all the same to us. It doesn't matter which language. So I propose that we work out a new language here, a universal language, like Volapuk or Esperanto."

Judging by the "Bravo" cries and the clapping it seemed that the Territorialist's proposal about Volapuk or Esperanto had won our general support. Largely because it meant opening the door to doing something, an undertaking, an enterprise, a job of work. Something to keep us busy—creating a new language, a very engaging and pleasant task. Very possibly we would have sat down that same day, all of us, in our Political Club, under a tree, on the hill, and started work inventing new words with new names. The thought suddenly entered my mind that I ought to say a word now myself. As a matter of fact, being a writer I should have had the first word on this language question. But I'm the sort of man who loves always being last. I go along with the view that both in eating and in speaking it is always best to be the last.

"Rabosei! Friends!" I said, speaking an ordinary Yiddish. "I must admit that I agree with the last speaker, the Territorialist. In fact, I agree with all of you. But I agree more with him than with all the rest. For us Thirteen United States of the First Jewish Republic there is no better, no finer, no more fitting and proper language than Volapuk or Esperanto. I only want to make one remark—that our Volapuk, our own, presents no problem. There is no more work for us to do. It's all finished, ready. I mean our Volapuk, which is Yiddish, our widespread folk tongue, which people call Jargon."

"Jargon? That ugly mixture of gutter speech, that synagogue and Tze'ena Urena talk, ghetto dialect! Thieves' slang!"

This is the sort of language that was now flying at me from all sides. I took it calmly and went on:

"I knew that sort of talk was coming! I was prepared for it. And I don't mind. Do you know why I don't mind it? Because I know that when you have heard what I have to say you will agree that I am right. Let's consider it carefully. What is Volapuk? A language made up of short words. No grammar. Easy to learn. What other language have you with so many short words as you have in what you call Jargon? With a one-syllable word like *et* or *nu* you can produce ever so much meaning, express what you want to say in what would in any other language require a lot of words, a whole dictionary of words. And if the question is one of grammar, what language has a grammar as practical as our Jargon? As for easy to learn, what can be easier than a language you don't need to learn? Isn't it really absurd? Which of us thirteen on our island doesn't understand Yiddish? Everywhere, over the wide world, wherever you go, you can talk to Jews in Yiddish. I myself have traveled the world with Jargon. I've been in America too and, thank God, people laughed—they understood me. So I tell you, Rabosei, our language is Volapuk. Our Yiddish is the Volapuk you want, our folk tongue. Long live the Folk! Long live the folk tongue! Hurrah!"

"Hurrah!" three quarters of our assembly chimed in. Two were silent—the Capitalist and the Assimilationist. The American cheeky one wasn't content only to stay silent. He found it necessary to put his two fingers in his mouth and whistle derisively. But I took no notice. My proposal, "Yiddish-Volapuk," was adopted with applause. The Proletarian came over to me and kept shaking my hand and thanking me.

The next thing was an argument which Jargon we should use. That started something! Everyone of us wanted to speak. As always, the first speaker was the Capitalist. His point was that if it was to be Jargon it should at least be pure, refined, adorned with pure German words. And with proper German pronunciation—not *vos* but *vas*, not *dos* but *das*. It's nicer.

The Socialist butt in with a proposal that everyone should be free to speak the way he likes. He was followed by the Orthodox Jew with a claim that the best Yiddish is that spoken in Lithuania, by the Litvaks (he is himself a Litvak). He took as an example the two words vos and dos. That, he said, was how Litvaks pronounced the words—correctly.

That must have infuriated the Assimilationist (the Pole of the Mosaic Faith) who hotly repudiated the vos and dos pronunciation. He insisted it must be vas and das. And he exploded violently against the Orthodox Jew. Called him all the names in the calendar—Litvak! Ox! Idiot! Nonentity! I never thought so devoted a Pole could also be a Jargonist!

Naturally both sides had adherents and opponents. Some supported the Orthodox Jew, that the true Jargon is that spoken by the Litvaks in Lithuania. Others agreed with the Assimilationist, that the best Jargon is that used in Poland. As was his habit, the Atheist, the impudent American, had to have his say. As he saw it, both the Lithuanian and the Polish Jargon were no good. The only proper Jargon was that used in the United States. "What sort of Jargon," he wanted to know, "is this that you have in Europe? Look at your names for example. You call John, Jonah, Charlie you call Chaim, Abe you call Abraham, and Ike you call Mordecai."

Understandably his speech rubbed all the rest of us the wrong way. Not so much the actual things he said, but his air of superiority, of knowing everything better and despising our way of seeing and doing things, telling us how we ought to speak and write our language, Yiddish. People got very hot under the collar. There was quite an outcry, a lot of shouting, and God knows how it would have ended but for a remarkable happening, something that put a stop to all our discussions and all our activities, and to our whole Thirteen United States.

ix
Thirteen Captives

If I were one man alone on the island, as Robinson Crusoe once was, I could also tell a lot of stories, marvels and miracles, things that never were on land or sea. But now, when we were thirteen Robinson Crusoes on one territory, I had to be completely credible, trustworthy. I must stick to the facts, to what really happened to us. I must be a true reporter, even, perhaps, against my own wishes. For I am sure my colleagues, the other twelve, will be reading my story, and if they catch me spinning a yarn, just inventing things, drawing on my imagination—

In the name of my colleagues, and in my own name, I must now confess that we, the thirteen Robinson Crusoes on Thirteen Island, made a dreadful mistake, committed a terrible error. Behaved stupidly. We fooled ourselves.

As soon as the sea had cast us up and we had come round, we should, all thirteen of us together or each of us separately, have gone out exploring the terrain, its length and breadth; perhaps we would hit on traces of human habitation. We shouldn't have depended on bananas and nuts that grow on trees, and on goat's milk. Thirteen of us together, not just one by himself, would have been a force to reckon with. We should have been on guard.

But what was the good of being sorry now for what we hadn't done? There is an old saying, sense comes with the years. Everybody knows that, but no one acts on it. We thirteen Robinson Crusoes, thirteen representatives of the Thirteen United States of the First Jewish Republic, felt on our island that we were there in possession. We were busy day and night with our organizing work, with drafting a proper constitution. It seemed to us that the whole world— meaning our island, our territory, our little Jewish Republic—the whole world besides us, the thirteen presidents—we felt there was nobody else in the world. The fact is that all people are like that. Each of us imagines that God created the world only for him. For him alone God drew the blue heaven over it, set the sun and the moon and the stars there, sowed the earth with grass, with corn, flowers, and trees, brought in cattle and beasts, fowls and birds in the air, fish in the water, and so on and so on. Nobody wants to know that there is someone else in the world, who too must enjoy these things. People have divided themselves into families, societies, kingdoms, empires, republics, states. And each of them knows only itself and no other. We too, Thirteen United States of the First Jewish Republic, we too locked ourselves away in our little world. Busy, hands and feet, with our own interests, we wouldn't look to see what was happening on the other side of the hill. Which of us could have suspected that there were on the other side of the hill settlements, houses, palaces, hovels, delightful gardens, and gloomy prisons? Which of us could have suspected that on the other side of the hill life flowed like a stream, seething and boiling as in a caldron, wheeling, dealing, facing and chasing, loving and hating, kissing and quarreling, toiling and moiling, rejoicing and lamenting, dancing around and falling sick, praying, blessing and cursing, living and dying—like everywhere in the world.

The first to give us a bang on the head with the news that we were in a place occupied by living people was our Proletarian. He had told us several times that he had heard shots from the other side of the hill. And of course, we laughed at him. The things a plain uneducated man imagines! He came to us once with a story that some of the goats were missing. How had we taken it? Probably in at one ear and out of the other. He came with another story a day or two later. "What is it this time?"

"The missing goats are back."

"Mazel Tov!"

"It isn't that," he said. "They've come back with red ribbons on their horns."

I don't know what there is to laugh at in that. But we all rolled about, fit to burst with laughing. His next complaint was that someone was drinking our milk at night.

"Must be spooks about!" one of us laughed. And all the others laughed with him. "What silly stories this man believes in!"

I don't know why, but the Proletarian had more trust in me than in the rest of us. He confided to me that he heard footsteps in the night. He swore to me that for some days now, first thing in the morning, he saw footprints on the soft grass. Somebody was stealing things from us. Things went missing. Whoever it was drank our milk. Ate half our bananas. Ate all our nuts. He was going to catch that thief, if it meant being up all night watching out for him!

Truth to tell, I didn't believe much either in his stories. And my colleagues believed them even less. We were busy with more important things just then. We were in the midst of our presidential election. My readers will remember from the previous sections how the campaign ended—we all thirteen presidents of our thirteen states had become presidents—thirteen presidents. Yet there was still some dissension. Such an important matter as a presidential election, even if we had cleverly side-stepped the issue by giving the honor to everyone, couldn't pass without leaving some bitterness and anger. Moreover, we still had a final task before us—working out a constitution for the Thirteen United States. And then it would all be done, finished with! We all turned up, each with his platform, with his constitution. Thirteen presidents, thirteen constitutions. But we managed to arrange things. We adopted all thirteen platforms. We took out the essentials from each constitution, the best bits, the finest, the prime. In this way we created a sort of fruit salad, tutti-frutti. Only one small task remained to do—to transfer it to paper. That's when the language question arose. What language should be used to publish the manifesto announcing the constitution? And which language was to be our ruling language? Each of us, naturally, stood up for his own tongue. For irrespective of the fact that we were all thirteen (not to mention it!) Jews, thirteen children of one People, we all came from different countries, had grown up in different cultures and with different languages. It went so far that one of us had proposed we should create a new language, our own language, a kind of Volapuk or Esperanto. Then one of us had got up (that was me) and discovered America. He said we already had a language of our own, Yiddish, which people call Jargon. It roused some small opposition from those who tremble at the word Jargon, to the devil with them! But it got much more support—and Jargon won the day. That's when the real trouble started. Which Jargon? The Litvak Jargon or the Polish Jargon? Or the half-Russian dialect, which is more than half-Goyish words. Or the American Jargon, where out of ten words you can hardly find one which is Jargon—"All members of our society darfen watchen our advertisements in di papers."

Whoever wasn't with us while we were debating the language question in our Political Club under the tree on the hill on our Thirteen Island has missed something! Every one of us was sure that only his point of view was right, that he alone understood, and the others didn't know a thing. Every one of us was ready to tear the others limb from limb, fling them all into the sea. And then it happened. Suddenly—

From somewhere—we had no idea who, what, how—an unknown somebody appeared. And immediately at his side another, and yet another. Strange creatures, big burly fellows with tall hats on their heads and holding long whips. They looked like wild herdsmen. Fierce, angry faces. Long beards. Like wild Turkish Bashi-Bazouks as they are pictured in the pictures you can buy by the dozen.

My readers can imagine what we looked like when we saw these Bashi-

Bazouks. Instinctively we all turned to the only defender we had in our territory—the Proletarian. His whole outfit of weapons were a long stick with some big stones that could easily crack the skull of the biggest Bashi-Bazouk, provided there was only one Bashi-Bazouk, and he let you. What could we do with a whole company of Bashi-Bazouks, wearing tall hats and holding long whips, who had suddenly pounced on us, without warning that they were coming? We did what the great Napoleon did in 1812, when he realized that he had blundered into a mess. Or what Admiral Rozhdestvenski did at Tsushima, when he saw his fleet was in danger. The only difference was that Napoleon and Rozhdestvenski came to their senses when they had already got knocked out, while we, the thirteen presidents of the Thirteen United States, threw down our arms immediately and surrendered ourselves into the hands of the enemy.

The first to speak was, as always, our Capitalist. He turned very courteously to the Bashi-Bazouks, and speaking in his best High German, asked them who were they, and what did they wish. If it was a matter of money, a contribution, he could give them a check on Berlin, Paris, London, St. Petersburg. His entire speech was wasted. It seems the Bashi-Bazouks didn't know German. The Socialist came forward next, the Russian-Jewish student with the black shirt, and he spoke to them in Russian. Short and to the point: "What do you want?"

"Why do you speak to them in that barbaric tongue?" said the American, who was also the Atheist. And he went on in English, repeating the same words, gentlemen and dollars, over and over again.

Then Madam addressed them. In French, of course. She smiled at them ingratiatingly. I don't know what they made of her smile, but it was clear they didn't understand French. After the first few words they cut her short and, pointing to the goats, said something unintelligible to us, in an unknown language. But from their behavior it was clear that they were complaining about us milking their goats.

"Do you know what I'll tell you," said our nationalist. "How do we know that they are not Jews like us, sons of Israel? I once read something about groups of Jews like this in the Caucasus. As for their language, I wouldn't be surprised if it turns out to be some corrupt form of Hebrew. Perhaps you would try them with Hebrew?"

"Sure! Sure!" cried the Zionist and the Orthodox Jew both together. The Nationalist went over to the leader of the Bashi-Bazouks and addressed him with a long passage from the Hebrew prayer book. It seems that the Bashi-Bazouks found our Hebrew as unintelligible as their language was to us. They were as ignorant of Hebrew as an Anglo-Jewish reverend or a small-town Russian state rabbi. They listened to the Hebrew speech to the end, and then they pointed again to the goats. After that they cracked their whips and said: "Heidah!" which we took to mean that we should go. Another time we would have held a meeting to decide who should go first. This time we didn't want to make a long business of it, and incidentally we didn't want to invite another order for us to move on. So we all thirteen captives put on a brave front and followed the Bashi-Bazouks uphill, with the whole herd of goats trailing behind us.

We went, as they say, through forest after forest, each of us full of his own thoughts. What the others thought I can't tell you. What was in my mind was that lovely story I had been reading on the ship—how Captain Coribaba had gone out looking for diamonds and blundered into the Island Kukuroso, where the wild men of the Taratuta Tribe who eat human beings dwell. There is a saying, "Regret is never too late." I am saying this in regard to that delightful and highly interesting story which I have already mentioned as having been written, printed, and published, where they print and publish all good, highly interesting stories, in America. There are people who put no trust in these delightful, highly interesting stories. I confess I was myself one of these. But now when such things could happen to me, to myself, I beat my breast in penitence and regret. From today on I'll believe everything that is written there.

True enough, the Bashi-Bazouks didn't tie us up, didn't put us on the fire to make beefsteak out of us, like those wild men of the Taratuta Tribe, as recorded in the delightful, highly interesting story which was composed, printed, and published in America. It could all have happened. Who prevented them, for example, from turning the Thirteen United States into a roast? From sticking a spear into each of us, right into our hearts, and dancing round us, singing wild songs like those savages of the Taratuta Tribe. Of course, each one of us thanked God every minute, every second, that he had escaped death, that he was still alive. We walked quietly, with bowed heads, not saying a word to one another. We had no idea where they were taking us.

x
The End of the Thirteen

The whole world can't be mad. If the world has assumed that a certain number is a bad thing, there is probably something in it. I know people, for instance, who will not live in a house numbered thirteen. Not for a load of gold. They won't go out of the house on the thirteenth day of the month. Not for any amount. They believe that it is unlucky to have thirteen children. I believe that too. I have proof of it, with what happened to us, how everything went wrong from beginning to end. When we first became acquainted on the ship, there were thirteen of us. Afterwards, in the storm and the shipwreck and when we were cast up on the island, we were the same thirteen. Looking round to see where we were on this seemingly uninhabited island, we were again thirteen Robinson Crusoes, and we had named the place Thirteen Island. We had established thirteen colonies, united them in thirteen states, we had elected thirteen presidents, composed thirteen constitutions in thirteen different languages. And now we were thirteen captives. In a word, any move we made was bound to cause trouble. Wherever we set our foot we came up against that luckless figure thirteen. True enough, we can't know if we would have done better had we been twelve or fourteen. Quite possible, we would have done worse. Gamzu l'Tovah (this too is to the good) is a fine dictum. I could give you example after example of how people kept themselves alive with only this one phrase. It would take too much time however, and I must hurry on to finish the story of the thirteen.

So there we were! We, the thirteen presidents of the Thirteen United States turned into thirteen martyrs. Wild men, Bashi-Bazouks, monstrous beings with big beards and long whips fell on our peaceful colonies, gabbled at us some unintelligible gibberish, and ordered us, by your leave, to walk together with a herd of goats, good friends who had served us loyally on our island by supplying us with milk. We put up no resistance. We went along with them to the place they led us to, quietly, with bowed heads, like the dutiful goats. We didn't speak a word among ourselves. For to whom could we compare ourselves? To the unfortunate princes driven from their kingdom and put into prison. Our sad past lay behind us. Our future was hung over with a black curtain. We didn't know what might happen to us before the sun had set. That was why we were all so sad. It was dark as night. Silent and sad all around us. The only sound was that of our footsteps, the bleating of the goats, and the Bashi-Bazouks cracking their whips, wanting us to move faster. How far we walked like that I can't tell you. Surely not more than five miles, perhaps less; and all the time uphill. All forest and stone. As soon as we got out of the forest on the other side of the hill, we saw a new world, with streets and houses, factories and trains, and people, living people. Deplorable though our state was, we rejoiced at the sight, were ready to fall on each other's necks and kiss each other. Whatever might happen, there was now a living spark of hope in us, that in the end each of us would very soon see our homes and our near and dear ones. We thirteen Robinson Crusoes had grown accustomed to a quiet, peaceful life on the other side of the hill, so that the noise now from the trains and the factories and the people appeared to us wild. It dazzled us, buzzed in our ears, and snapped in our heads. We saw children coming from school, their satchels on their backs, and their books in their hands. It brought tears to our eyes, good tears, tears of joy, of thankfulness. Children! The coming generation! Our youth!

And "our youth," when they saw thirteen prisoners, unknown folk, walking along with a herd of goats and a guard of Bashi-Bazouks, let out a howl, a shriek of derisive laughter, a mock ovation; they followed us all the way, singing and whistling and shouting, "Hurrah!"

Young people everywhere have such a power in them that they attract older people to join them in any prank they are playing. You may be a Tolstoy even, but as soon as you see a crowd of youngsters out on a spree, you stop to look, and before you know where you are, you have been drawn into the circle, and you are one of them. So you can imagine what a wild bunch we had around us

by the time we reached the city square. So we counted ourselves lucky when
we were at last taken into a big courtyard, we and the goats, and the gates were
locked behind us, so that the crowd couldn't follow. We were saved!

They received us very courteously in the courtyard, except that they
searched us for arms, a very natural precaution. When we saw that they were
not treating us in the way Captain Coribaba had been treated in the Island
Kukuruso, where the cannibals of the Taratuta Tribe live, we found our tongues
again and tried staging a protest. The first to do it was our Socialist. Speaking in
his queer mixture of Russian and Yiddish. He said it was a shocking thing they
had done, to fall on us, a group of peaceful citizens. The American gentleman,
who had been quiet as a mouse all day, suddenly turned heroic—in speech. He
informed them, in his confused way, that he was not the same as the others. He
would present a petition to the Ambasssador of the United States of America,
stating that he, an American citizen, had been evicted from his country and
been treated no better than a tramp, or the worst pickpocket. . . . As an
American citizen he would lodge a protest with the State Department.

All our protests, of course, were useless. They took us into what appeared to
be a courthouse. We were surrounded by a group of gendarmes, who also wore
those funny tall hats; and they carried truncheons. I happened to look round,
when one of those truncheons descended on me. I felt it.

In the courtroom they gave us nice, comfortable soft chairs to sit in. Thirteen
of us in thirteen lovely chairs. We were received by an old man, looking very
gentlemanly, with a flower in his buttonhole. This was their president. The
governor of the island. He spoke to us in their mad language, which we couldn't
understand. He repeated the same words three times to us. Apparently asking
a question. And we didn't know what the question was. Finally he pressed a
bell and spoke to one of the gendarmes, who left the room and returned with
someone who turned out to be a linguist, an interpreter. A tiny little darkish
man, with a bald head and glasses and a thin mustache. A real European. He
tried several languages on us. Probably knew more than thirteen languages. He
admitted as much to us himself. Must be a Jew, for who but a Jew would know
so many languages?

It took some time before we understood the linguist and before the linguist
understood us. And of all the languages he knew it so happened that the
language he found easiest was our own Yiddish, Jargon. So he admitted to us.
Because, he said, it contained elements from all the languages in the world.
Take, for instance, the language used here. You would find words in it very
similar to Yiddish. He gave us a number of examples; words in both languages
almost identical. For instance, the word for fire and for frying pan. And another
word, tippish, which with us means fool. So it does here. I don't know what
possessed one of my colleagues, one of the thirteen captives, the Nationalist, to
suddenly stand up for the honor and dignity of our holy tongue, Hebrew. He
had support from two other colleagues, the Zionist and the Orthodox Jew. "It
isn't true!" he cried out. "Tippish is not Yiddish. Tippish is Hebrew!" In the

end, confronted by three to one, our linguist-interpreter climbed down. He said that he knew that tippish is not Yiddish. But it didn't matter. Tippish was still a fool in any language.

It is superfluous to repeat here all the questions that were addressed to us and all our answers to those questions. It would be enough to give the essentials, the essence. We discovered that under the laws of the country we were criminals, on three grounds: (1) we were spies, come to spy out the land; (2) we had taken possession of a part of their territory; (3) we had trapped a herd of goats and used their milk for our purposes.

We had no idea, of course, of the punishment that would be meted out to us for these crimes. But it was clear that it wouldn't be much fun. The worst of it was that they believed us to be spies. Even highly civilized countries deal drastically with spies. There was only one good thing about it—they gave us the right to defend ourselves. And we did all we could, through our linguist interpreter, to tell our whole story, from A to Z—the storm at sea, and our being cast up on the island, with no knowledge that it was inhabited. We didn't know in what country we were. We had no idea of the name. We were like Robinson Crusoe castaways in what seemed a deserted island. Lucky for us that we had found the bananas and the nuts and the goats which had given us milk. Else we would have starved and gone to that land from which there is no return.

That governor of the island listened to our story intently. He made no attempt to interrupt. Then he put to us a whole row of questions for us to answer. I repeat here the questions and the answers, faithfully, exactly.

Governor: Why did you spend all your time on the other side of the hill? Why didn't you explore the country, go a little higher?

We: We didn't know the country.

Governor: What did you occupy yourselves with?

We: We organized our society.

Governor: What was the nature of this organization?

We: We organized ourselves in thirteen colonies, founded Thirteen United States, elected thirteen presidents, drafted thirteen constitutions in thirteen different languages.

Governor: You belong to thirteen different nations? Thirteen different religions?

We: No! We belong, all thirteen of us, to one nation, and we have, all thirteen, one religion. We all serve one God.

Governor: How do you come to have thirteen languages?

We: The fault of our history. We are scattered and dispersed over the whole world. We live in different countries, among different nations, speaking different languages.

Governor: What kind of nation are you? What God do you serve?

We: We are Jews.

Governor: Israelites?

We: Israelites.

Governor: Then you are descended from Abraham, Isaac, and Jacob? It was you
who created the book that is called the Bible? It was you who had a land
named Zion? A king named Solomon? A prophet named Isaiah? A holy
Temple, that the Romans destroyed, and you were driven into exile in all
the four corners of the earth? I have read much, ever so much about you in
our library. We all of us have read your Bible. We hold it holy! Swear to me
on your Bible that all you have told us now is true, and I shall let you go
free!

Of course, we all swore as he asked, all of us, even the American Atheist,
who kept telling us that he didn't believe in God, and the Socialist too, who was
very little of a believer himself. We swore, all of us, that all we had said was
true, not God forbid, exaggerated, and that we were all of us not guilty.

After hearing us swear to the truth of what we had said—even the cheeky
American Atheist—the governor wrote something on a piece of paper. Then he
wrote and read out his decision, after which the linguist-interpreter translated
it for us, word for word:

"I had thirteen aliens brought before me today. They were caught in our
country, on the other side of the hill, with a herd of stolen goats. The charge
against the thirteen consisted of three parts: (1) that they are spies, come to spy
out our land; (2) that they seized our territory without our knowledge; (3) that
they raided our pastures during the night and took away our goats.

"I listened to their arguments through an interpreter, and:

Taking into account that they are descendants of the People of the Bible, who
wander around the world for thousands of years because of their great sins, and
have no Fatherland;

Taking into account that the unhappy wanderers suffered badly in the storm
and were cast up on our territory by the angry sea and assumed that it was an
uninhabited island, and therefore they organized thirteen colonies and a state,
a tiny republic of Thirteen United States, till fate would look down on them,
and they would be seen by a passing ship, or some other miracle would happen;

Taking into account that our silly goats themselves blundered into the area
taken over by the thirteen wanderers, who had no other way of keeping alive
but with the goats' milk and with fruit from our trees;

I find that the thirteen accused emigrants were (1) not spies, (2) seized no
territory of ours, (3) I therefore order that the thirteen accused emigrants are
freed from imprisonment.

Having read out his verdict, the governor ordered us to be taken into an
adjoining room and given good and drink. The linguist-interpreter came with
us. A big, comfortable, bright room, with long tables at which they seated us,
the thirteen emigrants, and told us we could order anything we wanted, each of
us whatever he desired. According to his taste. Naturally, we acted on this
indulgence. Our Capitalist, for instance, wanted a beefsteak. The Orthodox

Jew asked for boiled eggs. The Nationalist asked for chopped liver. The Pole of Mosaic Faith wanted fish prepared in the Jewish (Zydowskie) way. The Zionist called for a bottle of Carmel wine. Our American wanted a couple of sandwiches and a steak and plum pudding. A glass of brandy. And two oranges. Also a bottle of ginger beer and a bottle of lemonade. And a Havana cigar. That was all. So he said. Madam, the only woman in our group, wanted a few biscuits, an ice cream, and some delicatessen.

After the meal they took us to the governor's private room, where he introduced us to his wife, a real grande dame. He told us that he was impressed knowing who we were, the great grandchildren of Abraham, Isaac, and Jacob, the People of the Bible. And here we were offered nuts and bananas which, to tell the truth, we had long got fed up with.

But we nibbled at them, forcing ourselves not to offend our hosts. In fact, we even had a word of praise, which we passed on through our interpreter, for the fine fruit their island grows. Each of us felt it would be only politic for us to pay a compliment or two to the governor and his wife. Several of our colleagues found this paying at compliments so much to their liking that instead of a few words, they ended up with long speeches. Especially our American, who repeated several times over that he considered the governor of this island the finest gentleman in the world, next, of course, to the president of the United States, Franklin D. Roosevelt.

Our American was followed by the Orthodox Jew who urged the governor to come on a visit with his lady to the United States of America, where he would be given a reception such as is given only to the great men of the world. "We, my colleagues and I," he said, "will always bless the governor for his humanitarian approach to us, like a brother." As he had already said, he and his colleagues would always bless the governor and his lady wife and their children.

The interpreter, before translating the remark about children, told us that the governor and his wife appreciated our remarks so far as they were concerned, but unfortunately they had no children.

"Then," the Orthodox Jew declaimed, "then we shall pray for the governor and his wife to be blessed with children."

Next the Territorialist thanked the governor again for his help and his understanding of their plight in what they had thought was an uninhabited island, thinking themselves marooned for life. He asked the interpreter to tell the governor that he, the Territorialist, would be proceeding to the forthcoming Congress of Territorialists, and he would inform the congress of the help and friendship they had received on the island and of the governor's personal kindness. He would submit to the congress his opinion that they could find no better place than this island on which to settle our poor suffering Jewish people. He was full of hope that his colleagues in the territorialist movement, headed by Israel Zangwill, would act on his report and send an expedition to this island to search out the potentialities.

The governor acknowledged the speeches and thanked us for the kind things that had been said about the island. When he came to the Territorialist's speech, he asked the interpreter to explain to us that while he had no objection to immigration, and according to the laws of the island, it was open to everyone who wished to live there, he had to make it clear however that a territorialist settlement would not be feasible. Not, he said, because we have anything against the Jewish People. On the contrary, you have every reason to be proud of your descent from the biblical patriarchs, and that you created the Bible, that you built the holy Temple, had a king like Solomon, and prophets like Isaiah. There were nevertheless real reasons against it—the fact that your land, Eretz Israel, has been given to strangers, and that you wander over the earth for centuries, in exile, scattered and dispersed—it all shows that God does not want you to have your own land, your own territory. You must have sinned terribly against God. And we can't go against God's judgment.

That was how the friendly governor ended his explanation, with a hypocritical smile. Then he ordered one of his men to blindfold us and put us, all thirteen of us, on board a ship sailing for some foreign port.

Afterwards, I was sitting in a corner on the ship, lost in thought about the great God we have, who created this vast world, which has no bit of space, not the smallest corner of it, for his chosen people, Israel.

From Menachem Mendel's Letters to His Wife Sheine Sheindel (1913)

Sheine Sheindel in Kasrielevky to Menachem Mendel in Warsaw

For the favor of the well-beloved, learned, munificent, and distinguished benefactor

First, I have to tell you that we here are all, thank God, in the best of health, please God, to hear the same from you, no worse, for the future.

Secondly, I write to inform you, dearly beloved spouse, that I suffer shame and disgrace because of you. I can't show myself in the street without some cheeky youngsters stopping me, wanting to be told the whereabouts of my husband, the turncoat, who has suddenly been transformed into an Angolanik. They mean the country Angola that you dug up for their good, somewhere at the back of beyond, where you are working out all sorts of projects. They are Zionists, and they are annoyed because you have abandoned Eretz Israel. They say Eretz Israel is a better place, and Eretz Israel, they say, is ours. While Angola is somewhere at the ends of the earth.

They say you have damaged their cause. They were going to give you a letter to Vienna, where there is to be a Zionist Congress. As you are going to Vienna anyway, it would have saved them money, not having to send someone specially. As Mother says—a kosher pot with a kosher spoon! But as you have turned apostate—may they all be apostatized, every mother's son of them, one by one—as you have become an Angolanik, they have been left without a spokesman. Now really, was it necessary, Mendel? Did you need this? I'm only a woman, and I don't know about these things the way you do. But it seems to me—and Mother says the same—that our own is not somebody else's, and someone else's is not our own! But what's the use of my writing to you, poor me! If you get a mad idea into your head, anything they tell you, you say O.K. You take their word for it! Have you been to Angola? Have you seen the place? What makes you praise it to the skies? You listen to everything those go-betweens, the middlemen tell you. Some project they want you to take up. What do those middlemen know? All they want is their fee, their commission for introducing the client. As soon as they pocket the money, they lose interest. And if you have any thought of fooling me and the children and Mother, may she be with us for a long time, into coming with you, put it out of your mind. I

213

tell you here and now, my dear beloved, we're not coming! I'll follow you to the ends of the earth, but not to Angola! Let the rich philanthropists you spoke about in your letters go first! You said they would come there, in God's good time. If they will settle there and get over the early hardships, the birth pangs, and they write to us a letter that everything is good and fine and ready for us to come, then we will begin to consider it, only then and not before. Now, we don't go! Nonsense! Your rich folk will prefer to stay in Yehupetz, in wealth and comfort, or go to Warsaw or Baku, and tell you to go to Angola and do all the hard work, preparing the ground, making it ready for the future settlers. It's easy to learn barbering on somebody else's beard! I'm afraid your Angola and their Eretz Israel will both end up a fiasco, like all your dreams, and the world will stay the way it is. The moneybags in Yehupetz will go on having a good time, may they choke on it, while we here in Kasrielevky will have the same rotten time that we're having all along, cooped up one on top of the other, choked and stifled, aping everything they do in Yehupetz. We've got to the stage when we can say with fair certainty that there isn't a thing in Yehupetz which isn't the very same with us in Kasrielevky.

Sheine Sheindel

Menachem Mendel in Warsaw to His Wife Sheine Sheindel in Kasrielevky

To My Spouse, the dear, wise, and chaste Mrs. Sheine Sheindel,

I want to inform you that I am, thank God, sound in life and limb. May God help us always to hear only good tidings from one another, good news, peace and comfort on all Israel.

Secondly, be advised, my dear spouse, that your Kasrielevky Zionists are very much mistaken if they suppose I have become an apostate, that from being a Zionist I have turned Territorialist. So what? I never was a Zionist, I never was a Territorialist. I always was a Jew, and I shall always remain a Jew. Though I don't wear the Zion emblem, and there is no Shield of David branded on my forehead; yet you fear that I may not be going like all the Zionists to the congress in Vienna. When I hear the word Zion or the word Jerusalem, I am transported! Something catches fire in me, and I am filled with longing for our ancient home and for our state. My soul faints in me for something that is our own, at least a Jewish policeman, or our own Jewish passport with Jewish lettering—"This passport is the property of Mr. Menachem Mendel of Eretz Israel." May we live to see it! And to tell the truth—why fool ourselves? If they gave us thirteen Angolas with eighteen Galvestons and the whole of America, supposing it was all offered to me, we would give it all back for one bit of land in Eretz Israel! Isn't it stupid? What will we do, for instance, with the prayers, "To Jerusalem Thy city return in mercy"? Are we do delete it from our prayer books? No, my dear spouse, there is nothing nearer and dearer to me than

Eretz Israel. But—you will say—all your efforts now for Angola? That is because Angola is offered to us for next to nothing. And at this moment I see no other land anywhere open for Jews. Not one!

My dear, let them find another land for us tomorrow, and I'll write for that land at once, without asking which is better and which is worse, so long as it is a land where we can live—for we are all on fire, and when there is a fire people run. That's the usual way of people. What can you compare it to? To one found lying in a field, near death. Three days without food. And we come and ask him, "Tell me, friend, what would you rather have, meat or milk?" Don't ask him questions! Give him meat, give him milk, anything, but don't let him die of hunger! I wish—can you hear me?—I wish we had enough money, enough to cover the costs, and we would have enough emigrants both for Eretz Israel and for America and for Angola as well. And for some other land on top of it. That's the old trouble again. Fragmenting us, breaking us up into parts. It means being scattered and dispersed among the nations. Yet it's better than sitting around, crowded together, ready to eat each other alive.

In short, let them first get acquainted—your Kasrielevky Zionists—with my project for Angola, and my project for Eretz Israel, and then let them say if I have become an apostate, as they allege. Or if I am not really their own true friend. I'm not going to boast to you the way others do. I don't claim to be a great diplomat. But I am a Jew who is saturated day and night in politics. I sit, as you might say, at the fount, and I meet all sorts of people, and I pick out the best bits from each of them, as they may be of use to me. Take a man, for instance, like Chaskel Kottick. Say what you will about him, and your Kasrielevky smart-alecks may poke as much fun as they like at his organization for aiding poor brides. But I come back to the words of our sages in Ethics of the Fathers—"Who is wise? He who learns from all men." I have picked up from this man much that is of real value. More than I can estimate. You ask me what. I'll tell you.

I learned from Kottick that every project a man has should be put on paper, divided into paragraphs. Each subject a separate paragraph. Everything carefully considered. Weighed and measured, so that no questions come up afterwards, no here or there. My project made for Angola has over a hundred paragraphs. It consists of two parts. The first part is how to run the enterprise, how to settle people on the land, the management. The second part deals with the money side—seeing that the money is there. Impossible, my dear, to recount to you the whole project in full. It takes over twenty foolscap pages, written on both sides. But I can give you a summary, the gist of it, the essentials. And then you will see for yourself how skillfully it has all been put together. Couldn't be better!

I arranged things so that the land is divided into colonies. Not just colonies helter-skelter, a hotch-potch. Everything is carefully calculated, so that each colonist will have not more than two hundred deciares of land, with each colony comprising fifty such colonists, who will all engage in agriculture. All the fifty colonists will be like one family, each sitting in his own homestead, with his own goods and chattels. Only when he goes out into the field to work, he will not go alone, but with the other forty-nine colonists, all as one man. Why, you may ask, all as one man? I'll tell you. This thing agriculture, you must understand, is hard work. You must not only know. You must also pull the plough. We don't deny that. It's not what a Jew was created for. He is not fitted for rough, tough labor.

There is a way out. The English have invented a machine that ploughs the earth. The things this machine does! No need of horses! Nor oxen! Nor people. Only one man to climb into the seat, to start the wheel, and the machine moves along and ploughs up two hundred deciares of land in the time it takes you to say Shema Yisroel! And the same with the other agricultural work. There are machines for sowing and for binding the sheaves. I sit in my seat on the machine and say my prayers, or repeat a few Psalms, and the machine does the work. Only one trouble with the machine. It costs money. A lot of money. In our currency it works out at something like ten thousand roubles. But what is that compared with fifty colonists? Two hundred from each of them, and you've got it. It needn't be cash down. You can get the best machines now on part payment. Even with the big machines. Not only the small. They can all be the same communal property. It's no longer the custom to milk a cow with your hands. One machine can milk fifty cows in the same time. A farmer with two hundred deciares can't have all the machines. But fifty farmers can.

This alone will show you that my project has been planned and calculated, thought over and taken account of all the snags and difficulties from the least to the most. I have calculated everything carefully, so that each colony of fifty families working the land has its own shochet and its own Beth Hamedrash, its own baths, its chadarim, even its market place. Everything provided for. Fifty such land-working colonies link together in tens. That constitutes a town. Every ten colonies, one town. The town can find housing for several thousand families engaged in trade, in building—houses, factories, mills, railways, shops for buying and selling grain and speculating on the Bourse the way it is customary in big towns, stores selling food—bread, milk, butter, cheese, potatoes, onions, radishes, all sorts of things grown in the ten land-working family colonies. After the town you get again another group of ten fifty-family agricultural colonies. Then another town of several thousand families, with factories, mills, shops, bourses, markets, and the rest, and so on over the whole area of the country. The agricultural colonies are under an obligation to keep the towns supplied with money and with people. Meaning taxes which every resident must pay. And by people we mean soldiers. All men at twenty-one will have to register for military service, in the event of a war or invasion. Or in the police force. Money raised by taxation would go to maintain the Jewish colleges and universities, with unrestricted admission for all, Jews and non-Jews, with no percentage norm for "aliens." Please note that my project does not contain the word alien. I don't know such a thing as an alien. Since God, bless his name, created the first man, all people are equal in his sight.

But all I have written here is but a fraction of a fraction of my project, which comprises everything. I did not omit the smallest detail, the least triviality. That leaves only one matter more—money. I have provided for that too. How, you will ask. I don't know if you will understand this. Because my plan is connected with speculation. And I remember you were always against speculation. But I'll try to explain it to you, in short concise words.

There's a bank. With shares. The shares are sold, and the money goes into the bank, which then buys the land in its own name, and all the other things needed. It builds houses, buys livestock, buys agricultural machinery. And it sells all these things to the colonists at a higher price, to be paid off in instalments. The bank profit is divided in halves. One half goes to buy more shares. The more shares there are, the more the bank pays the shareholders annually. In addition to dividends the shareholders gain from the rising value of the shares. As the dividend grows more will people want to buy shares, and more money comes into the bank. That means more money for the agricultural colonists, and so more people will want to become colonists. The more colonists there are, the more the country develops. The more it is developed, the better for the whole country.

Do you follow me? It's a wheel, and the wheel keeps turning. There are, of course, all sorts of details, and more details, and still more details. But I haven't time to go into all that. So I'm cutting it short. My next letter will give you more particulars, more details, everything more fully. May God give us good fortune and success. Keep well. Kiss the children, and give my greetings to Mother-in-law, and the whole family. Each one separately.

Your husband, Menachem Mendel

I forgot the main point:

The Angola matter occupied my mind so fully that I completely forgot about the Turk and his Adrianople. Let him stay there as comortable as he likes. So long as he doesn't tread on my crop, he may bang his head against the wall. I wouldn't even dream of interfering. And who was right—he or I—that we'll go into later. Only let's get a week or two older and hear what happened to the supervision under the Bucharest Peace, and how Sazanov received the envoys that Adrianople sent about this time to Petersburg. There are six members in this delegation, and two are said to be Jews. Would be worth while finding out whether they gave a thought before they left to whether they would under present laws be allowed to live in Petersburg. Or are they expecting a miracle?

Menachem Mendel in Warsaw to His Spouse Sheine Sheindel in Kasrielevky

First I have to inform you that I am, thank God, well. May God help us always to communicate good news one to another.

Secondly, I want you to know, my dear spouse, that I am going to Vienna, and without any question about it, to the congress. Not alone! I am taking with me a complete plan for Eretz Israel, a much bigger and a much better plan than the one I wrote about to you, about Angola. Angola is Angola, and Eretz Israel, if you can follow me, is Eretz Israel. That name alone is enough to warm a Jewish heart. It makes one burn with shame and longing that all nations have a home, but we drag around like beggars at other people's wedding feasts, picking up scraps from under the table. They grudge us even that, set their dogs on us. Chase after us with sticks and stones. Good God, the Bulgars, the Serbs, even the Montenegrins. What are they compared to us! Herdsmen, boors, rough creatures, yet each of them will sacrifice himself for his country, will give his sons, will offer his last possession in his country's need. And we? The oldest of the nations, God's Chosen People—what have we done till now, nearly two thousand years—for our country, Eretz Israel? Our own land, where our patriarchs lie buried, where we had our own Temple, our own priests and Levites, our prophets, our kings, kings of the House of David! No, say what you will, no one will open his mouth, not even our worst enemies, to deny us our right to this land, which is soaked with our sweat and blood and our tears. Indeed, it belongs now to the Turks. But that, my dear, is a good thing. It would be much worse if it belonged to anyone else. Say what you will about the Turk—Red Fez, Blue Pants, Thousand Wives—he is after all one of us, a cousin, of the same stock, our own flesh and blood, a descendant, like us, of Father Abraham. I agree, not the same mother. Our mother was Sarah. His mother was Hagar. A servant and a concubine. So what? Doesn't it show the hand of Providence was in this, arranging things so that Eretz Israel fell into the hands of Ishmael, our own kin, so that it can pass on, in time, to us!

Of course, my dear, you will be asking silly questions. Like: How? How is it possible? Well, we're not like other nations. We're not going to attack the Turk one day, suddenly in broad daylight, and run off with our Eretz Israel. The only thing we can do is to buy it from him. First, we have to ask the other side. Perhaps he doesn't want to sell. And secondly, if he is willing to sell, what will the other governments say? Dealing with the Turk, they all have a finger in the pie.

Now suppose there is no trouble from that quarter, you'll be asking me another silly question—where will we Kasrielevky paupers find all that money? Please, my dear spouse, don't worry your little head about that. Read my letter to the end, and you will find the answer to all your questions. You will yourself admit that, with the help of God, I have taken all precautions so that everything will be fair and square.

To begin with, about not wanting to sell. let's see now, what are the reasons for which the Turk may not want to sell? Of course he'll sell. It's as clear as the day to me! There has never been a time like now. Why now, you'll ask. For that you must know what is going on in politics. You must know the history. The Turk's entry into Adrianople and his refusal to leave have done him much more harm. He doesn't know himself how much. More than he can calculate. He has made people in high places rack their brains—they want him out of there; but they don't want bloodshed. They would like to do it by the new method of boycott, with money. The governments reckon to make an agreement not to lend him any money, not a bent coin. There's a story going round that Petersburg gave him a warning long ago that he was not to expect any more loans. No more money. That means we (where have we the money to lend—we need somebody to lend us money!) will get our friends to do it, our friends the French. They'll listen to us, and we'll refuse to discount a single Turkish bond, not a single one.

When the French do that, you may as well get yourself a beggar's bowl and go knocking at the doors. We know that from past experience. I wish we had the money we owe the French. They say about eight billion in our money—a good fat sum, eh, sweetheart? Chaskel Kottick says he reckons that if that amount of money had been given to Adam at the Creation, in single rouble notes, he could have sat counting it twenty-four hours a day, doing nothing else the whole time, not even eating or drinking or sleeping, only sitting and counting the one rouble notes, and he would still have a very long life span ahead of him before he was finished. Now do you understand?

In short, this is truly now an hour of decision. And it calls to us to use this opportunity, to make something of it. There's only one thing! Where are we Jews to find all that money? Even counting the Rothschilds and the Schiffs and the Brodzkis and the Poliakoffs. All the money to be enough to buy Eretz Israel from the Turk! That's bad, isn't it?

But I've had an idea. We can do it. And I think you will yourself admit that it's the best idea that any man's brain could have hit upon! What is this plan? Very simple! A leasehold plan. He'll lease Eretz Israel to us, with a proper leasehold contract. Say for ninety-nine years. Of course, we'll be having a lot of arguments, a lot of squabbling, diplomacy, politics. This one won't like it. That one will be against it. The English will have objections. The French will be upset. But what can they do to stop us signing a leasehold agreement? It's a private arrangement between us. We're not buying the land. We're not taking it away from anyone. We're leasing it for a period of ninety-nine years. We'll make it quite clear that the land is the Turk's and remains his land.

He'll be the king there, the sultan, as he was before. No change! Only one thing—as the leaseholders we want to use our own language there, to keep our own customs, to have our own schools, chedarim, Bathei Midrash, colleges, universities. We will live in accordance with our own laws and regulations, our Dinim. With our own judges, our police, our district governors, even our own ministers. It is all discussed at length in my project for Eretz Israel. I have even had in mind the right people to appoint to these posts, I shall be in Vienna at the Zionist Congress, and I'll be seeing some of the people on my list. For the present they are my candidates.

The head of it all, the president, should in my view be no other than Max

Nordau. He is an orator, I tell you! A lion! A giant of a man! They say that when he speaks the very walls shake. The vice-president should be Wolffsohn. He is a fine-looking Jew, David Wolffsohn, a man with a noble appearance. A presence. Reminds you of Herzl. And he's a man of means. And no fool. He speaks like a man! In plain Yiddish, in Jargon. Like you and me. Not like the other Germans to whom Yiddish is unclean, like pork.

And if we're looking for ministers, we have no lack of them. We couldn't find a better Minister of the Interior than Ussishkin. That's a man with character, with a will. When he says something, it must be as he says, though the whole world turns upside down. Dr. Tchlenow wouldn't make a bad minister, either. Except that he's too gentle a man. He would make a first-class diplomat. I'd make him Minister for Foreign Affairs, if Sokolow wasn't there. Sokolow is my first choice! A man who knows languages! How many languages he knows! His Hebrew is marvelous! Shmaryahu Levin would be Minister of Education and Culture. What a man! With nothing more than his five fingers he established a polytechnic in Eretz Israel. He's been in America, and he got money there for stipends, anything you want.

But all these ministries are unimportant. The important post, the one that matters, is the Ministry of Finance. For as we say where there is no food there is no Torah. Got me? Well then, we have a Finance Minister too, thank God. A man against whom all the Finance Ministers everywhere must take a back seat. Zlatopolski! Take my word for it, my dear, he would make a wonderful Minister of Finance. He would put even the great Witte in the shade. He has only one fault—too smart, up to every trick. And he's a gambler. Though that may be his chief advantage. Finance and the Bourse go together, and the Bourse is gambling, speculation. One gambler loves another gambler. I was one myself, worse luck, got myself involved in that kind of mess, so I should know! But these people are not the only possible ones. There are more candidates. We have no shortage of manpower.

Once we start sending our representatives all over the world—to a peace conference at The Hague, or to an arbitration somewhere, in London or Paris, Berlin or Moscow (if they will admit a Jew), there will be someone to look up to, someone to talk to. And the world will see who we are and what we are, and they will beat their breasts in penance. Mark my words! They'll regret the way they treated us, always leaving us to the last, the least of the last. They will consider it a privilege to have us as their guests. They won't know how high to seat us, to show us off—no small matter, the representatives of the new Jewish land, Eretz Israel!

I'm only surprised that no one thought of this before. Where were all our big men before, our champions? I mean the idea of taking a lease on Eretz Israel. Zionists made a lot of noise, begging your pardon, but it never entered their minds that we might be able to get a lease under the charter, or through plain, ordinary colonization. It never occurred to them. For that they needed a man like me, a man who deals in merchandise, a trader. That's what your

Menachem Mendel is—a trader. I'm not saying that I'm a genius or a Herzl. I'm just an ordinary trader, with a nose for such things. You'll see that in the second part of my plan. It's a good thing to have a lease in your hand. Every Jew knows that. The question is, how do you get the lease? How do you arrange things so that it should be to the advantage of the Turk to give us the lease on Eretz Israel rather than sell it? And—this is the main point—where do we get the money from, the sponduliks! That was the problem I sat up with for three nights running, writing and writing, till with God's help I set up a structure that will make you kiss your fingertips with delight. Only I have no time now—I must go and see about my travel passport for going abroad. So I'll cut it short. I'll tell you more in my next letter.

For the present, may God give us luck and good fortune, prosperity and success. Keep well! Kiss the children and my greetings to Mother-in-law and to the whole family. Give greetings to each separately, most cordially.

Your husband, Menachem Mendel
I forgot the main point.

If God wills it, I reckon that on my way back from the congress, I'll break my journey and come to see you all in Kasrielevky, you and the children and the whole family; not for long, of course, just a couple of days. For I am a man in bondage. And I won't be coming straight from Vienna. I must first be in several other places, big cities like Yehupetz, Odessa, Moscow, Riga, and other such places. They want me there, want me to address them about my projects for Angola and for Eretz Israel. Naturally, not for nothing. They are offering me very handsome fees. And they'll look after all my expenses. It wouldn't be a bad idea for me to deliver the same address in all those places. There are, let me say, seventy-six provinces with at least ten towns in each, and we get a total of 760 towns, without counting the small townships and the big villages. That should bring me a total of seventy thousand roubles. Nothing to sneeze at. It would help me no end in earning my living as a writer. What do you say?

Menachem Mendel in Warsaw to His Wife Sheine Sheindel in Kasrielevky

To My Dear Wise Chaste Spouse Sheine Sheindel

First I have to inform you that I am, thank God, in good health, body and soul. May his Holy Name help us always to hear good news one from another, good news, comfort, and salvation. For all Israel, Amen!

Secondly, I want you to know, my dear spouse, that I already have my foreign passport. It isn't an easy matter, sweetheart, for a Jew to get such a passport! And tomorrow evening, or the morning after, no excuse, if I have no interruption, I shall be on the train traveling direct to Vienna, going to the congress. I can imagine what will be happening there. The Zionists will learn about my plan to take a lease on Eretz Israel. Till now, every Zionist thought that by announcing himself as a Zionist he was doing a favor to the Jewish

People. Or he thought that by buying a shekel or a share he was absolved from anything else. To say nothing of the man who promised that he would go to Eretz Israel and buy a plot of land there. You'll never get him to say that you have shown him sufficient appreciation and gratitude. He expects you to write about him in the press, and if it isn't extravagent enough, you'll never satisfy him. He would like the Jews all over the world to give him a gold medal, half a ton in weight. For it's no small matter, is it, for a Jew to sacrifice himself, turning his back on the country he lives in, where they love and cherish him, spoil him with kindness, giving him every right a citizen should have, he and his children and his children's children. Doesn't a Jew like that deserve a pat on the back?

No, dearest spouse—if only my plan is adopted, the plan to take a lease on Eretz Israel, and you will see, all Jews will have become Zionists and will be tracking to Eretz Israel. Unless they are real anti-Semites, or they are cripples who can't go traveling and must stay where they are. Or perhaps they are meshumads, apostates. For consider it yourself—who will reject something like that? They take you and bring you to your own country and settle you there, build a house for you, and get farm machinery for you on hire purchase, for you to pay off in instalments—your very own man! They sow your fields or plant your vineyard, and they say to you, "Here you are! All ready for you! You can run a farm, or breed poultry." A man must be mad to say that he'd rather die of hunger three times a day and stay in Kasrielevky.

That leaves us with only one question—how do we get the cat over the water? Meaning, how can you shift millions of Jews, wives and children, bedding and Passover crockery, across to some other place? Yet even a child knows that you can't do that sort of thing in one go. Odessa wasn't built in a day. We'll do it slowly, bit by bit, transport ourselves gradually, one by one. The first to go will in general be those who are better off, our big men, the Brodzkis, the Wisotskys, the Gunzburgs, the Poliakoffs, the Halperins, and all the other millionaires. Next, the less well-to-do, the middle class, house owners, well-established people. After them the lower ranks, small community officials, artisans, business failures, paupers. For the world is a market place, a great big fair. It stocks all sorts. And that's how it is with human beings as well. A country must have everything. As long as there are rich men, plutocrats, millionaires, there must also be the poor, beggars, paupers. If there were no poor, who would need the rich? You'll say we could do without them now. I'd agree to that! Believe me, on my conscience, I would not object to depriving the rich of all their millions and dividing the money among the poor, share for share, so that they would all have the same. The trouble is only that we must ask the rich also before we do anything, and they won't have it! They won't allow it! Under no circumstances! On the contrary—the more millions a millionaire has, the more he wants. If he had his way, he would swallow up all the millions in the world. That's how it is since the Creation. I put no trust in the people who tell me that there will come a time when we will all be brothers, and there will be no millionaires, and there will be no poor. Fools! Don't they know that our Isaiah said that thousands of years ago? Only Isaiah said it with an *if*. It will happen, he said, at the end of days—when Messiah comes.

So now we have got to emigrate—transferring our Jews to Eretz Israel. That's easy enough. Leaving us again with only the same old trouble—money. Where can we get all that money, you ask. Then I must remind you, sweetheart, of something I wrote to you in one of my earlier letters. Must I remind you that there is a remedy for that trouble—shares. The biggest millionaire, the very biggest, the very top even, let's say Rothschild, can't do business without having partners, without shareholders. Those big loans Rothschild makes to governments—he never makes them by himself. Always with partners. When it comes to putting the money on the table, they bring in Bleichroeder and Mendelssohn in Berlin, and Jacob Schiff and Vanderbilt in America, and all the other big fish on the Bourse, and they have a meeting in London or Frankfurt or Vienna or Paris, and Rothschild stands up and says a few chosen words—this or the other state needs a loan of so many billions, to this or the other date, at so much or so much interest. I'll take half a billion, and you can have the rest. Agreed? Mazel and bracha!

And if it's a good business, with more than the interest alone to attract people, Vanderbilt from America gets up and says, "What's the matter with you, Mr. Rothschild, taking the fattest portion for yourself, half of all that's going, and leaving the other half for us beggars? Are you aware, Mr. Rothschild, that I, Vanderbilt, can take on my shoulders this entire loan, the whole five billion?"

Rothschild answers gently, diplomatically. "I believe you, Mr. Vanderbilt, that with your appetite you could easily swallow five times five billion. But you mustn't forget what our Torah says, and we have it translated into your English as, 'Live and let live'."

That annoys Vanderbilt, who isn't a Jew. A Christian. This Jew, Rothschild, teaching him how to behave! So he answers back, also very courteously, diplomatically, that though he hasn't the honor of being a Jew, like Rothschild, he still knows what is written in the Jewish Torah, in the Bible, just as well as Rothschild. While so far as appetite goes he, Vanderbilt, didn't think that the Rothschild appetite was much less than his own. Of course, Rothschild couldn't leave it at that. Paris is not Moscow. Rothschild isn't used to being told off. There is another Jew at this meeting, Jacob Schiff, a man with a head on his shoulders and a sharp tongue. He ups and makes peace between the two, reconciles them. He finds a compromise.

You would suppose this would be the end of the matter. They would divide the shares between them, pay cash for them, and that's that. Not a bit of it. They pay the money, but soon take it back. How? Simple! Each of these Leviathans and the Great Ox comes back home and starts a rumor, mostly in the press, that he has just made a big loan to this or the other government. A real stroke of big business! Fantastic! This is followed up with praise for the government, for its monetary policy, as a result of which its finances are firm as rock. That starts a furor on the Bourse, and people rush to buy the shares. Now shares have a habit, that as soon as you reach out for them, they rise. The shares are snapped up at the increased price. So that Rothschild finds himself left without a single share for himself.

So what does Rothschild do? With the money? He wants to advance another loan, to another government. Not his own. Through the same go-betweens, through the same diplomats. With the same partners, the Leviathans and the Great Ox. Another meeting is held. And again there are shares. Once again the shares are put on the market for the general public, and again with a good profit for the men at the top.

In short, it appears that all these loans that the governments take from the Rothschilds are in reality made by no one but you, by the whole Tribe of Israel, by the whole world. It turns out that everybody who has any money has a share in the loan. Even those who have no money have a share. How is that possible? I'll explain it to you in a few words. For instance, you buy meat from the butcher and bread from the baker. With your money the butcher and the baker buy a dress for the wife and shoes for the children. Again with your money the butcher and the baker buy various goods. The grocer and the shoemaker, too, buy their goods from the factory or the warehouse, and it makes the manufacturer a rich man, and he buys shares. Doesn't that mean that you have a share in them? That brings me to my point, what I wanted to say to you, that there is no such sum of money that the world can't cover. So it shouldn't frighten anyone, that the Turk would demand a high price for the Eretz Israel lease. And in case he insists that we pay several years instalments in advance, I wish that this was our only obstacle, and we could now go on to the next step, to signing the contract for the lease, under the plan that I have with God's help worked out. So as you see we have reached the real point, what I wanted to tell you, about my plan for the lease. But as I have no time now, I am cutting it short. My next letter, written on my way back, will give you a fuller explanation. For the present, may God give you mazel and bracha, with prosperity and success. Keep well! Kiss the children. Convey my greetings to Mother-in-law. And my friendliest greetings to everyone separately.

Your husband, Menachem Mendel

Menachem Mendel in Warsaw to His Spouse Sheine Sheindel in Kasrielevky

First, I am informing you herewith that I am, thank God, well and in good spirits. May God help us to hear always good news from each other, and from all Israel comfort and salvation, Amen!

Secondly, I want you to know, my dear spouse, that I am going to the congress. Not just telling you the same story again, that I'm going. I am now on my way! In a few hours the train will be making the journey to Vienna, and I already have my ticket in my pocket. I mean to say we'll soon be leaving for Vienna. That is to say, I haven't actually got the ticket. But it's as good as in my pocket. The editors of my paper have promised me a ticket, for I am going on their expense account. Did you suppose I would be going on my own account? No! There are several staff writers on the paper going like me, expenses paid. A whole crowd of us. A very different thing when you're traveling as one of a crowd. You sit with other people. You talk of this and that, tales of long ago. Like a busy fair up there! And all the time your train is running on its way, and you hardly notice how fast time flies. In short, we're on our way to Vienna, to the congress. What I mean is, we are ready to go. We're packed for the road. Not I. My colleagues are! I have no need to pack. I have no luggage. I'm taking only my tallith and tephilin. And my pen. I have a pen that writes by itself. So keep well! What is important is that I am taking with me something of greater moment than all their writing stuff. I mean my project to take Eretz Israel on lease. I've sewn it into a safe place so there is no need to worry on that account. After all, we're in a train. But you never know! I don't want this crowd to have any suspicion of what a treasure I am carrying with me to Vienna. They are scoffers and cynics. They love to make a mockery of everybody and everything. Even of themselves. And of each other. That's the way with our writers. We've got one of them with us in the same carriage, one of the real giants in our literature, a good chap, really, but he loves pulling your leg, poking fun at everybody. He's stuck a fancy name on every one of us in the party. For me he has found a new name for each day of the week, Bismarck, Vanderbilt, Witte. Now he's found another name for me, Theodor Mendel, or Menachem Herzl.

It's all to do with the congress. Everybody talking about the congress. I'll give you an example. In our own editorial office. I walked into the office one day and found a gentleman there, a fine-looking man, elegantly dressed, well-spoken, gold watch and chain, like a cantor in the synagogue on the Holy Days. He greeted me with a smile. Spoke to me. What do Jews say to each other in the synagogue? Talk about our children. His son. His only child. A young man of talent. Nobody like him in the whole world. He could teach our leader writers how to do their job. When he goes into a contest, he comes first, ahead of all our established writers. All the other students are jealous of him. He carries off all the prizes. And when he gets up on the platform, he sweeps everybody off their feet. A marvelous young man. And if that isn't enough, he's just finished a list of all the subjects he's taking at the university. I tell you, a prodigy, a treasure, a man in a thousand. And you should see his Hebrew writing!

Well now, this proud father pitches me a yarn about his son, his clever son, this marvel of a young man, this nonpareil. There's only one thing wrong with him—it shouldn't happen to anyone! A man has one only son, and suddenly that son with all the abilities in the world goes mad. He's not violent. He doesn't hit out with his fists. Nothing like that. His madness is Zionism! He suddenly became, just like that, without any warning, mad on Zionism. He wants everyone to become a Zionist, a real Zionist, to go to Eretz Israel and work on the land there, a common farm laborer! The fool! It's true enough, as he says, that people go to Eretz Israel, to dig the earth! As long as it's the earth in Eretz Israel!

You can't argue with him! You can't talk him out of it! Kindness won't do it! Anger won't help. A tragedy! One only son—good-looking and clever, and with all his studies completed, and there's nothing he wants to do, only go to Eretz Israel. As a common farm laborer! What a fool! True enough, as he keeps saying, he wasn't wanted here. Unless he turned Christian first, apostatized. So what! Is there no other answer than to get up on your hind legs and run off to the other end of the world? To dig the earth? Where? In Eretz Israel—a wild, untamed land! Run by barbaric Turks! With Chalukah Jews! Shnorrers! Mendicants! Beggars!

And the poor father went into a rage, fuming, furious.

That really annoyed me. The impudence of the man! Shouting and swearing at a country without rhyme or reason. He just doesn't like Eretz Israel. So am I supposed to leave him unanswered? Say nothing to counter his wild outburst? So I gave him what for!

"Aren't you ashamed of yourself talking like that?" I said. "Wouldn't it be better if you left this kind of jabber to your enemies? Let them talk to you! How dare you talk about Eretz Israel like that! Who do you think you are! You're just one of the rabble, the Erev Rav, the mixed multitude! The mob! Do you know when Jews like you will go to Eretz Israel? When your children will all have been baptised. And your millionaires will all be paupers! That's when you will remember that there is a country called Eretz Israel; but by that time it will be too late!"

In short, I gave it to him good and proper! As he deserved. I don't know how the words came to me. And this Jew listened to me, and with a smile and a wink, said: "And who may you be?"

"I?" I answered. "I am a Jew."

"That I can see! I can see that you're a Jew, not a Russian Goy," he returned. "What is your name?"

"Menachem Mendel," I told him.

My Jew didn't answer, not a word. He licked his lips, buttoned up his capote, turned to face us all, and said, "Good day to you!" and out he went.

What shall I tell you, sweetheart? It was superb! The whole editorial staff complimented me. "Bravo! We had no idea, Reb Menachem Mendel, that you're such a fiery Zionist! We always thought you were a Territorialist!"

I thanked them for the compliment, and I said, "Stop worrying about what I am. I'm neither a Zionist nor a Territorialist. I am a Jew." And I went off to my work on the project for a lease on Eretz Israel, putting it into shape, and completing the whole plan of which I will give you more of a summary, so that you will see that your Menachem Mendel doesn't waste his time with empty dreams.

Firstly, I propose sending a deputation to the sultan, the same people I suggested as candidates for ministerial posts in Eretz Israel. I gave you the names before. All men of standing and position, who have achieved something in the world, men with education and with brains. Men with a name. Not youngsters! Men who will make an impression when they walk into the sultan's chancellery.

What they have to do in the first place is to present themselves to him—who they are and what they are, where they come from, who sent them. Not sparing of words. Not to try to say everything at once. And each one separately. One at a time. Tell him the whole story. What they had come for. Just in the ordinary way, to congratulate him on his victory at Adrianople. And gradually come to the matter they want to discuss with him. Only at the very start they must make it clear to him, not to frighten him, not to make it seem they have come to demand, to claim a right, reminding him that Eretz Israel had once belonged to us. Today? That's a long story. There's God's hand in it! God asks no questions. At this point they may recall a fable, a Midrash, or a text somewhere. No difference what. Till they can tell him that they have come about a business deal, something to his advantage. What business? Now it's time to explain. It is common knowledge that the sultan, the Turk, that is, is hopelessly in debt. He needs money, lots of money, which he can't get on the international loan market, not because he is a security risk. Far from it! Only the financial world doesn't like his policies and is threatening him with a boycott. We have a way out for you, Sultan—not only to get the big loan he needs desperately, but to put him on his feet properly, to clear him of all his debts, wipe the slate clean, absolutely clean.

How? Let him only sign a contract for Eretz Israel, giving it to Jews on a lease for ninety-nine years. The money for the lease would be paid promptly, on the dot. Without fail. If he wished, he could have a large sum in advance, on account. Nor was that all. They could offer him something else that would be very attractive to him. What? Well, you know that Jews are the biggest Leviathans on the Bourse. We can give you a list of names—Rothschild, Mendelssohn, Bleichroeder, Jacob Schiff. In short, they would say to him, the Jewish delegates, that is, we'll see to it that our bankers would take over your debts, and they will advance you a big new loan. After all, he had only just come out of a war, Adrianople, and the Balkans. True enough, he had won that war. But even a successful war is a costly business. A new loan would clear him, would put him straight.

That is the language to use with the sultan. Not mincing words. You must talk to him straight from the shoulder. And after that, almost in the same breath, off to London, from London to Paris, from Paris to Berlin and to Vienna, to speak to the big guns, to the Great Ox and the Leviathans, but mostly to the Rothschilds, to show them the plan, the whole plan for the lease and to say to Rothschild—"We have come to you, the whole Jewish People have come to you, not, God forbid, to beg for alms, but with a business proposition, an opportunity that comes only once in two thousand years! A business deal that would bring you a fine percentage profit on the capital, and which would give employment to twelve million Jews, at this hard and bitter time for Jews, oppressed and persecuted, mass flight, apostasy, Mendel Beilis—for heaven's sake don't forget Mendel Beilis and the ritual murder case spun round him. The Rothschilds are themselves Jews, aren't they? They have Jewish hearts. They run kosher kitchens. I am told they fast on Yom Kippur. And they still have a synagogue in Frankfurt, where poor Jews hold services, Mincha and Maariv, day after day."

Having finished with the Rothschilds, we next turn to our own kind of Jews. They mustn't run away with the idea that this is a game. That they can just sit by and wait for the miracle. Our first approach must be to the men of wealth, to our millionaires. We must be short and sharp with them as well. We must tell them, if you are Jews, show it! Transport yourselves and your capital, your money, to our land, our own land. Don't worry. If you have money, you won't do worse in business than you do here now. You don't want to go? It isn't convenient? You don't want it? Your children haven't completed their studies? All right, stay here! But with one condition—Discard the name Jew! Let them stop throwing you up at us! Let's have an end to our suffering for your sins! Here, the delegates can work in a parable from the Kelmer Maggid, or a story from Mottke Chabad. No need to spare them, even if they are millionaires. And no need to go soft with the others, the ordinary Jews, the plain simple Jews. They mustn't suppose that because they are not rich they are privileged, are free from obligations. Nothing for them to do. And they may forget everything that has happened till now and start again from the beginning, from Ma Tovu, as our parents did.

If Abraham, Isaac, and Jacob could descend to herding sheep, they may pocket their pride and dig the soil, plough and sow, reap and thresh in Eretz Israel, keep cattle and poultry, do all the things that have to do with agriculture. It won't hurt them! On the contrary—it will elevate them, crown them in the eyes of the world. Take my word for it—I'm not mad! I'm not saying that all the twelve million Jews, every one of us, must go out into the fields to work. There is enough to do in Eretz Israel besides farming and wine growing. There is trade. There is shipping. There is the Bourse. Work enough for all of us! I've got it all written down in my plan, paragraph by paragraph. But I haven't the time to go into all that now. So I must cut it short. And I'll write to you about it all more fully, when I'll be already at my destination, journey's end.

For the present, blessings and good fortune for you! Keep well! Kiss the children! Regards to Mother-in-law! And greetings to the whole family, each and every one, specifically, each separately.

Your husband, Menachem Mendel.

I forgot the main point:

As I am now on a journey out into the world, and I reckon to be home for

Succoth, I feel like bringing back a present for you, as well as something for the children and for Mother-in-law. For each one something separately, specially suitable. I have with God's help been in America and have come back safe and sound; I got a job which gives me a living and enables me to do some good also to the world at large. So it is only right that you, too, should get a little joy out of it. So I am asking you, my sweet spouse, to write to me plainly and legibly all that is in your mind, what you want and would like to have and write to me in Vienna at the Zionist Congress.

Menachem Mendel in Vienna to His Spouse Sheine Sheindel in Kasrielevky

First of all I want to know that I am, thank God, sound in mind and body, may his Holy Name help us to have always good news from each other. And from all Israel. Amen!

And secondly, be advised, my sweet spouse, that I am now in Eretz Israel. Easy to say Eretz Israel! The fact is that I am for the time being in Vienna, but I feel as if I were in Eretz Israel. No small matter—Jews walk about free and openly with Magen Davids in their buttonholes, talking Hebrew in the street, kissing and embracing; and I like all the others. On arrival in Vienna we went at once into the town, to the places the Zionists had prepared for us long ago, and we registered. It seems that they issued warnings some weeks back that there would be difficulty in finding apartments for all of us. They worked hard at it, till they found billets at last for us all. They arranged it so that the delegates from this town stay here, and the delegates from that town stay there. All written down on paper, with our numbers according to the alphabet. Only due to haste and there being so many people to deal with, so many Jews, bless them, arriving all at once, there was a bit of confusion, a mix-up of delegates and hotels. So we had to do some running around.

What do you think, sweetheart, the way we had to lug our suitcases about from one hotel to another. All the hotels were packed full. Till finally with God's help we found a place, not much before nightfall. So that we could at last stretch and relax. Our host was a German, and we couldn't understand his language. And he couldn't understand our language. Though we spoke ordinary Yiddish, and more than half our words were German. But that wasn't the worst of it! So what, if the German didn't understand us! We were not going to marry into his family. And we were not going to stay in his lodgings for evermore. Sooner or later the congress would end, and we would, with God's help, be on our way from here. I wish we could be delivered as easily from the Golus! And from poverty and want!

If things get too bad we can always show a German a coin and hold up two fingers, and he understands perfectly. It was hard and bitter for our own language, Yiddish, which must not be used here. Here we must speak only Hebrew. And what can we do about it? If everybody talks Hebrew! Ussishkin is said to have issued a slogan—"Hebrew or Russian!" And when Ussishkin says that, it's the last word. Nothing more to be said. You'll ask me, of course, what do those delegates do who don't know Hebrew. What do you suppose! Poor people! They sit there with their mouths shut. Can't say a word! A human being isn't a dumb creature. Especially if you've come as a delegate to a congress. You move away into a corner and carry on a conversation very quietly in Yiddish, so that Ussishkin shouldn't hear you. But wait! That isn't the end of it! The ban on Yiddish wouldn't be so bad if they let you talk Hebrew the way Jews talk Hebrew. But they heap one ban on top of the other. We must talk Hebrew not as Jews talk Hebrew in our parts, but the way Turks talk it in Eretz Israel. Sephardic, they call it. You know, my dear, I'm not an ignoramus. I went to cheder, and I was a bright scholar. Yet I have a hard struggle to put my ear to catch the sound of the Separdic. Nonetheless it's a pleasure to listen to the sheer sound of it, the way they speak it.

The other day there was a young girl went up on the platform and delivered a speech in Sephardic Hebrew that warmed all your bones. And there is a delegate, from Odessa I believe, a dear man! Pure gold. They call him Jabotinsky. Vladimir Jabotinsky. Vladimir. A Goyish name. But what a devoted Jew he is! Fire and flame! A young man still! And when this Jabotinsky speaks, when this Vladimir stands up and speaks—in Hebrew—what can I tell you! It's a taste of Heaven, Paradise, Garden of Eden! I'd give you all the best cantors in the world! You could sit all day and all night listening to him. You'd never tire! Even though you understand no Hebrew. You couldn't tear yourself away! That's the power of the man! And don't forget that this is only the pre-congress, a conference. You'll ask me, what is a conference? What is the difference between a conference and a congress? Let me explain. You know what a congress is. Well, when the delegates arrive and the congress hasn't started yet, you get together every day or every second day, those of you who have arrived, and you talk together and you argue and bicker and quarrel. And you adopt a resolution. You get hold of the general lines of the congress before the congress opens. Understand?

The first conference we held here led to a clash over the language. A dispute over what language to use at the congress, so that we should understand each other. To my mind, it was a very unnecessary argument. Jews come together and want to talk things over. Why shouldn't they? Let everyone talk as best he can. And if you want the others to understand there is surely no better way than to talk plain Yiddish. What Jew doesn't understand Yiddish?

But no! There are such stubborn people about, especially our Russian Jews from Petersburg, from Odessa, and from Bochislav, who tell you categorically that they don't understand one single Yiddish word, chop their heads off if they do! "Yiddish? No understand!"

Poor Jews! You must feel sorry for such people. All they know is Russian or Hebrew! What can I tell you? It started such a row, you wouldn't believe. There was one suggestion that we should use three languages—Hebrew, Russian, and Yiddish as well. They turned it down. They said two languages are enough. We'll stick to Hebrew and Russian. No Yiddish! We don't understand Yiddish! The chairman saw it was an endless wrangle and decided the only thing was to take a vote on it. "Those in favor of two languages, Hebrew and Russian." And a forest of hands shot up. Of course, my hand was not among them. Would I repudiate my language, Yiddish? It looked like the bigger half allowing us to use Yiddish as well. But there was one man, a delegate from Yehupetz, who hit on an idea and instead of holding his hand up once, held up both his hands, and so he got a majority against it. I know the man. A fanatical Hebraist. He raised his right hand and his left hand. And that decided the issue. No Yiddish! Yiddish at this congress banned!

So you see, they buried our Yiddish language alive. All because of one hand raised when it shouldn't have been!

It hurt me very much. I was mortified. So many Jews have been speaking Yiddish for years, for hundreds of year, and there was nothing wrong with it. No one has died yet because he spoke Yiddish. And now suddenly, a ban against Yiddish. It's a crime to speak Yiddish. More's the pity! They killed Yiddish, those Zionists have! Those Zionists!

I was on the point of jumping up and shouting at the top of my voice, "What are you doing? You want us to talk to everybody in Hebrew? Or in Russian? When I can't say what I want to say properly in Hebrew, and he can't properly understand what I'm saying in Hebrew! Think of the millions of Yiddish-speaking brothers we have who know no other language, only Yiddish!"

But what sort of wrathful prophet am I! Aren't these Jews too, aren't they Zionists as well, trying to spread Zionism and drowning it without realizing what they are doing? Don't they see into what dangerous waters they are steering! Look, there was this young man, Vladimir Jabotinsky, going up to the platform to speak. And I tell you, when he spoke in Hebrew, all my anger vanished, and I had to agree with him, I had to confess that he was right in wanting all Jews to speak Hebrew. He said a Zionist who can't speak Hebrew has no excuse whatever—Let him learn! He gives us two years to learn Hebrew, till the next congress, in two years time. He's right! Two years should be enough to teach and learn the language. Why shouldn't we learn Hebrew! Vladimir Jabotinsky himself couldn't speak Hebrew two years ago. And now listen to him! When I come back home, I'll take up learning Hebrew. One hour or two hours a day, perhaps three. The more hours the better. And when I have learned Hebrew, I'll speak no other language, only Hebrew. In the editorial office, in the hotel. Everywhere!

So you see, all my anger had gone, and I was able to talk to the Hebraists like one of them, even to the delegate from Yehupetz who had held up both his hands against Yiddish. He came up to me. No, I went up to him. He complimented me. Said he admired the way I spoke. He had heard all my speeches at the conference. And he couldn't praise me highly enough. What can one say to a man who talks like that? He told me all about himself. I could tell you a lot about our talks together, the two of us. But as I have no time for that now, I must leave it to my next letter, when I shall tell you more about these things, more fully.

May God give us mazel and blessings, health and prosperity! Keep well! Kiss the children! And greet Mother-in-law and the whole family! Each one separately, in the most friendly way.

Your husband, Menachem Mendel

I forgot the main point:

I knew it! I knew it would turn out like this. What else? They want to murder our language and get away with it! It wouldn't be right! Protests started rolling in from all over the place. The first outburst came from Smargon. "Smargon protests in the most vigorous way against the twenty-seven hands that were raised against our Yiddish language!" Smargon was followed by Bochislav, who sent their protest straight to me! "What's the idea!" they demanded. "Wanting to shut our mouths, to stop us speaking in our language! You are our delegate in Vienna, and if your hand was among the twenty-seven raised against Yiddish, may your hand wither!"

Next came Oshmiani. They also wrote to me. Though we were not on terms of acquaintance, they said, we had a friend in common, Shmuel Mattes of Oshmiani, who is now in Baikon. And on those terms of acquaintance they asked me to advise them, as their friend—what should they do about this issue? Hebrew? The children don't understand! Russian? The parents don't know it!

And I received a sharply worded protest also from Kasrielevky. They went for me hammer and tongs! Where had I been! Why hadn't I spoken up! If I had let them down, if it was my fault, they'd make me feel sorry that I had been so negligent! I wouldn't dare to show my face in Kasrielevky. There was no signature to the letter. Just two words—Some Jews! And I got a rudely-worded protest from the highly-placed Yehupetz, signed by all the richest people there, our millionaires. "You know very well, Reb Menachem Mendel," their letter began, "that we are elite, the millionaires in Yehupetz, and we have no great love, are no great Hasidim of your Jargon, no great readers of Yiddish booklets and newspapers and the like. In the first place, where would we get the time for so much reading. It's as much as we can manage to get through a Russian newspaper and all the telegrams and quotations on the Bourse. And you expect us to read Yiddish books as well. Besides, it doesn't suit us. It doesn't fit in with our status. How do the French say it? Noblesse oblige! Position has its responsibilities. You know that yourself. You were once one of our Yehupetz residents. We are fond, very fond indeed, of having someone tell us a Jewish joke or a Jewish anecdote and tell it in Jargon. Telling it in Hebrew would spoil it. So what are those people doing about it, your Zionists! They'll only make a mess of it."

And that is how the protest letter ended. With the signatures of all the bigwigs following, the Brodzkis and the Halperins and the Gunsburgs, the Zeitsevs and the Poliakoffs.

Your husband, Menachem Mendel

Menachem Mendel in Vienna to His Spouse Sheine Sheindel in Kasrielevky

First, I want to tell you that I am, thank God, sound in body and mind. May his Holy Name help us to hear always good tidings from all Israel, Amen!

Secondly, be advised, my dear spouse, that things are desperate here; everything is upside down. Everybody running around, everybody talking, everybody excited, everybody clapping bravo, and I like all the others. The conference is over, you understand, and what we have now is the full congress. Impossible to describe what the congress is like. You must be there yourself to see and feel it. Imagine a huge hall, the size of the big market place in Kasrielevky, or even bigger, and this hall is packed full of delegates, pressmen, and visitors—visitors from every part of the world, so many that it is impossible to count. The result is that the place is cramped, overcrowded, everybody pushing and shoving and making a terrible noise. And unbearably hot. That's the inside. You have no idea how many people were left outside. They couldn't get in. No more room! Is there a hall big enough anywhere in the world to take all those who would like to be there as visitors? In order to reduce the crush they hit on an idea, a method (trust a German to find a method!) They counted the number of seats and printed that number of admission tickets, for delegates, for pressmen and for visitors. Just so many tickets for so many seats. No more! No more room! Except some seats for sale to visitors.

The result was that some ticket holders who came late found themselves crowded out. Other visitors had taken their seats. A good many of those who were crowded out were pressmen—I was one of them. And the pressmen made a terrible row. The man who made the most noise was the delegate from Yehupetz, the one who had voted out Yiddish. He is a pressman as well, like me, the correspondent of one of the Hebrew papers. He went for those Germans who had made the seating arrangements! The way he shouted at them! And not as you might think in Hebrew, but in good plain Yiddish, in Jargon. And how do you think it all ended? They let us all in! How else? People have respect for a writer, my dear. Everywhere, especially when he raises his voice and has a say. True enough, by the time we got inside, there were no empty seats left. But that didn't worry us. So we stood on our two feet the whole time. But we were inside, where we could see and hear. And we could join in the clapping, like everybody else.

That's the way it is at a congress. Everyone who mounts the platform is greeted with a burst of applause. When he starts speaking, he gets another burst of applause. Can you imagine what it sounds like when an audience that size—about ten thousand—starts clapping, keeping time. Most of the applause went to Sokolow. It went on for nearly five full minutes. And when he mentioned the name Mendel Beilis and spoke of the way that poor innocent man is suffering in prison for a crime he never committed, for all the crimes he is accused of, there was such an outburst of clapping and crying out his name, that if he had been there and had seen and heard it, he would have felt that all he had endured there in prison was worth it. Beilis, Beilis! When I think of that Jew Beilis, it breaks my heart. And there is a thought hammering at my brain— how does one recompense such a man who has been tortured for all Israel, made a victim, a sacrifice for all Israel?

What do you suppose, my dear, a congress looks like? A congress like this, with thousands of Jews, all in formal dress, and all with one idea, with one thought in their mind, Zion! It gives the gathering a festive air. Good to know that there are still countries in the world where Jews may assemble and proclaim freely and openly and in a loud voice all the things on our mind and in our heart. You should have been here when they read out all the telegrams that we sent to the old man, Emperor Franz Joseph, congratulating him on attaining his advanced age and wishing him still longer life, grateful for his treatment of the Jews under his rule, and the reply he sent us. Or seen the sea of people who flooded the streets of his capital city Vienna, when we all went in a body to Herzl's grave, here in Vienna. The orderliness and the hushed silence. You would have said that this congress is a true ingathering of the tribes, a pilgrimage like in the olden days, when Jews all over Eretz Israel congregated in Jerusalem. But for the fear of profanation I would say that the Shechina, God's Spirit, rests now in Vienna.

The Jew who has not been at least once at a Zionist congress doesn't deserve to tread this earth. As long as I live, I have never felt so much, so intensely that I am among Jews than here at this congress. I seem to have been newborn here; I have grown wings here, and I fly! The only trouble is that the congress won't go on for more than one week. What is one week? I dread to put the words on Satan's tongue—I keep thinking, when will I reach the great moment here? When will the auspicious moment come when I can stand up and read out my projects, when I know the available time has all been divided up among the would-be speakers. I can't see my turn coming! Yet with God's help I may still snatch a few minutes between one speaker and another and get my name on the list of speakers. You'll want to know why I put so much stress on this. I'll tell you. I want to get up on that platform and say something. And they won't let me! The speakers list was compiled a long time ago. I know that. The list is full. But it may still happen that somebody whose name is on the list will get so fed up with waiting that he will give up any expectation of being called on, that I'll be able to get my say. It's very rare for all those whose names are on the list to wait until they get a few minutes at the end. It wouldn't be possible for everyone who wants to speak to get the chance. Not even if the congress sat longer and sat all day and all night, all the twenty-four hours together, without a moment's respite to drink or sleep.

To come back to the congress—I haven't the words enough to describe to you what sort of a thing such a congress is. I want to tell the congress all I have in my mind. For as God is my witness, I only want to do good, to put forward my projects. But I can't go into all that now. There is no time. So I'll cut it short.

Keep well! Good fortune and blessings on us all. Kiss the children. And give my greetings to Mother-in-law. And my regards to all the family, each one separately and most warmly.

Your husband, Menachem Mendel

I forgot the main point:

You would think Heaven had fallen to the ground—not a single person took up the cudgels for Yiddish! No, there was one. Not only one but two. You want to know who they are—one is an engineer from Yehupetz. The other a lawyer from Warsaw. They are both still young men—daredevils! What's on their mind is in their mouth! God save us from such! They didn't half give it to the enemies of Yiddish, our Jargon! They gave them what for! Fire and brimstone! They tore the guts out of them. Only one thing wrong with them—why didn't they take a stand like that before? Why didn't they say the same thing in Yiddish? Everybody would have understood! There still is some hope for our Yiddish tongue! At the hands of Vladimir Jabotinsky! He is supposed to have said that when the Twelfth Zionist Congress is held, he will address the assembly only in Yiddish! Stop him if you can! Please God, work a miracle! Let him do it! If he wants to, he is the man to do it! And do you think Ussishkin couldn't speak Yiddish? Of course, he could! He can speak very good Yiddish. But he won't! A caprice of his! Let Ussishkin do it! Then Jews would all speak Yiddish, freely and openly. An end to the Golus! What do you say to that? There is a time for everything!

Menachem Mendel in Vienna to His Spouse Sheine Sheindel in Kasrielevky

First, I want to inform you that I am, thank God, alive and well, may his Holy Name help us always to hear good news, one from another, only good news for all Israel, Amen!

Secondly, be advised, my dear spouse, that we have already got to Ne'ilah, the concluding prayers. The congress will end tomorrow night. And my project hasn't had a chance yet. I'm still at the beginning. No wonder. So little time, and so much to do! I really don't know how we'll manage to conclude all the items on the agenda, not to be left stuck in the middle. We still have to elect the new president, for the next two years. I look up to the platform, where our bigwigs sit, and I think to myself, who of them is to be our new president? With so many candidates, and all excellent choices. They would all do well, make a good president. Of course, the Germans are sure the new president must be one of themselves, a German. They are all good at calling out orders. None of them would refuse the post. Then there's the language question. Imagine me as president, addressing the congress in ordinary plain Yiddish. It would be drab, colorless. Prosaic. True, they would understand what I was saying. But what would it sound like? Dull and unexciting; like any plain meeting. It would be a different story in Hebrew, except for one problem—Sephardic! "Rabotei" (rabosei) . . . the "Congrett" (congress) . . . in Odetta" (in Odessa), etc. Who would understand anything? And can it be compared to German? When a German stands up on his feet, folds his arms, and says, "Ladies and Gentlemen," or "Distinguished Congress!"—the words ring out like a bell. No, say what you will, we do not have anywhere near as many candidates as the Germans have. When you look at the present president, David Wolffsohn, you feel in every fiber of your being that the Almighty himself decreed that he be president. The way he sits, stands, and talks, his pleasant smile, his look, the way he gestures with his hand—he's like a king. And what do you think of Bodenheimer? A bad president? Or Warburg, or Hantke? Or Simon? Or Jean Fisher from Antwerp? In brief—not to talk about the Germans, but about our own, the Russians: there's Sokolow, for instance, I should only have such a president! Or Tchlenow, or Ussishkin—doesn't he look like a president, sitting there on the dais? Or Dr. Shmaryahu Levin. Or what's wrong with Dr. Weizmann? Or Rabbi Maaze, of Moscow? Or Temkin of Elizabethgrad? They wouldn't make good presidents? Or Jabotinsky, the one called Vladimir, even though he is still rather young, don't you think he would do well? For my part you could even vote for Dr. Passemanik, if he did not belong to the Opposition.

The "Opposition" are the ones who are always shouting, criticizing, always finding fault. All they do is look for the failings in every one, and for the bad in everything, and tell you it is no good. It is this way in every parliament in the world, and that's the way it is with us at the congress. A man gets up to speak, or to make a proposal, and we immediately look over to the opposition, to Dr. Passemanik. What will Dr. Passemanik say? It seems that the speaker is doing so well, speaking with such charm, such conviction—gold and silver—but Dr. Passemanik will certainly not approve. And so it is. The speaker hasn't even finished, and Dr. Passemanik is already writing himself notes, getting ready to ask for the floor. The speaker has barely finished, the applause still sounding in the hall; he has barely had time to catch his breath and wipe the perspiration from his brow, and he is already beaten, wounded, crushed, trampled—a wreck! Dr. Passemanik is the one who did him in. He has some mouth—may God protect us from it!

We have others in the congress, just imagine, other wreckers like him. There is David Treitsh, from Cyprus, a Dr. Kahn, from the Hague, and others like them, but I am not as afraid of any of them as I am of this Dr. Passemanik. This Jew puts the fear of death in me! I know in advance that he will destroy my

Eretz Israel project, will grind it into dust and pound it into the ground. But I don't care. When my turn comes everything will be all right. What do I care about the Opposition when the audience, the people, that is, are with me? How do I know? From my new good friend from Yehupetz, the one who slaughtered Jargon at the conference. You cannot begin to imagine what a dear man he is, and what relations have developed between us. We are like one soul. We are always together. In the group pictures of delegates we are also side by side. And in one picture we are all alone, just the two of us, embracing each other. I am sending you the picture with the inscription he himself wrote on the bottom: ". . . the lovely and the pleasant in their lives, and in their death they were not divided . . ." (2 Sam 1:23), which means that those who really love can be parted only by death.

He goes nowhere without me, nor I without him. And thank God, there are places to go. We have a Jewish theater here, where they perform in Hebrew. We even have our own Jewish cinema, where for half a crown, that is twenty kopecks, you can see all of Eretz Israel with Judea and the Western Wall, alive and moving right before your eyes. If you could only see the tears we shed at the sight of these things! He was not just babbling when my dear friend said to me, in Hebrew of course, that it would have been worth coming to Vienna just for that. I don't know why, but I am very much attached to this Jew. On the Sabbath, we went together to the German synagogue. However, because neither of us has high hats, they did not let us in. Among the Germans, the high hat is more important than the tallith. When they see a Jew in the synagogue without a high hat they get the shakes. As a result, we had to look for a Jewish synagogue, and since Vienna is very big, we walked very far.

While we walked, I explained my whole Eretz Israel project to him, and he liked it so much he almost went out of his mind. "It's a pity," he said, "that it is written up in Jargon, not in Hebrew. In Hebrew, it would look entirely different. But," he said, "not to worry. I take it upon myself to translate it into Hebrew—without making a vow on the Sabbath—and without charging a penny!" He wants me to dictate it to him in Yiddish, and he will translate it into Hebrew, word for word. It is as easy for him as smoking one cigarette, but writing is like mud in the streets—you dip the pen, and write. Especially Hebrew, which is his mother tongue. We were going to get right to work on it, but we had no free time, not even one second!

We have to approve a university in Jerusalem—not a simple matter. We almost have it passed already. Money is spilled out here like beans. Fifty-thousand, seventy-thousand, one-hundred thousand. The heart expands and the breath rejoices when you see how the rich toss their donations about— hundreds of thousands. That's not nothing! With this kind of giving, it would not be a surprise if we have everything very soon. We already have almost everything. We have our own gymnasia in Jaffa. We have our own polytechnic in Haifa, and now our own university in Jerusalem. What more do you want? All that remains to be done is to move a few Jews there, and we're all set. This is something I have worked on, and for this they'll need me; my plan, that is. They won't escape me, please God, and with His help.

Right now I have to run to the congress hall, it is the last day, that is: my day, when I have to appear. And since I have no time, I must be brief. In my next letter I'll write in detail, God willing. Meanwhile, may God give us mazal and blessings, with good fortune and prosperity. Be well and kiss the children, long may they live, and greetings for Mother-in-law and all the family, each in the most friendly way.

Your husband, Menachem Mendel

I forgot the main thing: I kept this letter in my pocket all day. I thought that my turn would come and I would read my project, and then I would be able to write to you about that, too. It turned out that the whole business, including the congress itself, is all over, and I am still holding on to my project. I held on to the last minute. What did I think? That when it was time for Ne'ilah, when it came time to close the congress, then, without waiting for any turn I would march up to the bimah, pound my fist in the table, and say:

"Listen, Rabosei, the fact of the matter is this—you have had a congress full of success and effect, so many thousands of people listening for eight whole days and nights, and now it's all over, finished. You have, thank God, done great things! But one thing, Rabosei, you have not done. You have forgotten one thing—Eretz Israel! How do we get to Eretz Israel? I have a plan"—and here I would undo my pack of papers, to read out my whole project from Ma Tovu to Oleinu, from beginning to end.

That's how I thought it all out in my own mind. But man proposes, and God disposes! At the very moment when I was walking up to the platform, the president, David Wolffsohn, banged his gavel on the table and said: "Ladies and Gentlemen, I have now to announce that the congress is closed. Next Year in Jerusalem!"

That brought a burst of applause, and the whole vast assembly stood and sang Hatikvah, the Zionist anthem, "Our Hope!" All of them singing, and I singing with them all. What shall I tell you, my dear wife? One who has not heard this singing has not heard anything worth listening to in his life! Who has not seen this way of saying goodbye, the kissing, the shaking of hands. And I like all the others. Now we have to think how to scrape together the money for the journey back home. The Germans have emptied our pockets to the last heller. Never mind! I'll think of something. I'll manage! The editors won't leave me stuck here! But what will the others do? Like my new friend from Yehupetz. He hasn't said anything about it, but I notice that his pocket is pretty thin. It doesn't even have the small change he needs to get him back to Yehupetz. He boasts that he has legs. "It's all right," he says, "to go to the congress on foot." And he laughs. A strange Jew! There are so many rich men at the congress, real tycoons, well-rounded Jews with fat bellies. Does it ever occur to them, for example, that someone else may not have? May need help, God forbid? . . .

Listen to what I tell you: our world is a nasty world; an ugly world. Take me, for example, with my projects. They knew very well that I did not come here with empty hands. Did it occur to any one of them to come up to me and say "Reb Menachem Mendel, please, show us what you have?" No, each one prefers to think of himself. Each one brought something of his own, and each one wants to be heard . . . On second thought, perhaps it is better this way? I am going to tour the world, and I'll read this project along with my other projects to my audiences. I'll have all the time in the world, I won't have to rush. I won't have to ask for the floor, and I won't have to worry about Dr. Passemanik. I know that if God wills the audience will love me, especially when I come out with the new project that is weaving itself in my mind, a new plan, a brand new combination—I tell you, a real brain-wave! For this reason I can certainly say, "this too is for the best."

Menachem Mendel in Vienna to His Wife Sheine Sheindel in Kasrielevky

First, I have to tell you that I am, thank God, sound in body and soul. May his Holy Name help me always to hear such good news from you and from all Israel.

Secondly, be advised, my good sweet spouse, that I am still here in Vienna. All the delegates and all the visitors left immediately after the closing session. Only a lot of pressmen and writers, with me among them, stayed on for a few more days, not just so, for the fun of it, but to do a very necessary job, to do something for ourselves. We thought it over and came to the following conclusion: The congress decided everything. We elected a committee, a very fine committee, thank God. As for presidents, we have now two presidents, Professor Warburg and Dr. Tchlenow. We have our own bank. We also have a university, and we speak Hebrew. We took care of everything and everybody. Why shouldn't we writers do something for ourselves as well? Why shouldn't we have a fund? As it is we haven't even the beginnings of a fund, a fund of our own. All the writers the world over have a fund. Only we Jewish writers haven't anything like it. How are we worse than ordinary workingmen? Tailors and shoemakers, hatters all have a fund. Why shouldn't there be a fund for Jewish writers?

Now you'll ask me, what is a fund? What do we want a fund for? So I'll tell you! There is a famous Jewish writer named Mordecai ben Hillel Ha-Cohen. Mordecai, the son of Hillel, and he's a Cohen. Now this Cohen sits all alone in Eretz Israel and is said to feel very much at home there. Yet he has us on his mind too, all his colleagues, the writers outside Israel. So he thought it over and sent a project to the congress to secure the living conditions of us, the writers, when we grow old or we fall ill or we die, God forbid. We should have a fund to look after us, after our wives and our children. You'll ask, where's the money coming from. There will be money enough. Don't worry about the money. It will come in the first place from us writers ourselves. And secondly, from lectures and concerts that we'll arrange in all the towns and cities wherever Jews live. Those functions alone will bring in thousands. Then voluntary contributions, offerings, bequests. Wouldn't there be in this town or the other one or two millionaires who will remember before they die that there is such a fund for Jewish writers? And then plate and bowls placed in the synagogue on Yom Kippur Eve for the worshippers to make a contribution for charity. There are so many plates and bowls. There would be one plate more. And weddings, Bar Mitzvas and circumcisions and funerals. The funerals are the most likely means of getting money. When a man thinks of death, he dips his hand in his pocket, very fast.

We've got it all worked out, very carefully thought out. No need for you to worry about money. The only thing is that we should be united about it. In our own interest. We're not just anybody! Not tailors or shoemakers! We're writers, who talk about union and peace, and castigate the common folk, and preach high morality to them. We should be united, with one mind and one soul.

That very minute, as though my thinking about it had brought it about, as soon as the congress closed, the writers, myself among them, were called to a meeting to discuss the proposal made by that writer who lives in Eretz Israel, all of us, whether we write in Hebrew or in Jargon—all Jewish writers. And the letter calling us together was signed by none other than Bialik himself. Not the Bialik from Yehupetz, the timber dealer, but the famous Bialik, the great poet who lectures in Hebrew, publishes books and shakes the world!

So we got together, all of us who write from right to left, all the famous writers, each in his own branch, about thirty of us in all. Our first item was to elect a chairman. That started a bit of a clash. The Hebraists wanted one of their own. The Jargonists were against that. They were afraid it would lead to bias, one-sidedness. We found a way out of that difficulty by electing a man who was both on this side and on that side—Reuben Brainin. This Brainin is a famous Hebraist. He had gone so far as to make the long journey to America for the purpose of spreading Hebrew there. While he was there, he had meanwhile become editor of a Yiddish paper. To earn a living. What else could the poor man do?

There was no better man as chairman. So having elected him we started the meeting. Very well, then. What happens now? Up jumps a little scribbler, one of the young Hebraists who had been raising the cry, "Hebrew or Russian! No Yiddish! No Jargon!" And he started a new revolt—"No! I won't sit with the Jargonists! I don't want to get mixed up with them! I wouldn't give one Russian for ten thousand Jews who speak Jargon!"

Now what does one do with a man like that? And he was followed by another and another—Out with Jargon! Wipe out the memory of it! It's unclean! Worse than pork or ham!

They went so far as to introduce a paragraph that the fund would be only for those of us who write in Hebrew.

That roused us. That started a storm among the Jargonists. And I right in the middle of it: "Outrage! Inhuman! Malicious!" One Jew to exclude another because he speaks Yiddish! As though the Hebraists were the only true Jews, and we were Karaites! Or Meshumadim! Apostates, God Forbid! Enemies of Israel!

The row went on for a long time, till a few of us, who love, peace, and quiet intervened, and most of all the president, Reuben Brainin, the famous Hebrew writer, who is the editor of a Yiddish paper in America, and we agreed on a compromise—long life to them for that! We agreed on a compromise, that we, though we write in Yiddish, are nevertheless Jews like all the others. Only since there is a difference of opinion, and some can't stand us because of our language, we'll take a vote on it.

"Who is against Yiddish?" And the result was that, out of the nearly thirty who were present, fifteen voted for Hebrew, and fourteen for Yiddish. That started a worse storm than before, more shouting, more tumult. We almost came to blows.

You want to know the result? There wasn't one. We dispersed without a yes or no. The Hebraists left separately. And we left separately. And we decided— we the Jargonists—we decided to split, to break away and establish our own fund. Let them live, to a hundred and twenty years, and we'll manage, with God's help, without their favors. But we feel no grudge against them. "To show what we mean," Nomberg said, "let one of them come to us to ask to join our group, because he may need help from our fund, and we'll accept him gladly." That's the sort of man Nomberg is. And the kind of men we all are. We take the line that when God created the world, there was no Hebrew language yet. No Yiddish either. God, Bless His Name, doesn't mind what language people use to speak to him. A woman who doesn't know a word of Hebrew comes to him weeping, with an ordinary Yiddish prayer book. Doesn't God listen to her? And Reb Levi Yitzchok, the Rabbi of Berditchev, on Yom Kippur Eve, used to contend with God in Russian. And let's think of it, how will it be in a hundred years time when we die? They will bury us both alike, the Hebraists and the Yiddishists, deep down in the ground. So what have we to be so stuck up about? I said that to one of them, a famous writer, a thinker, the editor of a paper, named Klausner. He signs himself Doctor Klausner. He listened to me attentively, thought for a while, smiled, and said that my words contained a thought that had been once expressed by a very great philosopher—he told me the name, but I've forgotten it now. When it came to saying goodbye, he gave me his hand and said he knew that I write sometimes also in Hebrew. He hoped therefore that one day I would become a Hebrew writer completely. We parted the best of friends. With everybody. That's my way, thank God, always. I don't like quarreling, as you know. Jews should not quarrel! There's nothing to quarrel about! And now I am on the point of leaving Vienna. I've got the money now for the journey. My editors sent it to me.

Meanwhile my head is buzzing with thoughts and ideas, with all sorts of combinations and arrangements. How does one arrange for our fund to have more money? For the more money a fund has the better, both for the fund and for its members.

As I have no time now, I am cutting this letter short. My next letter will tell you everything in full detail. For the present, may God give us mazel and blessings, with good fortune and prosperity. Keep well and kiss the children, and greetings for Mother-in-law and for all the family, each one in the most friendly way.

Your husband, Menachem Mendel